The Semiotics of
Russian Cultural History

The Semiotics of Russian Cultural History

Essays by

IURII M. LOTMAN

LIDIIA IA. GINSBURG

BORIS A. USPENSKII

TRANSLATED FROM THE RUSSIAN

Introduction by BORIS GASPAROV

Edited by ALEXANDER D. NAKHIMOVSKY
and ALICE STONE NAKHIMOVSKY

CORNELL UNIVERSITY PRESS

ITHACA AND LONDON

First published in 1985 by Cornell University Press.
Published in the United Kingdom by
Cornell University Press Ltd., London.

International Standard Book Number (cloth) 0-8014-1183-1
International Standard Book Number (paper) 0-8014-9294-7
Library of Congress Catalog Card Number 84-45152
Printed in the United States of America
Librarians: Library of Congress cataloging information
appears on the last page of the book.

The paper in this book is acid-free and meets the guidelines
for permanence and durability of the Committee on Production
Guidelines for Book Longevity of the Council on Library Resources.

Contents

Preface

The essays that make up this collection focus on stages of behavior in Russian history—ways of acting and viewing the world that are characteristic of specific periods of the Russian past. The authors are well known, and their broad understanding of semiotic theory and literary analysis is much in evidence in this book. Their backgrounds, and their theoretical biases, make them at home with the formation of literary characters and literary style, and also with biographical and historical sources. The result not only sheds light on certain problems of Russian history but on a more theoretical plane, reveals unexpected aspects of the relationship between literature and the world beyond it.

The essays have been arranged in chronological order to follow the historical periods they describe. The opening essay, Lotman and Uspenskii's "Binary Models in the Dynamics of Russian Culture," is a broad overview of Russian cultural history that identifies certain dominant themes at work in both the pre-Petrine period and the eighteenth century. The second essay, "The Poetics of Everyday Behavior in Eighteenth-Century Russian Culture," provides additional detail and anecdotal material to develop the analysis begun in "Binary Models." In the third essay, "The Decembrist in Daily Life," Lotman crosses into the nineteenth century to focus on the behavior of the following generation, the noblemen involved in the abortive Decembrist uprising. The fourth essay, "Concerning Khlestakov," takes up the development and peregrinations of the group that came of age in the aftermath of the Decembrist movement. Finally, Ginsburg's essay deals with the intertwining of literature and life in the 1830s and 1840s, the generation of Belinskii, Bakunin, Stankevich and Herzen.

To an American eye, the considerable scope of these essays makes them seem, at times, a kind of intellectual three-ring circus. It may therefore be helpful to point the reader toward some of the things that are going on in them. First is a reevaluation of certain historical events in terms of the participants' behavior: the activities of the Decembrists and Decembrist wives ("The Decembrist in Daily Life"), Radishchev's suicide ("The Poetics of Everyday Behavior"), Chaadaev's early abandoning of a brilliant career ("The Decembrist in Daily Life"). The articles on the eighteenth and nineteenth centuries view behavior as a phenomenon of a particular era, often as a corollary of literary plot; the essay on "binary models," which discusses an earlier and much broader stretch of Russian history, concentrates on explaining why certain categories of behavior lasted in spite of superficial refocusing and renaming. A second major concern is the relation between literature and the extraliterary world, which reveals literature both as a reflector of behavior and as one of its formative influences. The use of literature as a historical document must take into account the distorting lens of literary structure, and Lotman offers extremely interesting observations on the relationship of neoclassicism and romanticism ("The Decembrist in Daily Life," "The Poetics of Everyday Behavior") and romanticism and realism ("Concerning Khlestakov") to the extraliterary world. Finally, the authors have presented and analyzed selections from numerous sources that in some unexpected way encapsulate an era. Some of these are well known; others, like the two separate descriptions of a landowner's ritualized reordering of daily life, have been unearthed from undeserved obscurity and stand out in their own right as extended and extremely curious historical anecdotes.

The American reader of these articles may find it helpful to know something about their academic context. The rules of academic discourse in the Soviet Union are different from those of the West. In the Soviet Union, the primary mode for communication in the humanities is oral: conversations, seminars, talks. A published article is a record of thoughts that have been put forward elsewhere. It is accepted as a kind of shorthand for work in progress, and the way it is written—as opposed to what it says—is not subject to particular scrutiny. Lidiia Ginsburg is a writer of great elegance, but Lotman and Uspenskii do not try in their writings for a particular precision of expression, nor do they see it as their task to do so.

In preparing these essays for the English-speaking reader, we have tried to interfere as little as possible with the original texts. Some material from the footnotes, in particular extended selections from interesting and otherwise unobtainable memoirs, has been transferred to the main text. As a result, the footnote numbers in the original and the translation do not agree. A different problem was presented by the authors' wide-ranging references to Russian cultural figures, both fictional and real. In the occasional places where we felt some explanation was needed, we have inserted brief glosses within the text. In the majority of cases, this is a matter of separating fictional characters (Griboedov's Molchalin) from historical figures (the Decembrist Ryleev) and supplying references to citations from Pushkin and Tolstoi. In some instances, the gloss is slightly longer: thus, instead of "translating" the Russian *Paleia* as the Greek/English "Palaea" and referring the reader to a footnote, we have left the word untranslated, inserting the explanation "a rendering, with commentary, of Old Testament texts." Such explanations proved necessary only for the essays by Lotman and Uspenskii—the essay by Lidiia Ginsburg presented few problems of this nature, and where necessary, the translator has supplied his own footnotes.

We express our deepest thanks to Boris Gasparov and Irina Paperno. It was with their advice and collaboration that this collection was conceived, and they played a crucial role in selecting articles, solving difficult problems of translation, and disentangling knotty references. Boris Gasparov, himself a prominent representative of the Tartu school now teaching at Stanford, kindly agreed to write the introduction. For this, and for all services unnamed, we are immeasurably grateful.

We also thank Judson Rosengrant, both for permission to use the first chapter from his translation of Lidiia Ginsburg's *On Psychological Prose* (to be published by Princeton University Press) and for long and instructive discussions on the art of translating. Ilya Serman of the Hebrew University, Jerusalem, Hugh Olmstead of Widener Library, Harvard University, Wayles Browne of Cornell and Agnes Langdon of Colgate University provided much-needed help in finding references. Patricia Ryan was, as always, our indomitable typist. This project was partly supported by a Cornell Humanities Faculty Development Grant, and also by the Cornell Soviet Studies Committee and the Colgate Research Council, whom we thank for their great generosity.

A. D. N.
A. S. N.

Hamilton, New York

The Semiotics of
Russian Cultural History

Introduction

BORIS GASPAROV

Literature and all the social mechanisms associated with it—literary movements and criticism, literary circles and debates about the role of literature in society, all that can in sum be called "literary life"—have played an exceptional role in Russian culture during the past two centuries. Russian literary life has been far more than one component among the many that make up social life. In the nineteenth century in particular, it served as a replacement for those political, social, legal, and even economic phenomena that could not develop fully in Russian society. Literary works and literary debates were seen as a substitutes—if not complete, then at least symbolic—for all the activities whose normal manifestations were blocked by political conditions, and perhaps also by psychological difficulties created by the social structure. As early as the mid-eighteenth century, and particularly after Pushkin, many educated Russians saw their literature as an all-embracing "guide to life." Literature was regarded, and even regarded itself, as containing the solution to moral problems and the answer to cardinal philosophical questions. It was a political program for the transformation of society, a codex of individual behavior, a way of understanding the national past, and a source of prophecy about the future.

What can be termed the sanctification of literature (an attitude that often included the santification of the writer as well) became a conscious element of Russian nineteenth-century society through the writing of the critic Vissarion Belinskii (1811-1848). Over the next century, despite the enormous changes in both life and art, this dominant theme of Russian culture remained unaltered. The so-called "realistic critics" of the 1860s sought to explain to the public those aspects of real life which were present, or, in their opinion, should have been present, in contemporary poetry and prose. Much later, the symbolists, with their idea of "life–building," endeavored to transform every detail of ordinary life into an artistic sign. For all their apparent differences, the two schools are variations on a single principle: the expansion of literature into life. And in both cases, the realization of this idea was carried to an extreme that shaded into the grotesque.

The intensity with which the literary process was experienced had its negative aspects. The reading public, the critics, and sometimes even the writers themselves concentrated on the secondary functions of the literary work. Trying to establish the closest possible ties between the literary text and life, they formulated the mythologized image of literature as the "guide to life" and missed the purely artistic message of the work—the meaning inherent in and unique to its artistic organization.

Russian formalism of the 1910s and 1920s was a natural reaction to this tradition; its radical nature matched the strength of the tradition against which it was directed. Formalism emphasized the structural relations inherent in literature and literary life, which kept the latter separate from nonliterary reality. The formalists isolated any literary fact—from the construction of a single work to the origin and competition of literary movements—from the tangle of real-life phenomena in one way or another connected with it, and examined it solely from the viewpoint of its internal structure. Boris Eichenbaum and Victor Shklovskii replaced social and psychological analyses with the question of how a work was "made." In the same way, the formalists explained the development of literature over time not in reference to the influence of external factors, but as a series of innovations peculiar to literature itself whose purpose was to "defamiliarize." Eventually, these "defamiliarizing" innovations themselves became canons of mass literary culture, creating in their stead the necessity for further decanonization (Iurii Tynianov).

In the 1920s, formalism was seen as a movement radically opposed to traditional views of literature. This oversimplificaiton gained wide acceptance at the same time that the formal method itself, in complete accord with Tynianov's law of literary evolution, became a standard tool of intellectual production. In the late 1920s and early 1930s this process was hard to see because of the extremely unfavorable external situation. But in the 1960s and 1970s, when the main principles of formalism had been taken over by the school of structuralist poetics, the tendency to canonize the formal method appeared in full force. The canonization, naturally enough, generated a search for a new way to "defamiliarize" the point of view of the researcher-observer, and the result was a partial restoration of ideas that had been pushed to the sidelines by the now ascendant formal school. (It has to be kept in mind that the idea of "ascendancy" in literary life, and especially in Russian literary life, is by no means always associated with numerical or institutional supremacy. More often it involves largely symbolic indications of cultural prestige, whose role in society may nonetheless be quite important. In fact, possessing an understated and unfixed nature may make their authority that much stronger).

During the 1930s, Tynianov, Eichenbaum, and Boris Tomashevskii wrote commentaries for collected editions of the Russian classics, and did research on the historical contexts in which those works were written, the daily life of the past. Their turning in such a direction may, of course, be written off to political pressure. But it is also possible that external pressures encouraged a tendency that was already present. In any event, such pressures played no role whatsoever in the analogous path taken some thirty years later by Iurii M. Lotman. As early as 1968, Lotman had organized a Tartu University seminar in the study of Russian daily life at the beginning of the nineteenth century, thus making the move from structural analysis in isolation to the study of the interrelationship between a literary work and its real-life context. This new phase— which may be called post-formalism or post-structuralism—resulted in the works presented in this book.

As it turned out, the structural method not only did not rule out an examination of extraliterary context; it even enriched that context with ideas. The positivist, teleological approach of the nineteenth-century "realistic critics" had admitted literature's role in society only to the extent that literature reflected the society's actual life or ideals. But the relationship between literature and society appears in a completely different light when viewed from the formalists' premise that literature, unlike everyday life, possesses a high degree of internal organization. If the structural ties that exist among the elements of a literary work are imposed onto the chaos of everyday life, they reveal in that chaos a certain *model* with a distinct structure and meaning. When the highly organized and conscious world of a literary work touches the endless continuum of human life, certain of the latter's discrete and interlinked elements are singled out. These elements are considered by society to be *relevant*. They are seen as having specific functions, and they are kept distinct from an enormous number of other facts, which, though no less important for everyday life, remain beyond society's field of vision because they are not essential to the model that the society, influenced by literature, has chosen for itself. What might have been seen—without the aid of literature—as a disorderly series of acts or even as the complete absence of any acts is immediately recognized by members of a particular culture as the configuration of "the superfluous man," "the romantic," "the decadent," "the natural man," "the rouge," and so on. Lidiia Ginsburg writes about this role of literature in the introduction to her book *On Psychological Prose*: "Art is always organization, a struggle with chaos and nonbeing, with the transitory flow of life."[1]

Such a process is possible only when a literary work possesses features in which many readers can recognize their real-life experience or thoughts. But no matter how precise the correspondence between literary plot or character and an actual social phenomenon, a work of literature always has something that is missing in real life: the intentional selection of all the elements that compose it, and the structural ties among them. It is this distinctive quality of literature which determines its influence on society. Literature does not fulfill its role as the "guide to life" (more precisely, the "model of life") *despite* its purely artistic qualities but rather by virtue of them. Studying the structure of a literary text is therefore an important means of analyzing social life—first because artistic structure influences life directly, and second because this structure is an ideal model which can be used to describe the much more complicated and multifaceted processes that take place in society.

Such are the basic ideas behind the studies which arose out of structuralist poetics in the 1970s. Their effect has been the definition of a new discipline, a blend of structuralist poetics, social psychology, and anthropology. This discipline, which could be called *the semiotic aspects of social behavior*, examines social life as the realization of cultural codes developed by society. Cultural codes are systems of more or less conventional signs that a member of a given society must internalize in order to participate competently in that society's life. The possessor of such a cultural code is able to distinguish within the flow of raw experience those elements

[1]Lidiia Ginsburg, *O psikhologicheskoi proze*, 2d ed. (Moscow, 1976), p. 14. English translation of the first edition (Leningrad, 1971) by R. Judson Rosengrant forthcoming from Princeton University Press.

significant from the point of view of his culture, identify their value, and react to them.

Like any native language, the codes of social behavior are not consciously created or learned, they are acquired during the ordinary practice of social relations. Any system with a heightened and deliberate internal organization will tend to play an important role in this process of internalization. In the European context of the past two centuries, literature has been one of the most significant systems of this type. Patterns that organize real-life materials within a work of literature have an influence on the cultural codes of everyday behavior that can be compared to the influence of highly organized literary language on ordinary speech. For this reason, the study of the structure of the literary text and the mechanisms of literary development provided a necessary foundation for work in the semiotics of behavior.

Thus, a critical school that began in radical opposition to the teleological approach eventually took up the question of literature's social role. Though the methods of study have completely changed, the question itself has once again assumed a dominant role in Russian cultural life. The pioneering works that overcame the canonization of structuralist methods have unexpectedly returned us— although on a different level of analysis—to the ideological tradition of Russian literary criticism, and the view of literature as the "guide to life."

The first explicit formulation of the new approach appeared in the works of Lidiia Ginsburg.[2] Ginsburg belongs to the younger generation of Russian formalists, educated by the founders of the formal school at Leningrad's Institute for the History of the Arts. Characteristic of her work is a heightened interest in texts that lie on the border between literature and nonliterary documents: memoirs, diaries, correspondence, descriptions of the rituals of life within artistic groups. This interest she shares with many of the older formalists, particularly Tynianov, who saw the "peripheral" genres as an important source for bringing about the renewal of stultified and canonized literary forms. In some periods—the Russian 1830s and 1840s, or the age of symbolism—such genres were at the center of literary life; in other periods they were pushed far to the sidelines and ceased to be viewed as literary texts. Their fluctuation between literary and nonliterary status gives documentary genres a partic-

[2]This approach was also implicit in G. Vinokur, *Biografiia i kul'tura* (Moscow, 1927).

ularly important role in the process through which literary models influence codes of social behavior. Ginsburg first took up this problem in 1926 in her article on Viazemskii as a man of letters,[3] and then later in 1957 in her study of Aleksandr Herzen,[4] but its fullest exposition appears in her book *On Psychological Prose*, which was itself an important stimulant to the development of the semiotics of behavior.

The central theme of the book, as formulated in the introduction, is "the correlation between a given historical period's concept of personality and its artistic representation."[5] At first glance, this seems like a direct continuation of the ideas of Vissarion Belinskii and the other proponents of the Russian "natural school." Even the book's title is reminiscent of the Russian critical tradition of the last century. However, this unabashedly traditional theme is presented in a completely new way. For Ginsburg, "psychological prose" is not a secondary reflection or description of actual human consciousness; it is a highly organized artistic model with a powerful reverse influence on society's self-conciousness. The primacy of life in relation to literature is the primacy of raw, chaotic material. Defined and structured by a literary model, this material is given a new idealized existence in the minds of members of the society. Ginsburg writes: "A highly organized aesthetic system is a powerful force for a movement of culture. Tolstoi, Dostoevskii, and the other great novelists showed what a 'secondary reality,' thought up by a genius, can become for the spiritual life of humankind."[6]

Ginsburg's book is represented in this collection by its first chapter, an examination of Russian literary life of the 1830s and 1840s. These decades were a period of diaries and correspondence that aspired to literary expressiveness, and also of literary circles with highly ritualized social forms. These circles had a decisive influence on such important cultural figures as Mikhail Bakunin, Herzen, Dostoevskii, and Nikolai Nekrasov. Belinskii took up the "natural school" and "realistic criticism" during this period, and the *raznochintsy*, the plebeian intelligentsia, became established as an alternative to aristocratic culture. All these factors played a formative role in the development of literature and the synthesis of a spiritual life for society as a whole. Ginsburg documents the formation of

[3]Ginsburg, "Viazemskii-literator," in *Russkaia proza* (Leningrad, 1926), pp. 102-134.
[4]Ginsburg, *Byloe i dumy Gertsena* (Leningrad, 1957).
[5]Ibid., 2d ed., p. 5.
[6]Ibid., p. 32.

literary models of personality types, situations, and social relations, showing the decisive importance of these models for contemporary behavior and self-consciousness.

Russian literary models had a number of European sources: the life and art of Jean-Jacques Rousseau; the idealist philosophy of Fichte, Schelling, and Hegel; and German romanticism. These sources coalesced with purely Russian social and artistic problems, emerging in the creative work of people who had been drawn into the process of spiritual "self-organization." The process resulted in the appearance of literary models like that of the prophet-messiah who combined "demonism" and titanic "rebelliousness" with the role of "man-god"; such a prophet was invariably surrounded by a group of infatuated women. The model was worked out and realized in life by Mikhail Bakunin. Another example is the "teacher," passionate and shy, an idealist-*raznochinets* who dies young from poverty and illness. Such was Vissarion Belinskii. Then there is the model of youthful romantic friendship, devoted to the service of humanity (Aleksandr Herzen and Nikolai Ogarev), and finally that of the disenchanted young man, whose indignation leads him to destroy romantic "chimeras" (Ivan Turgenev). These ideal representations, borrowed from books or spontaneously created in the process of literary life, were transformed into real behavior and actual life histories. Their reality became, in turn, inseparable from their artistic representations in letters, diaries, roles adopted by members of artistic groups, and finally literary images. Art and reality, the model and its projection in real life, are in continual interaction, creating a complex cultural fabric with no clear line between "literature" and "life."

Iurii M. Lotman is widely known as one of the founders of structural poetics of the 1960s. Yet Lotman's first works, dating from the 1950s, were not stucturalist at all; they were descriptive studies of various phenomena in the history of Russian culture from the late eighteenth to the early nineteenth century. (Among the works of this period, his monograph on Andrei Sergeevich Kaisarov and the literary-social polemics of his time should be especially noted.[7] This period was followed by a decade of intensive work in the field of structuralist poetics and the general theory of sign systems, resulting, among other works, in two important books:

---

[7]Iurii M. Lotman, *Andrei Sergeevich Kaisarov i literaturno-obshchestvennaia bor'ba ego vremeni, Uchenye zapiski Tartuskogo gosudarstvennogo universiteta*, no. 63 (Tartu, 1958).

the lectures in structuralist poetics (1964)[8] and *The Structure of the Artistic Text* (1970).[9] Subsequently, Lotman returned to the problems of Russian cultural history, introducing into this field the ideas and methods that had come together in the process of his work in poetics. More recently, he has been joined by a group of scholars, many of whom had been participants in his seminar in Russian everyday life, which ran from the late 1960s through the early 1970s. Their work laid the foundation for a new discipline: the semiotics of social behavior and everyday life. The material for it was for the most part Russian culture of 1780 to 1830. In addition to the articles published in the present collection, Lotman's most significant contributions in this area include his volume of commentaries on *Eugene Onegin*,[10] particularly the section called "A study of noble life in the Onegin period"; his article on theater and theatricalness in Russian culture of the early nineteenth century;[11] and the commentaries on Nikolai Karamzin's *Letters of a Russian Traveler*.[12] An important work relating to the same period of Russian cultural history is Larisa Vol'pert's study of the correspondence of the Pushkin circle.[13]

Lotman has consistently been interested in the dynamic relationship between the social norm and its violation in individual behavior. His interpretation of the structural approach does not absolutize the structure of the social code, but includes the anomalies in its realization among the factors necessary for its existence. Variations from accepted norms are important not only because they may lead in time to the changing of these norms, but also because they could not be perceived apart from the background of a working normative code. For this reason, anomalies serve as a confirmation, albeit a negative one, of the existence of a social

[8]Lotman, *Lektsii po struktural'noi poetike* (Tartu, 1964).

[9]Lotman, *Struktura khudozhestvennogo teksta* (Moscow, 1970; English translation, *The Structure of the Artistic Text*, translated and with a foreword by Ronald Vroon (Ann Arbor: Michigan Slavic Publications, 1977).

[10]Lotman, *Roman A. S. Pushkina Evgenii Onegin: kommentarii* (Leningrad, 1980).

[11]Lotman, "Teatr i teatral'nost' v stroe russkoi kul'tury nachala XIX v," in Lotman, *Stat'i po tipologii kul'tury*, no. 2 (Tartu, 1973), pp. 42-73. Translated in *Semiotics and Structuralism: Readings from the Soviet Union*, edited and introduced by Henryk Baran (White Plains, N.Y.: International Arts and Sciences Press, 1976).

[12]Lotman, *Pis'ma russkogo puteshestvennika N. M. Karamzina: Literaturnye pamiatniki* (forthcoming).

[13]L. I. Vol'pert, "Druzheskaia peripiska Pushkina Mikhailovskogo perioda: sentiabr' 1824 g--dekabr' 1825 g, *Pushkinskii sbornik* (Leningrad, 1977), pp. 54-62. An extended version appears in Vol'pert, *Pushkin i psikhologicheskaia traditsiia vo frantsuzskoi literature* (Tallin, 1980), pp. 6-41.

code: "A norm and its violation are not locked into a static state of contradiction, they are continually changing places. Rules arise for violating rules and violations appear that are essential to norms. A person's actual behavior will vacillate between these poles."[14]

Lotman's approach to the subject goes back to Tynianov's theory of literary evolution, which perceives the literary life of any period as the juxtaposition and interaction of standard ("canonic") and substandard phenomena. These opposing poles do more than simply struggle for ascendancy, periodically changing places in the functional hierarchy as the "younger branch" becomes the new canon. They also need each other, since one pole cannot be perceived without reference to its opposite. Lotman's system differs from Tynianov's theory on two accounts. First, he has radically extended the scope of Tynianov's theory, not limiting it to literature, but expanding it to cover the entirety of culture. Second, he has made consistent use of the concept of langue versus parole, borrowed from structuralist linguistics. This analogy permits a precise formulation of the relation between the ideal rules of social behavior and the way these rules are put into practice. More precisely, Lotman sees the real life of a society as a text ("parole") organized according to a specific cultural code (its language).

The analogy with language has a more than methodological significance. In their studies of Russian cultural history, Lotman and Boris Uspenskii have demonstrated the actual parallelism and relationship between social processes and the state of the standard language. Thus, the "duality" of eighteenth-century Russian culture following Peter's reforms, with its hierarchical division into public and private (domestic) spheres of behavior, has its correspondence in the division of language into two styles, with the use of each style strictly regimented.[15] The debate about language in the early nineteenth century reflects the changes taking place in psychology and behavior.[16] Finally, the shape of social behavior in the period from 1810 to the early 1820s is closely tied to the cultivation of various genres of spoken language, from oratory to improvisations among friends. In this sense, Lotman's article on

---

[14]Lotman, "Dekabrist v povsednevnoi zhini,"*Literaturnoe nasledie dekabristov* (Leningrad, 1975), p. 26. Translated in this volume as "The Decembrist in Daily Life."

[15]Lotman, "Poetika bytovogo povedeniia v russkoi kul'ture XVIII veka," *Trudy po znakovym sistemam*, no. 8 (Tartu, 1977), pp. 65-89. Translated in this volume as "The Poetics of Everyday Behavior in Eighteenth-Century Russian Culture."

[16]Lotman and B. A. Uspenskii, "Spory o iazyke v nachale XIX veka kak fakt russkoi kul'tury," *Uchenye zapiski Tartuskogo gosudarstvennogo universiteta*, no. 358 (Tartu, 1975), pp. 168-254.

the function of spoken language in the cultural life of the Pushkin period,[17] and an article by Irina Paperno on reconstructing spoken language from written sources which considers the language of literary circles and subliterary genres in the Pushkin period[18] are important additions to the study of the everyday behavior of the Decembrists presented in this volume.

Using the concept of "parole" to cover the observed facts of culture provides a methodology for work with source materials. The meaning of the information appearing in these sources must not be taken literally. Such sources are realizations of a given cultural language and can be understood only on the basis of that language. Reading them becomes an exercise in cultural "translation" from the appropriate language of cultural signs, hypothetically reconstructed by the researcher. It is essential to follow this rule even when using relatively reliable sources, oriented toward the objective presentation of facts. On the other hand, provided it is read with an understanding of the appropriate cultural language, even the most fantastic and unreliable text can give valuable information about a cultural period. In recent years, Uspenskii, Lotman, and some of Lotman's students have provided brilliant examples of the semiotic reading of "compromised" sources. Among the most notable are Uspenskii, "Historia sub specie semioticae";[19] Lotman, "On Foreigners' Impressions of Russia as Source Material;"[20] K. A. Kumpan and I. A. Paperno on deciphering the memorist's position, examining the treatment of Paul I in the papers of N. A. Sablukov;[21] and M. B. Plukhanova on Kreshkin's history of the youth of Peter I.[22]

[17]Lotman, "K funktsii ustnoi rechi v kul'turnom bytu pushkinskoi epokhi," *Semiotika ustnoi rechi–Lingvisticheskaia semantika i semiotika II, Uchenye zapiski Tartuskogo gosudarstvennogo universiteta*, no. 481 (Tartu, 1979), pp. 107-120.

[18]I. A. Paperno, "O rekonstruktsii ustnoi rechi iz pis'mennykh istochnikov: kruzhkovaia rech' i domashniaia literatura v pushkinskuiu epokhu," *Semiotika ustnoi rechi—Lingvisticheskaia semantika i semiotika I, Uchenye zapiski Tartuskogo gosudarstvennogo universiteta*, no. 442 (Tartu, 1978), pp. 122-134.

[19]Uspenskii, "Historia sub specie semioticae," in *Materialy Vsesoiuznogo simpoziuma po vtorichnym modeliruiushchim sistemam*, 1(5) (Tartu, 1974), pp. 119-130. English translation in *Semiotics and Structuralism: Readings from the Soviet Union*; and also in *Soviet Semiotics*, ed. Daniel P. Lucid (Baltimore: Johns Hopkins University Press, 1977).

[20]Lotman, "K voprosu ob istochnikovedcheskom znachenii vyskazyvanii inostrantsev o Rossii," *Sravnitel'noe izuchenie literatur* (Leningrad, 1976), pp. 125-132.

[21]K. A. Kumpan and I. A. Paperno, "K deshifrovke pozitsii memuarista: Pavel 1 v zapiskakh N. A. Sablukova," *Trudy po znakovym sistemam*, no. 7 (Tartu, 1975), pp. 112-119.

[22]M. B. Plukhanova, "Istoriia iunosti Petra 1 u P. N. Krekshina," *Uchenye zapiski Tartuskogo gosudarstvennogo universiteta*, no. 513 (Tartu, 1981), pp. 17-39.

The second article in the present collection, Lotman's "Poetics of Everyday Behavior in Eighteenth-Century Russian Culture," gives a semiotic interpretation of historical "texts" of this period of Russian culture. The ritualized imitation of Western cultural forms gave Russians of the period a self-conscious awareness of theatricality and "masquerade." Lotman writes: "Play-acting at everyday life, the feeling of being forever on the stage, is extremely characteristic of Russian gentry life eighteenth century. The emphasis on the artificiality of "correct" social behavior and the fact that its code had to be learned by members of the society as though it were a foreign language had a paradoxical result. The "Europeanization" of Russian society did not replace traditional, archaic cultural forms, but on the contrary turned them into an essential background for Europeanized social behavior: ". . . despite what is generally believed, Europeanization accentuated rather than obliterated the non-European aspects of daily life. In order to perceive one's own behavior as consistently foreign, it was essential *not to be* a foreigner: for a foreigner, foreign behavior is not foreign. What was needed was to assimilate forms of European daily life while retaining an external 'alien' Russian attitude toward them. In this way, in place of the traditional view of eighteenth-century Russian life as a superficial layer of Europeanized culture imposed on the thick stratum of national tradition, Lotman constructs a more organic model in which the two contradictory directions do not simply coexist, but presume and define each other. This model permits the rereading of numerous facts relating to various aspects of life at the time.

In "The Decembrist in Daily Life," Lotman takes up the behavior of the noblemen in and around the circle that organized the abortive uprising of December 14, 1825. The majority of Decembrists belonged to the generation of Russian nobles nurtured by the ideas of the French Revolution and the Napoleonic wars. It was this generation that brought to Russian society the political, ethical, and aesthetic concepts of the European enlightenment and early romanticism. Lotman's article about them is a model of a systematic description of the semiotics of behavior during a given period—in this case, the period from the late 1810s to the early 1820s. Characteristic of Lotman's work is the wide array of sources the article employs in creating a model to encompass factors that affect culture ranging from literary images and historical events to individual peculiarities in the personalities of some major figures of the period.

Among the most important features of the psychological and

behavioral model of the Decembrist, as Lotman describes it, is the insistence on the "seriousness" of behavior. Even the most "trivial" details of everyday life, which the preceding epoch considered culturally irrelevant, are brought into the sphere of public expression and take on semiotic significance. Thus the role of explicit self-expression is heightened, the oratorical pose and the public "gesture" are emphasized, and the influence of literary models increases. Particularly important were images and plots from antiquity, which the Decembrists took as their main source for evaluating actual situations and determining their own conduct. By reconstructing the cultural language used by the future Decembrists and their compatriots in the decade before 1825, Lotman is able to give a new explanation for certain features of the Decembrists' behavior which initially seem paradoxical. First among these is their contradictory attitude toward conspiracy: even as they conspired together and maintained secret societies, they nonetheless cultivated specific traits of public behavior that served to single them out as potential conspirators. Second is their confusion during the closed investigations that followed the failure of the uprising, because they were then in a situation in which they could no longer make use of the familiar stereotypes of theatricalized behavior and literary models. Finally, Lotman brilliantly demonstrates the role of the cultural code in creating the halo that came to surround the wives of the Decembrists who followed their husbands into Siberian exile.

The result of this study is a completely new understanding of the role of the Decembrists in the development of Russian culture. For Lotman, the significance of the Decembrists' ideas and writings was secondary to that of their creation of a particular type of character, a particular model of psychology and behavior. This model had a strong and protracted influence on Russian society, an influence that can be compared to that of Pushkin on the development of Russian literature. It was thus in the creation of a behavioral model that the "creative energy" of the Decembrists had its most significant results, while the "poetry of the Decembrists was to a great extent eclipsed by the work of their brilliant contemporaries Zhukovskii, Griboedov, and Pushkin," and their political ideas "had become outmoded by the generation of Belinskii and Herzen."

The essay "Concerning Khlestakov" examines the years immediately following the defeat of the Decembrists. Lotman uses Khlestakov, a central figure in Gogol's play *The Inspector General*, as an ideal model for reconstructing certain aspects of the cultural consciousness of the period. The era of Khlestakov witnesses the disintegration of the highly developed cultural type shaped by the Decembrists, and in this process various features of the preceding period reappear in grotesque guises and recombine themselves in extremely odd ways. This reshaping of the cultural code both generates the special social type of the "adventurer" and fosters the real-life existence of situations reminiscent of Gogol's comedy. The only difference is that in some of these situations the actors belonged to the highest levels of government and were responsible for the direction of the vast government apparatus.

The four essays just discussed provide a semiotic analysis of four contiguous periods of Russian cultural history. Each period covers from ten to twenty years; in their totality, they run from the second half of the eighteenth century well into the 1840s. That the stretch of Russian history selected for this detailed and systematic analysis should reach its end simultaneously with Russian literary romanticism is not accidental. Classical and romantic literature created active models for characters and situations which had a direct impact on the behavior and psychology of their time. The conventionality or "literariness" of these models is obvious, making it relatively easy to find examples of their influence on cultural phenomena of the approriate period. Performing an analogous operation on the second half of the nineteenth century, the period of literary realism, is much more difficult. Since the expressed aim of realistic literature is the maximally precise reproduction of reality, it is particularly hard to isolate the artistic model and analyze its influence on society. Discovering that realistic literature depicts an *imitation* of reality far more than it depicts reality itself requires a special effort. The apparent absence of an immanent artistic model is the mark of a specific type of model whose hidden nature makes its exceptionally complex. Any work of literature is a conventional artistic coding of reality. But on top of this, a realistic work performs another operation on the literary code, giving it the appearance of "natural" mimicry, an unconditioned imitation of reality. Lotman has this problem in mind when, comparing the literary codes of romanticism and realism, he notes that "in some respects it may be said that realism is more conventional than romanticism."[23] One can hope that the analysis of the literary codes of realism will result

---

[23]Lotman, "O Khestakove," *Trudy po russkoi i slavianskoi filologii*, no. 26 (Tartu, 1975), p. 52. Translated in this volume as "Concerning Khlestakov."

in studies that can show the influence of realistic literary models on Russian culture in the second half of the nineteenth century.

Lotman and Uspenskii's article "Binary Models in the Dynamics of Russian Culture" has a special place in the present collection. Unlike the other essays, which examine limited historical periods, this essay proposes a universal model for the development of Russian culture from the Christianization of Rus' at the end of the tenth century to the end of the eighteenth. The article can be read as a summary of a whole cycle of essays that the two authors wrote during the 1970s. It is closely linked with Uspenskii's work on Russian medieval culture and Russian cultural "bilingualism," as the cult of St. Nicholas viewed in a historical-cultural light,[24] and the problem of Christian-tribal syncretism in Russian cultural history.[25] A second source is Lotman's works on cultural typology, in which fundamental linguistic concepts—syntagmatic versus paradigmatic, syntax versus semantics, spoken versus written language, and so on—are used as parameters for a generalized semiotic model of culture. Note in particular his volume of articles on the typology of culture[26] and the essay concerning two models of communication in a cultural system.[27]

Like much of what they wrote separately, the article on binary models attempts a semiotic interpretation of the entirety of Russian history and culture on the basis of one dominating invariant factor which the authors see as sharply differentiating Russia from the West. This factor is the duality of Russian culture: the division of cultural life into two contradictory spheres, one of which functions as "elevated" (sacred) and the other as "low" (profane). The actual content of the two contrasting spheres can be changed completely from one historical period to another. Moreover, the functional status of cultural phenomena can change with time: what was once "on top" (in the sphere of the sacred) can be "down below" in a different historical period (and here we may note once again the influence of Tynianov's theory of literary evolution). But the existence of two spheres and hence of two contrasting behavioral codes is a constant and immutable law that applies to the most

[24]Uspenskii, "Kul't Nikoly na Rusi v istoriko-kul'turnom osveshchenii," *Trudy po znakovym sistemam*, no. 10 (Tartu, 1978), pp. 86-140.

[25]Uspenskii, "K probleme khristiansko-iazycheskogo sinkretizma v isttorii russkoi kul'tury," *Vtorichnye modeliruiushchie sistemy* (Tartu, 1979), pp. 54-62.

[26]Lotman, *Stat'i po typologii kul'tury*, no. 1 (Tartu, 1970).

[27]Lotman, "O dvukh modeliakh kommunikatsii v sisteme kul'tury," *Trudy po znakovym sistemam*, no. 6 (Tartu, 1973), pp. 227-243.

varied cultural phenomena. This law not only permits but demands that "native speakers" of Russian culture radically change their behavior and their reactions as they move from one situation to another, in accordance with the appropriate cultural sphere and behavioral code. Russian "double faith"—the maintenance of pagan patterns within the Christian consciousness as an alternative type of behavior; Russian–Church Slavonic bilingualism; the juxtaposition of Europeanized and traditional Russian forms of behavior—all these are concrete realizations of the invariant cultural plan in different areas of culture and different historical periods. This pattern, in the opinion of the authors, makes Russian culture markedly different from that of Western Europe, where the dominant role belongs to a "middle," semiotically neutral sphere of behavior, viewed by society as neither sacred nor profane.

To engage in this order of generalization is not without a certain risk, since the skeptically inclined reader could come up with numerous counterexamples in both Russian and Western culture. It is enough to remember the "carnivalization" of Western medieval and Renaissance society (to borrow Bakhtin's term), in which the presence of binary rules of behavior and the ability to make radical shifts from one system of rules to the other are clearly evident. Certainly Bakhtin's ideas were a direct influence on this model of cultural typology. What is paradoxical is that these ideas, developed by Bakhtin in his analysis of François Rabelais, should give rise to a theory which aims to describe the specifics of Russian culture.

Like any typology, a typology of culture cannot take account of all the details that would be pertinent to a description of a single historical period. For this reason, the numerous examples from both Russian and Western culture that contradict a binary typology do not in themselves constitute a powerful argument against it. It is far more important, in my opinion, to consider the theory's accuracy in re-creating the traditional outlook of Russian culture on the West through the language of semiotics.

The characteristic Russian view of the Western world can be observed in Russian cultural history beginning no later than the sixteenth century. It involves the defining of the West in strictly negative terms, making it into a mythologized "antiworld" whose parameters are determined from Russian culture—or at least from the image of Russian culture in the minds of its "native speakers"— by a process of inversion. Over the course of history, Russian culture has ascribed both good and bad qualities to itself, but no matter what the state of its self-image, it always saw the West as either lacking those particular qualities, or as possessing diametrically opposed ones. A typical example is the nineteenth-century debate between "westernizers" and "slavophiles." Though they came to opposite conclusions, both sides held an image of the West that was a purely automatic antipode to their conception of Russia. Indeed, Lotman and Uspenskii may be said to depart from this perspective only in that their exclusive purpose is the reinterpretation of the past, while the primary goal of earlier formulations was prophecy about the future. Their article is a brilliant analysis of certain phenomena reflecting this Russian attitude toward the West. Paradoxically, the very model they construct in the course of the analysis reflects a cultural bias no less than the material it seeks to explain. This binary model is in fact not so much a metatex—a description or interpretation—as it is a *text* of Russian culture; it does not interpret and explain so much as it spontaneously reflects the deep structure of the Russian cultural consciousness. In considering this theory, one should remember Lotman's principle regarding the use of textual sources. For the meaning of the Lotman-Uspenskii theory need not be taken literally; it can be "decoded" with an eye to the specific cultural language that produced it. If the semiotic alteration is kept in mind, the works which develop the binary typological model become a valuable and unique source for two areas of study: the history of Russian culture and its contemporary state.

How then, does Soviet research in the semiotics of culture and behavior relate to other studies of culturally patterned behavior?[28] Because of the rigid and conservative compartmentalization of Soviet science, the whole field of cultural and psychological anthropology remains underdeveloped in the USSR, where "anthropology" means primarily physical anthropology and ethnology. In this situation, the semiotics of culture and behavior has taken upon itself functions that elsewhere belong in the domain of science (anthropology), but in the Soviet Union have not developed into independent scientific fields of research. The semiotics of culture, based mainly on the analysis of literary texts, fills this gap in the same way that literature itself replaced those aspects of

---

[28]For the following discussion I am indebted to Irina Paperno. See I. A. Paperno, "The Individual in Culture: N. G. Chernyshevsky, a Study in the Semiotics of Behavior" (Ph.D. diss., Stanford University, 1984). Irina Paperno contributed to this article in other ways as well. Many of the ideas expressed here arose from our conversations.

social, political, and intellectual life that were suppressed in nine-teenth-century Russia.

Soviet studies in the semiotics of culture and behavior cannot, of course, be considered a complete analogue of the Western fields of cultural and psychological anthropology. For one thing, the semiotic approach by and large excludes psychological considerations from the interpretation of personality and concentrates solely on those aspects of human behavior that are culturally significant. At the same time, the peculiar status of semiotics among other human and social sciences allows it to incorporate some of the strategies and dimensions of research which have not been emphasized by traditional cultural studies. Most important, the semiotics of culture has developed a sophisticated apparatus for the analysis of various cultural texts (both narrative texts and "texts of behavior") based on the methodology of contemporary structural linguistics, poetics, and literary analysis. Cultural anthropology, on the other hand, relies almost entirely on field research. Anthropologists seldom deal with written texts and, indeed, do not have an adequate technique for their analysis. As a result, anthropological studies are mostly limited to small, homogeneous non-Western societies and to contemporary Western cultures. Cultural anthropology remains ill equipped for the diachronic study of culture and the analysis of those aspects of contemporary cultures which are inextricable from literary activity and historical tradition.

Seen within the framework of cultural studies, the semiotics of culture and behavior provides a "missing link" between such forerunners of the field as Jacob Burckhardt, Nikolai Danilevskii, and Oswald Spengler, and modern cultural and psychological anthropology. It makes it possible to consider culture as lived by individuals within the traditional typological and historical study of complex literate civilizations.

Binary Models in the Dynamics of Russian Culture (to the End of the Eighteenth Century)

IURII M. LOTMAN AND BORIS A. USPENSKII

Culture in its broadest sense may be understood as a non-hereditary memory of a group, expressed in a certain system of prohibitions and commandments.[1] Such an understanding by no means precludes an axiological approach to culture: in fact, for the group itself, culture always appears as a system of values. The distinction between these approaches may be reduced to the difference between the external point of view of an observer and the internal point of view of a "native speaker" of a culture. The axiological approach always considers the internal point of view, a culture's own self-consciousness. Those who study a culture using an axiological approach will nonetheless occupy the dissociated position of the outside observer: the internal point of view is what is being investigated. But seen in this way, the history of culture is not simply the dynamics of various prohibitions and commandments. It is also the dynamics of a culture's self-consciousness, which to varying degrees explains the corresponding changes in normative positions (that is, commandments and prohibitions).

Thus, culture—a system of collective memory and collective con-

Translated by Robert Sorenson from "Rol' dual'nykh modelei v dinamike russkoi kul'tury," *Trudy po russkoi i slavianskoi filologii*, no. 28 (Tartu, 1977), pp. 3-36.

[1] Lotman and Uspenskii, "O semioticheskom mekhanizme kul'tury," *Uchenye zapiski Tartuskogo gosudarstvennogo universiteta*, no. 284, *Trudy po znakovym sisteman*, 5 (Tartu, 1971), p. 147. (Note translation in *New Literary History* no. 9 [Winter 1978]—Ed.)

sciousness—is at the same time a unified value structure for the group. A culture's need for self-description, coupled with the necessity, at a certain stage, for a unified structuring of its values, has a strong effect on the culture being described. In creating its own model for itself, a culture has an active effect on the process of self-organization; it organizes itself hierarchically, canonizing some texts and excluding others. Eventually this model becomes a fact in the culture's history, and, as a rule, influences the ideas of posterity and the conceptions of historians. Our purpose, however, is not to make past models of cultural self-description into automatic texts for historical investigation, but rather to turn them into a specialized subject of investigation, as a particular type of cultural mechanism.

The history of Russian culture in the period we have selected provides convincing evidence of the culture's clear-cut division into stages that replace one another dynamically.[2] Every new period—whether that of the Christianization of Russia or of the reforms of Peter the Great—is oriented toward a decisive break with what preceded it. At the same time, however, the investigator will encounter a good many repeated or very similar events, historical-psychological situations, or texts. The regularity of such repetitions prevents us from writing them off as coincidences with no deeper causes. Moreover, they cannot be attributed to the remnants of receding cultural periods: such a view is contradicted by their stability and their active role in the cultural system to which they are contemporary. Analysis shows that new historical structures in pre-nineteenth-century Russian invariably include mechanisms that regenerate the culture of the past. The more dynamic the system, the more active are the mechanisms of memory which ensure the homeostasis of the whole.

The specific aspect of pre-nineteenth-century Russian culture that interests us here is its essential polarity, a polarity expressed in the binary nature of its structure. The basic cultural values (ideological, political, and religious) of medieval Russia were distributed in a bipolar field and divided by a sharp boundary without an axiologically neutral zone. A particular example will clarify what we have in mind. In Western Catholicism, the world beyond the grave is divided into three spaces: heaven, purgatory, and hell.

---

[2]We have not touched on the controversial question of historical periodization from the viewpoint of the contemporary investigator; our interest is in the divisions which were obvious to people within the culture.

Earthly life is correspondingly conceived of as admitting three types of behavior: the unconditionally sinful, the unconditionally holy, and the neutral, which permits eternal salvation after some sort of purgative trial. In the real life of the medieval West a wide area of neutral behavior thus became possible, as did neutral societal institutions, which were neither "holy" nor "sinful," neither "pro-state" nor "anti-state," neither good nor bad. This neutral sphere became a structural reserve, out of which the succeeding system developed. Inasmuch as continuity is obvious here, there is no necessity to emphasize it structurally, nor to re-create it consciously and artificially.

The Russian medieval system was constructed on an accentuated duality. To continue our example, one of its attributes was the division of the other world into heaven and hell. Intermediate neutral spheres were not envisaged. Behavior in earthly life could, correspondingly, be either sinful or holy. This situation spread into extra-ecclesiastical conceptions: thus secular power could be interpreted as divine or diabolical, but never as neutral.[3]

The presence of a neutral sphere in the medieval West led to the appearance of a certain subjective continuity between the negated present and the awaited future. The ideals of antifeudal thinkers were drawn from certain spheres of surrounding reality—the extra-ecclesiastical state, bourgeois family life—and these ideas were carried over into the ideal space of social theory, where they were interpreted in heroic or moralistic terms. The neutral sphere of life became the norm, and the greatly semioticized high and low spheres of medieval culture were forced into the category of cultural anomalies.

Russian culture of the medieval period was dominated by a different value orientation. Duality and the absence of a neutral axiological sphere led to a conception of the new not as a continuation, but as a total eschatological change. It is significant, in this sense, that the typical Western contrast between the positive world of the family and the negative kingdom of evil was completely absent in Russian culture. In the West, the image of the Mother of God, presented through a poetic prism of private family life, was an important one for Renaissance painting. It had no echo in Russian

---

[3]Lotman and Uspenskii, "Spory o iazyke v nachale XIX veka kak fakt russkoi kul'tury," *Uchenye zapiski Tartuskogo gosudarstvennogo universiteta*, no. 358, (Tartu, 1975), p. 173.

art at the corresponding moment of the dissolution of medieval consciousness.

Under such conditions, the dynamic process of historical change has a fundamentally different character: change occurs as a radical negation of the preceding state. The new does not arise out of a structurally "unused" reserve, but results from a transformation of the old, a process of turning it inside out. Thus, repeated transformations can in fact lead to the *regeneration* of archaic forms.

Given such a consistent and cyclically repeated "negation of negation," the possibility of forward development is determined by the appearance of a new perspective. At each new stage, changing historical conditions and, in particular, external cultural influences lead to a new perspective on cultural development that will activate one semantic parameter or another. As a result the same conceptions can appear at each stage furnished with a new content, depending on the point of departure.

These underlying structures of development are what allows us to speak of the unity of Russian culture at the various stages of its history. It is in the transformations that invariants are revealed. To a great extent this explains why, over various historical periods, Russia has been characterized by reactionary and progressive tendencies and not by conservatism.

1. Among the oppositions that structured Russian culture from the conversion to Christianity straight through to Peter's reforms, one of the most stable has been the opposition between "the old and the new." The activity and significance of this opposition is so great that from the subjective position of the "native speaker" of the culture, it has at various stages included or subsumed other singularly important contrasts, such as: "Russia versus the West," "Christianity versus paganism," "true faith versus false faith," "knowledge versus ignorance," "upper classes versus lower classes," and so on.

This essay is in large measure devoted to the difference between the subjective experience of these conceptions in the consciousness of participants in the historical process, and the meaning they objectively acquire in an integral cultural context. Its subject, in other words, is the complex dialectic of the mutual transitions and their interrelatedness.

1.1. The decisive milestone in the self-consciousness of Old Russia was the conversion to Christianity. It is in connection with this event that we find in historical sources the first definitions of the Russian land as "new" and of the Russians as "new people." In the *Povest' Vremennyx let (Primary Chronicle)*, Vladimir says in a prayer after baptism: "O Christ, O God, who made heaven and earth, look upon these new people."[4] Hilarion, in his "Sermon on Law and Grace," calls the Russian land "new skins" into which the new teaching has been poured.[5] It is not important to us that the epithet "new," used to characterize newly converted peoples, has its origin in an external tradition: in Russian history over the course of time it acquired a distinctive meaning covering a broad range of concepts.

The way in which "the old" is replaced by "the new" has deep significance. As Evgenii Anichkov has convincingly demonstrated, an attempt at creating an *artificial* pagan pantheon preceded the conversion of Old Russia: it may be that for the creation of a new "Christian" Russia a consolidated and largely artificial image of "the old" was a psychological necessity.[6]

The conversion itself occurred as a demonstrative exchange of places between the old (pagan) and the (Christian) religions. An external but very significant manifestation of this reversal was the spatial transfer of shrines in the process of baptism. The idol of Perun was cast down from the hills of Kiev to the Podol, that is, to the site of the Christian church of Elijah (the Christian double of Perun). A Christian church was then built on the hill, on the site of the former heathen temple.[7] Thus there was a radical exchange of "top" and "bottom." Vladimir (like Peter in a later era) inverted the existing system of relationships, changing pluses into minuses. He did not simply accept a new system of values, replacing the old with the new, but rather wrote the old into the new—with a minus sign.

The conversion of Russia had the character of a broad cultural-political change and was connected with Russia's entry into the sphere of Byzantine influence. For this reason, the early tendencies

---

[4]*Povest' vremennyx let*, ed. V. P. Adrianova-Perets, part. 1 (Moscow/Leningrad, 1950), p. 81.

[5]Ludolf Muller, *Des Metropoliten Ilarion Lobrede auf Vladimir den Heiligen und Glaubensbekenntnis* (Wiesbaden, 1962), p. 87.

[6]E. V. Anichkov, *Iazychestvo i Drevniaia Rus'* (St. Petersburg, 1914).

[7]Vladimir's idols had been set up on a hill above the Dnieper, and the church of Elijah was on the Podol, that is, down below. Then Vladimir demonstratively *cast down* the idols into the Dnieper, and laid the foundation for the Christian church of St. Basil (his patron saint) "on the hill where once stood the idols of Perun and the rest." *Povest' vremennyx let*, part 1, p. 81; cf. p. 56. If the church of Elijah stood "over the Ruchai," then Perun's idol was dragged down the present Kreshchatik and the Podol slope into the Ruchai, and thence into the Dnieper. Cf. Anichkov, p. 106.

to move away from Byzantine influence and the attempt to place the Greeks and their empire hierarchically lower than the Russian land are all the more notable. It is significant that this attempt brought about the labeling of Byzantium as the "old" state in contraposition to the "new" Russia. As early a figure as Hilarion, celebrating Russia's entry into the world of Christianity, refers condescendingly to the long-baptized Byzantium, comparing it to the *Old* Testament and to Hagar, ruled by a coercive law; Russia is compared to Sarah and the *New* Testament's grace.[8] These tendencies were expressed with particular clarity in the period dominated by the concept of Moscow as the "third Rome": after the fall of Constantinople, Russia thought of itself as the only bulwark of Orthodoxy, and messianic attitudes grew stronger. One must keep in mind that the fall of the Byzantine Empire more or less coincided with the Russian liberation from the Mongols. Thus, while in Byzantium Islam triumphed over Orthodoxy, in Russia Orthodoxy triumphed over Islam. Byzantium and Russia in a sense changed places, and as a result Russia became the center of the Orthodox, and therefore of the Christian, world.[9]

Even earlier, the monk Khrabr had asserted that the Slavonic language was more holy than the Greek, inasmuch as Greek was created by pagans and Church Slavonic by holy apostles; his words enjoyed wide popularity in Russia. In a Slavonic article about the creation of Russian grammar, which was included in the Tolkovaia Paleia, a rendering, with commentary, of Old Testament texts (the article has also come down to us in other copies), Russian grammar along with Russian faith, is seen as divinely revealed and independent of Greek mediation:

> Let it be known by all peoples and by all men, that the Russian tongue took this holy faith from no one, and that Russian writing was not revealed by anyone, but only by Almighty God himself, Father, Son, and Holy Spirit. The Holy Spirit inspired Vladimir to take the faith, and from the Greeks came baptism and the other rites. And Russian writing appeared, given by God, to a Russian in Korsun'; Constantine the philosopher learned from it, and thence he put together and wrote down books in the Russian tongue .... As for that Russian man, he lived according to the faith, with fasting and virtue in pure faith,

---

[8] I. N. Zhdanov, "Slovo o Zakone i Blagodati i Pokhvala kaganu Vladimiru," in Zhdanov, *Sochineniia*, vol. 1 (St. Petersburg, 1904), pp. 70-80.
[9] N. F. Kapterev, *Kharakter otnoshenii Rossii k pravoslavnomu vostoku v XVI i XVII stoletiiakh* (Moscow, 1914); M. D. Priselkov, "Nekrolog N. F. Kaptereva," *Russkii istoricheskii zhurnal*, book 5 (St. Petersburg, 1918), p. 315.

35

isolated alone, and he alone of the Russian people first became a Christian, and unknown to anyone, from whence he came.[10]

1.2. The stable conception of the Russian land as "new" was paradoxically combined with the activation of extremely archaic cultural models. The very concept of the "new" was a realization of notions whose roots go far into the past. One may note here two models for the construction of the "new culture":

(1) The deep structure formed in the preceding period is preserved, but completely renamed, while all the fundamental structural contours of the old are preserved. In this case *new texts* are created while the archaic cultural frame is preserved.

(2) The deep structure of the culture itself changes. Even in changing, however, it reveals a dependence upon the cultural model that existed earlier, insofar as it is constructed by turning the preceding "inside out," transposing it through a change in signs.

A vivid example is the way pre-Christian ideas penetrated into the cultural system of Christianity. The pagan Gods had a double fate: on the one hand, they could be identified with devils, thus relegated to a negative, but perfectly legitimate position in the system of the new religion. On the other hand, they could be merged with the Christian saints who replaced them functionally. As devils they could even keep their names; as saints, only their function. Thus Volos/Veles turns into the "hairy" devil *volosatik*, a wood goblin, and so on. He is at the same time transformed into St. Blaise (*Vlasii*), St. Nicholas, or St. George.[11] Mokosh' continued to live as an unclean power of the same name (cf. the dialectical *mokosh'* in the meaning "evil spirit";[12] it is interesting that the same word in contemporary dialects means "indecent woman"[13] cf. *venera* [Venus] with the same meaning in the urban jargon of the eighteenth and nineteenth centuries). Mokosh' is at the same time

---

[10]O. Bodianskii, "Kirill i Mefodii: Sobranie pamiatnikov, do deiatel'nosti sviatykh pervouchitelei i prosvetitelei slavianskikh plemen otnosiashchikhsia," *Chteniia v. imp. Obshchestve istorii i drevnostei rossiiskikh pri Moskovskom universitete*, 1863, book 2, p. 31; cf. N. K. Nikol'skii, "Povest' vremennykh let, kak istochnik dlia istorii nachal'nogo perioda russkoi pis'mennosti i kul'tury," *K voprosu o drevneishem russkom letopisanii*, no. 1 (Leningrad, 1930), p. 80, note 2.

[11]Uspenskii, "Kul't Nikoly na Rusi v istoriko-kul'turnom osveshchenii," *Trudy po znakovym sistemam*, no. 10 (Tartu, 1978).

[12]M. K. Gerasimov, "Slovar' uezdnogo Cherepovetskogo govora," *Sbornik Otdeleniia russkogo iazyka i slovesnosti imp. Akademii nauk*, vol. no. 3 (St. Petersburg, 1910), pp. 3 and 56; *mokosha* means "unclean spirit."

[13]A. F. Ivanova, *Slovar' govorov Podmoskov'ia* (Moscow, 1969), p. 267; *mokos'ia* means "promiscuous woman."

plainly identified with the early saint known in Russian as Par-
askeva-Piatnitsa[14] and even with the Mother of God.[15]

In the same way, the sites where pagan temples had been could
have one of two fates. In the first instance, the function of sanctity
could be preserved with the replacement of the pagan divinity by
a Christian saint (in essence, by a renaming of the divinity). The
opposite could also occur. The nature of the divinity could be
preserved (sometimes including the name), but with the function
transformed into its diametric opposite: the place could become
"unclean," an abode of demons. There is an interesting example
of how both these viewpoints, existing in separate cultural groups,
could intersect, creating a kind of double "reading" of one and the
same cultural fact. On the one hand we have the well-known custom, established on the authority of St. Vladimir, of building Christian churches on the sites of pagan temples. On the other hand,
there is a revealing legend in the manuscript collection of the Kazan'
Spiritual Academy, which describes how a church was struck by
lightning during Sunday service, since it had been built on a "wor-
ship-place of idols," and a birch and rock remained behind the
altar.[16] Likewise in Novgorod, a monastery (the so-called Perun
Monastery) was built to replace the idol of Perun, which had been
thrown into the Volkhov River; at the same time, as late as the
sixteenth century, pagan orgies still occurred annually on the spot.[17]

Of course, while the former site of a pagan temple might be
perceived as uninterruptedly holy by the parishioners, the clergy
saw such construction as the sanctification of an unclean place and
the expulsion of a demon from his own territory.[18] Thus, the build-

---

[14]Viach. Vs. Ivanov, V. N. Toporov, *Slavianskie iazykovye modeliruiushchie semioti-
cheskie sistemy (Drevnii period)* (Moscow, 1965), pp. 90, 150, and 190; V. N. Toporov,
"K ob"iasneniiu nekotorykh slavianskikh slov mifologicheskogo kharaktera v sviazi
c vozmozhnymi drevnimi mifologicheskimi paralleliami," in *Slavianskoe i balkanskoe
iazykoznanie: Problemy interferentsii i iazykovykh kontaktov* (Moscow, 1975), p. 20.

[15]Toporov, pp. 19-20; V. I. Chicherov, *Zimnii period russkogo zemledel'cheskogo ka-
lendaria XVI-XIX vekov: Ocherki po istorii narodnykh verovanii, Trudy instituta etnografii
AN SSSR,* new series, vol. 40 (Moscow, 1957), pp. 55-62.

[16]"O bor'be khristianstva s iazychestvom v Rossii," *Pravoslavnyi sobesednik,* August
1865, p. 226.

[17]Adam Olearii, *Opisanie puteshestviia v Moskoviiu i cherez Moskoviiu v Persiiu i obratno*
(a translation from the 1656 German edition of A. M. Loviagin) (St. Petersburg,
1906), pp. 128-129.

[18]According to the chronicle, Vladimir addressed the Lord with the following
prayer immediately after the conversion of Old Russia: " . . . help me, Lord, against
our hateful enemy, that relying on thee and on thy kingdom, I may overcome his
evil designs. And so saying, he commanded that churches be built and put in those
places where idols had stood." *Povest' vremennykh let,* part 1, p. 81.

ing of churches on pagan sites is directly connected with the battle against demonic powers. Elsewhere the chronicler enthusiastically exclaims: "Where in old times the infidels sacrificed to devils on the hills, there now stand holy churches, golden-roofed and stone-built, and monasteries full of monks, ceaselessly glorifying God in prayers, in vigil, in fasting, and in tears, by whose prayers the world endures.[19] Note, however, that in both cases the site was not perceived as indifferent to the opposition "holy" vs. "unclean"; it stood in contrast to neutral territories. The possibility of an exchange of members in this opposition was confirmed by the transformation of the holy into the unclean: it is well known that abandoned churches were a favorite residence of unclean powers (see Gogol's "Vii").

Buildings like bathhouses, barns, and smithies are interesting examples of the fate of pagan temples in the Christian world. There is reason to suppose that the perception of these places as "unclean" is connected with their special sacral significance in the pre-Christian life of the Eastern Slavs, that is, with their specialized role as family or domestic temples. In other words, pagan temples continued to preserve their cult functions in the Christian period, though with a minus sign. Particularly revealing is the common notion that bathhouses belong not to Christian but to unclean powers. (In the Christian consciousness this is understood as the power of the cross having abandoned bathhouses and other "unclean" places: the efficacy of unclean powers is generally connected with divine acquiescence.) Correspondingly, on holidays, when people go to church, wizards, who are never seen there, go to the *bathhouse*.[20] The bathhouse also appears as the traditional place of divination, sorcery, magical cures, and, of course, incantatory healings; the cult role of the bathhouse also shows up clearly in the marriage rite, where bathhouse rituals are no less important than the church ceremony: each complements the other. In view of all these connections, it is quite natural that in Russian folklore the bathhouse could receive the name *bozhena* (from *Bog*, God),

---

[19]A. A. Shakhmatov, "Predislovie k Nachal'nomu Kievskomu svodu i Nestorova letopis'," *Izvestiia Otdeleniia russkogo iazyka i slovesnosti imp. Akademii nauk*, vol. 13 (1908), book 1, p. 264.

[20]N. A. Nikitina, "K voprosu o russkikh koldunakh," *Sbornik Museia antropologii i etnografii AN SSSR*, vol. 7 (Leningrad, 1928), pp. 311-312. Cf. the songs about Grishka Otrep'ev, where Grishka is determined to be a wizard on this basis.

meaning, essentially "temple."[21] Just as characteristic, and just as common, is the idea that people go to the bathhouse to *pray* to the unclean power (in essence, incantations pronounced in a bath-house may be viewed as a kind of prayer). Note how this belief is expressed in the following Belorussian song:

> In the middle of Wolchkovskii village,
> La, la (refrain with banging and stomping)
> Lo, lo, there stood an oaken *bathhouse*:
> Li, li, li (refrain with banging)

> People would go there to pray to God,
> Embrace the post and kiss the stove,
> Prostrate themselves before Sopukha,
> They thought: the Immaculate Mother of God,
> But Sopukha was the unclean one![22]

Thus, pre-Christian forms of behavior could be preserved in the life of Orthodox Russia as a type of legitimate antibehavior. In certain places and at certain times the Christian was *compelled* to behave "incorrectly" according to the norms of Christian behavior. Correct behavior in the wrong place and at the wrong time was perceived as blasphemous, that is, as sinful. At Christmas and at a few other points in the ritual calendar, in visiting "unclean" places both within the Russian land and in the land of the "infidel," a special kind of behavior was called for, behavior with norms op-posed to the "correct" ones.[23] In practice this custom led to the conservation of the norms of pagan behavior.

To a significant extent, the new (Christian) culture organized itself by way of contrast to the old one; thus the old pagan culture, as anticulture, was a necessary condition for culture as such. In this way the "new culture," which conceived of itself as the ne-gation and complete annihilation of the "old," was in practice a powerful means of preserving the latter. The "new culture" in-

[21]P. S. Efimenko, "Materialy po etnografii russkogo naseleniia Arkhangel'skoi gubernii," *Izvestiia Obshchestva liubitelei estestvoznaniia, antropologii i etnografii pri imp. Moskovskom universitete*, vol. 30, *Trudy etnograficheskogo otd.*, book 5, part 1 (Moscow, 1877), p. 104; cf. Igor Vahros, "Zur Geschichte und Folklore der grossrussischen Sauna," *Folklore Fellows Communications*, vol. 82, no. 197 (Helsinki, 1966), pp. 199-200.
[22]Petr Bessonov, *Belorusskie pesni s podrobnymi ob"iasneniiami ikh tvorchestva i iazyka, s ocherkami narodnogo obriada, obychaia, i vsego byta*, no. 1 (Moscow, 1871), p. 29.
[23]Uspenskii, "Khozhdenie za tri moria Afanasiia Nikitina na fone iazykovoi i kul'turnoi situatsii drevnei Rusi," forthcoming.

cluded both inherited texts and past forms of behavior, whose functions had become a mirror image of what they were before.

In sum, the everyday practice of orthodoxy is an undervalued source for the reconstruction of the Eastern Slavic pagan cult.

1.3. Polemics with opposing ideologies inevitably becomes an important element in the self-definition of any cultural phenomenon. In the process of such polemics one's own position is formulated along with a revealing transformation of the position of the opponents. The Christianization of Russia not only required the "new faith" to define itself in relation to paganism, but drew the Russians into the polemics between Eastern and Western Christianity. It became necessary to take a stand in the fundamental ideological debate of the era. Paganism and "Latinism" were, in principle, phenomena of different kinds. The Old Russian scribes were clearly aware of the difference; they could even affirm that the Latin heretics were worse than the pagans, "because one cannot guard against them, as one can against the pagans. The Latins have the Gospels and the writings of the Apostles and other sacred things, and they go to church, but their faith and their law are unclean; they have befouled the whole earth."[24] In other words, "Latinism," unlike paganism, was perceived as a blasphemous parody of genuine Christianity, externally similar but with a different content: a sort of Orthodoxy inside out. Paganism and Catholicism in this context contrast with each other as an absence of information (entropy) versus false information.

At the same time a fundamentally different understanding of paganism becomes possible, in which it is interpreted as a false faith. In this case paganism and Catholicism are merged, in the perspective of the Orthodox consciousness, because of their antithetical opposition to the true faith. Both pagans and "Latins" appear to the Orthodox Christians of Kievan Russia as bearers of an "alien" faith. They are polemically identified with each other, and certain common characteristics begin to be ascribed to them. The result is a certain syncretic image of an "alien faith" in general. Old Russian scribes could speak of "Khors the Jew" and "the

---

[24]"Voproshenie kniazia Iziaslava, syna Iaroslava, vnuka Volodimirova, igumena Pecherskago velikago Feodosiia o Latine," in Andrei Popov, *Istoriko-literaturnyi obzor drevnerusskikh polemicheskikh sochinenii protiv latinian (XI-XV veka.)* (Moscow, 1875), p. 79. The citation is from a copy of the second recension of Feodosii's speech, as found in the sixteenth-century Rumiantsevskii Typicon (Kormchaia) of southern Russian origin. There are various opinions about the authorship: some scholars ascribe it to Feodosii Pecherskii, others to Feodosii the Greek, a writer of the twelfth century.

Hellenic elder Perun."[25] Insofar as paganism was thought of as non-Orthodoxy, non-Orthodoxy began to be thought of as paganism.

This identification had interesting consequences. We have seen how Orthodoxy took on certain norms of pre-Christian life as forms of legitimatized antibehavior. Now the reverse occurred: the forms of antibehavior were ascribed to the "Latins," whose image was constructed from Orthodox ideas about the "unclean" world and forbidden activity. As a result, genuine features of Russian pagan behavior, along with other "impieties," were ascribed to Western Christianity. This circumstance makes polemical works "against the Latins" a source that must not be ignored in the reconstruction of Eastern Slavic paganism.

Thus, an Old Russian denouncer of the Latins, on the basis of the Russian expression "damp Mother earth," which had a distinct ring of paganism for him, confidently ascribed similar conceptions to the Catholics: "They call the earth mother." And from this starting point he without hesitation reconstructed the whole text of the myth: "If the earth is their mother, then their father is the sky."[26]

[25]A. N. Afanas'ev, *Poeticheskie vozzreniia slavian na prirodu*, part 1 (Moscow, 1865), p. 250. Moreover, both in the Old Russian tales about the battle with Mamai and in Innokentii Gizel''s *Sinopsis* (in the description of the battle of Kulikovo), Perun appears as a *Tartar* god: "Then Mamai saw his own destruction, and began to invoke his vain gods, Perun, Savat, Iraklii, Gurok, and his supposed great ally Mohammed." From Innokentii Gizel', *Sinopsis* (St. Petersburg, 1778), p. 163. Cf. also the corresponding place in S. Shambinago, "*Povesti o Mamaevom poboishche*" (St. Petersburg, 1906), *Sbornik Otdeleniia russkogo iazyka i slovesnosti imp. Akademii nauk*, vol. 81, no. 7, pp. 67, 118, 160, and 187.

[26]*Povest'vremennyx let*, part 1, p. 79; cf. Popov, p. 17. This entry, found in the chronicle under the year 988, must, judging by its content, belong to a later time.

See the large number of parallels in the juxtaposition of "sky-father" and "earth-mother" in Ivanov and Toporov, pp. 101 ff. and 207; S. Smirnov, *Drevnerusskii dukhovnik: Issledovanie po istorii tserkovnogo byta* (Moscow, 1914), pp. 262-263 and 266-268. It is curious that the corresponding ideas are even reflected in people's names: cf. "Mnikh Selivestr, nicknamed 'mother earth.'" in the Rumiantsevskii manuscript collection, no. 154, f. 375; see A. Diuvernua, *Materialy dlia slovaria drevnerusskogo iazyka* (Moscow, 1894), p. 95. The prohibition against men lying face down, or on their bellies, on the ground, which often figures in Old Russian penance-books, is very significant in this regard. In some texts the rule is explicated in detail: "If [he] curses [his] father or mother, or beats them, or lies face down on the ground, it is as if [he] had lain with a woman. Fifteen days [of penance]" (A. I. Almazov, *Tainaia ispoved' v pravoslavnoi vostochnoi tserkvi*, vol. 3, no. 44 [Odessa, 1894], p. 151, also pp. 155, 195, 275, and 279; Smirnov, p. 273, also the appendix, p. 46, no. 15.) One may compare mother-curses as an element of pagan behavior. It is not accidental that an Old Russian preacher, in denouncing foul language, says that the Mother of God is insulted by mother-curses, as is another, the one who bore you, and a "third mother—the earth, by whom we are fed." The connection between mother-curses and Mother Earth is plainly conditioned by pre-Christian ideas. In light of the above, it is characteristic that Old Russian didactic literature should often refer to mother-cursing as "Jewish language." (Smirnov, pp. 274 and 156).

This example is exceptionally revealing of the method by which the Old Russian consciousness reconstructed "Latinism." It is evidence that the antipagan orientation of Old Russian Christianity entailed the inclusion of mechanisms for independently producing correct pagan texts; in other words, paganism was included in the active cultural memory of Old Russian Christianity. Thus, if paganism was understood as an alien faith, Catholicism in turn actually acquired the characteristics of the *old* faith.

Another assertion is characteristic of the identification of Catholicism with paganism. The "Latins" were said to go to church in "Polovetsian garments" and "Hungarian hats."[27] Regardless of the historical accuracy of this information, it is significant that pagan Polovetsian dress and Hungarian Catholic dress are mentioned in the same breath.

We find a noteworthy example of the same kind in a denunciation of the Catholics in Metropolitan Makarii's *Menologion*: "On the first night the priest lies with his bride in the sanctuary behind the altar, having laid her on a rug. He makes the sign of the cross over the woman's shame and kisses it. And he says: 'Heretofore this was my mother, now it is my wife.' Thus he lies with her, and the filth having come out of the bride onto the rug, the rug is washed and burned, and people in the church are sprinkled with that filth."[28] It is hardly necessary to add that there were no Catholic parallels to the rite described. But it is no less obvious that beside the fantastic details, this evidence contains data about extremely archaic customs, with roots in the deepest past. Although some resemblance to archaic rites of this type may well have remained in the author's consciousness, a natural supposition is that the corresponding ideas were also generated independently by the mechanism of prohibitions. In this case one may consider that Kievan Christianity included within itself mechanisms for the generation of pagan texts for polemical purposes. In other words, it included a structural memory of the cultural experience of bygone times.

Not only did "the new" incorporate "the old" in a complex way;

---

[27]Popov, p. 25. The text cited is the more revealing in that it is apparently a reinterpretation of the "silk garments" and "horned hats" mentioned in other recensions of this composition (the story of Petr the Lisper); see Popov, p. 26 and also p. 22.

[28]Ibid., p. 81. This is inserted in the already cited "Voproshenie kniazia Iziaslava"; it is not found in other copies of the work, however, and probably belongs to a later interpolator.

it also generated "the old," while subjectively thinking of itself as its antipode.

1.3.1. Much later, too, and at widely differing stages of historical development, a polemical or negative orientation could lead to the generation of pagan texts and even the regeneration of pagan rituals. In a number of cases this result was conditioned by anticlerical tendencies.[29] Thus, in a demonstrative rejection of church ritual, Stepan Razin made couples who wished to marry to dance around a tree; that is, he regenerated the corresponding pagan rite, memory of which was preserved in folkloric texts, proverbs, and the like. The following description appeared in an anonymous foreign source, published in 1671:

> Later he [Razin] returned to the Don with his collaborators, where he again began his acts of villainy against the church. He drove away many priests, hindered divine service, and interfered in church affairs. Here is an example of a magnificent ceremony established by Sten'ka [Razin], the Cossack pope. Instead of the usual marriage rite, which in Russia is performed by a priest, he made the couple dance several times around a tree, after which they were considered married in Sten'ka's way. He also shouted various blasphemous things against our Savior.[30]

[29]Various kinds of folk sayings are quite revealing in this regard. They are often constructed on the principle of parodic travesty of a text of a traditional type (P. Shein, "Eshche o parodii v narodnykh tekstakh," *Etnograficheskoe obozrenie*, book 25, [1895], no. 2). In a number of cases this kind of travesty leads more or less organically to the actualization of pagan ideas. Consider the following rhyme from the Vologda region, for example: "This summer new testaments came, a young courier came running from the post office and brought the new testaments. Truth died, falsehood came alive, the lie walked away with a staff. It's written, it's written, from Uncle Borisov, and not from Roman, and no lies in it: Uncle Vlas came up, if I had had such power then, and a flock of sheep, I would have become his holy father, given him communion, taken his confession and stuck him in a pile. Would have made myself wheels, gone riding up to heaven. It's all different up in heaven, with churches made of turnips and the doors made of tripe. I grabbed some tripe, and hopped into the church. In the church it's all different from ours: the gods of clay, bald spots of wood, I knocked on the bald spot, ate some oats, and started to pick up the crumbs and started to invoke Father Yawnmouth. Father Yawnmouth, don't walk past my gates—I'll eat you up too" (G. N. Potanin, "Pesni i pribautki, zapisannye v derevne Aksent'evoi, v 3-x ver. ot gor. Nikol'ska," appendix to Potanin's article, "Etnograficheskie zametki na puti ot g. Nikol'ska do g. Tot'my," *Zhivaia starina*, 95, no. 4, [1899]. Features of paganism ("falsehood came alive") may be discerned here both in the image of the clay idol-gods, and in that of Vlas (Volos), the protector of sheep, and the like. We would like to express our gratitude to Aleksandr Belousov, who pointed out this text as well as the evidence cited in the following notes.
[30]"Soobshchenie kasatel'no podrobnostei miatezha, nedavno proizvedennogo Sten'koi Razinym," in *Zapiski inostrantsev o vosstanii Stepana Razina*, ed. A. G. Man'kov (Leningrad, 1968), pp. 108 and 116 (original English text on pp. 95 and 103).

In the death sentence passed on Razin, which was read at the place of execution on June 6, 1671, it was said:

> And in 7178 [1670], arriving at the Don, you, villain, together with the Cossacks obedient to you, having forgotten the fear of God, apostate from the Holy Catholic Apostolic Church, you said many blasphemous things about our Savior Jesus Christ, and forbade the building of churches on the Don and services in those which were there, and drove out all the priests, and if someone wished to marry, you made them walk around a tree in place of the usual marriage rite.[31]

In a similar way, after the revolution "there were cases when young people who wanted to do without a church marriage were afraid to tell their elders about it. They left their village as if for the neighboring one, to a church several versts away, but, without traveling that far, they stopped in the woods, got down from their wagon, and 'walked around a fir-tree with lighted candles.' "[32]

The fate of Aleksei Timofeev's song "The Wedding" is also characteristic. The romantic poet, whom Senkovskii called a "second Byron," wrote lyrics which naively opposed a romantic cult of Nature to the Christian marriage rite, and in so doing, apparently to his own surprise, regenerated a number of pagan ritual ideas. His text, set to music by Dargomyzhskii, was later perceived through the prism of women's emancipation and George Sand-ism. It became a favorite of the "people of the sixties," whence it entered the repertory of the Russian democratic intelligentsia of the end of the nineteenth century and the beginning of the twentieth.

The rebirth of pagan rites may be observed among sectarians, including some of the extreme branches of the "priestless" Old Believers. Aleksandr Belousov brought to our attention that among priestless sectarians who did not practice marriage, the rejection of church marriage led to the formation of the custom of abducting the bride, which continued until recent times. The custom of "marriage by departure" could, however, include a ceremony near a

---

[31]Ibid.

[32]M. E. Sheremeteva, *Svad'ba v Gamaiunshchine Kaluzhskogo uezda* (Kaluga, 1928), p. 109. Compare the expression "marry around a fir-tree, around a bush" (*venchat' vkrug eli, vkrug kusta*), applied to unmarried couples. Cf. Vladimir Dal', *Tolkovyi slovar' zhivogo velikorusskogo iazyka*, vol. 1 (1880), p. 331. Dal' provides the following note: "a simple jest, or a memory of paganism?"

tree or lake.[33] It is no less significant that several Old Believer sects bury their dead *in the woods*. This is where so-called unclean dead are usually buried;[34] but at the same time, the practice corresponds to the Slavic pagan custom of burial in forest or field, mentioned by so early a figure as Koz'ma of Prague.[35]

These and similar rites have been observed in those Old Believer sects that believe the Antichrist has already come: inasmuch as reversal is a primary feature of the world of the Antichrist, rejection of that world may in practice lead toward a return to pagan forms. Nonetheless, the rebirth (or continuation) of pagan burial rites is not found only among sectarians. A curious instance appears in the memoirs of Vladimir Pecherin, who describes how a priest refused to bury a suicide in the cemetery: "so they went and buried him in one of the burial mounds."[36] Here the alternative to burial in consecrated cemetery ground is a grave in a burial mound, which is thought of as a kind of pagan ("unclean") space. As in other cases of the burial of the unclean, this choice reflects essentially pagan behavior.[37]

---

[33]P. I. Mel'nikov, "O sovremennom sostoianii raskola v Nizhegorodskoi gubernii," *Deistviia Nizhegorodskoi gubernskoi uchenoi arkhivnoi komissii*, vol. 7 *Sbornik v pamiat' P. I. Mel'nikova (Andreia Pecherskogo)*, part 2 (Nizhnii Novgorod, 1910), p. 275.

[34]D. K. Zelenin, *Opisanie rukopisei Uchenogo arkhiva imp. Russkogo geograficheskogo obshchestva*, no. 2 (Prague, 1915), p. 581; Vas. Smirnov, "Narodnye pokhorony i prichitaniia v Kostromskom krae," *Vtoroi etnograficheskii sbornik, Trudy Kostromskogo nauchnogo obshchestva po izucheniiu mestnogo kraai*, no. 15 (Kostroma, 1920), p. 39. Smirnov also informs us that the flagellants (*khlysty*) buried their dead in the *swamp*, which is also a place where bodies that must be "put away" are buried. On the dead who must be "put away" and their burial in general, see Zelenin, *Ocherki russkoi mifologii*, no. 1 (Prague, 1916).

[35]Koz'ma Prazhskii, *Cheshskaia khronika* (Moscow, 1962), pp. 107 and 173; cf. A. Kotliarevskii, *O pogrebal'nykh obychaiakh, iazycheskikh slavian* (Moscow, 1868), p. 93. Cf. the word *roshchenie* (growth), signifying an ancient burial ground. The word is preserved in this meaning in Kostroma dialects; see Vas. Smirnov, p. 36; N. M. Bekarevich, "Dnevniki raskopok kurganov," *Kostromskaia starina: Sbornik izdavaemyi Kostromskoi gubernskoi uchenoi arkhivnoi komissiei*, no. 5 (Kostroma, 1901), pp. 335, 367, 396, 402, 406, 407, 416, and 425.

[36]V. S. Pecherin, *Zamogil'nye zapiski* (Moscow, 1932), p. 28.

[37]As late as the sixteenth century, the dead were often buried in pagan burial mounds rather than in Christian cemeteries. Thus in the Vodskaia district, Makarii, archbishop of Novgorod (and future metropolitan of Moscow), was told that instead of going to church or to confession, the adherents of ancient (pagan) traditions called in *arbui*, or heathen, priests, "and it is said they place their dead in the country on burial mounds or other burial places with these same *arbui*, and it is said they do not bring their dead to church to the cemetery to bury them." See the epistle of Makarii to the Vodskaia district about the extermination of pagan rites and rituals in the edition *Dopolneniia k Aktam istoricheskim, sobrannye i izdannye arkheograficheskoi komissiei*, vol. 1 (St. Petersburg, 1846), p. 28. One may suppose that it was not only among the Finnish population that such customs were preserved.

2. The later Russian middle ages, as distinct from the earlier period, to a great extent took "the old ways" as a slogan. The highest axiological criteria began to be associated with precisely "the old" and "the primordial." Were historians to accept this subjective orientation toward the past unconditionally, however, they would risk becoming victims of the sort of conceptual confusion already familiar to us.

2.1. Dissatisfaction with the whole system of Russian life, which was widespread among all levels of the population in the seventeenth century and was expressed in a number of popular movements, took the form of demands for a return to the past. The understanding of "past" that appeared in this context could sometimes be quite peculiar. Fairly common was the conception that contrasted God's beautiful world to the horrible disorder of the world of humans. A natural consequence of this view was the demand for a return to the primordial, natural order. The Kirsha Danilov collection of Russian folklore (the composition of the collection is seventeenth-century, the manuscript probably dates from the early eighteenth) is characteristic in this sense. In the collection is a triumphal stanza, repeated in three different texts, which affirms the breadth, space, and magnificence of the natural world: "Oh the height, the height of the skies . . . . " The function of this stanza, however, is revealingly transformed in each text. In the first, "About Salovei Budimerovich," it is in harmony with the basic content of the epic (*bylina*) and paints a picture of epic spaciousness.[38] In the second, the *bylina* "Agafonushka," it is turned inside out, resulting in a travesty:

> Oh how high, the height of the ceiling,
> Oh how deep the depth of the cellar,
> Oh how broad the expanse of the hearth before the stove,
> The open field—under the benches
> And the blue sea—in a tub of water. . . .[39]

"Spaciousness" in the epic world of the *bylina* is parodically contrasted with the "narrowness" of the real conditions of surrounding life. For the seventeenth century this "narrowness" was a transparent metaphor for social evil. To a certain degree it is based on a contrast between the nobles' takeover of land in central Russia

---

[38]*Drevnie rossiiskie stikhotvoreniia, sobrannye Kirsheiu Danilovym* (Moscow/Leningrad, 1958), pp. 9 and 292.
[39]Ibid., pp. 181-182 and 409.

and the spaciousness of "no man's" lands and waters on the far-away, unknown frontiers. This opposition evokes the third use of the refrain, a generalized juxtaposition of the good in nature and the evil that reigns in human society; of harmony and beauty in the former and the disintegration of relations in the latter:

> Oh how high, the height of the heavens,
> Oh how deep, the depth of the ocean-sea,
> Broad is the expanse of all the land,
> Deep are the pools of Neprovsk,
> Wondrous the cross of Levanidovsk,
> Long the rivers of Chevyletsk,
> High the mountains of Sorochinsk,
> Dark the forests of Brynsk,
> Black the earth of Smolensk,
> And swift are the rivers downstream.
> Under Tsar Davyd Evseevich,
> Under elder Makarii Zakhar'evich,
> There was great lawlessness:
> Old nuns in their cells bore children,
> Monks on the roads were robbers,
> The son takes the father to court,
> Brother rides upon brother in battle,
> Brother takes sister for himself.[40]

Ideas of this kind were also shared by the Archpriest Avvakum:

High mountains, cliffs of stone and very high; twenty thousand versts and more I dragged along, and never did I see such mountains any-where. On their summit are tents and earthen huts, gates and towers, and fences, all made by God. Garlic grows there, and onions bigger than the Romanov onion, and very sweet; there also grows wild hemp, and in the gardens fine grasses and flowers, very fragrant. There are a great many birds, geese and swans, that swim on the lake white as snow. And fish in the lake—sturgeon and trout, sterlet and salmon-trout and whiting and many other kinds. And the fish is very fat: you can't fry the sturgeon, or it would be all fat. The water is sweet, and in it are sea-calves and great sea-hares; when I was living in Mezen' I saw none such in the ocean. And all of this was made by Christ for the sake of man.... But such is man that he is given to vanity, and his days go by like a shadow: he leaps like a goat; puffs himself up like a bubble; he rages like a lynx; he seeks to devour, like a serpent;

---

[40]Ibid., pp. 159-160 and 479.

when he gazes on his neighbor's beauty, he neighs like a foal; he is crafty as a demon.[41]

The idea of the divine and beautiful natural order is also clearly expressed in Avvakum's story of how he prayed for the health of his hens. "God's hand is in everything: cattle and fowl exist for his glory."[42]

Thus the kind of thinking that rejected the whole existing social order in the name of the natural, concealing in fact a profound negation that presaged the ideas of Rousseau and Tolstoi, was subjectively experienced as a glorification of the past. All of human history was "the new"; "the old" was the divine, primeval order.

The image of "the old" was deeply antihistorical and oriented toward a break with actual historical tradition.[43]

2.2. The idea that forward movement is a return to a lost truth (movement into the future is movement into the past) became so common that it took hold of diametrically opposed social groups. The desire of Nikon and his followers to "correct" ecclesiastical texts was founded on the conception of a primary and correct (Greek) order. Subsequent history was seen as a process of gradual corruption and eventual regeneration.

An inversion of historical time is characteristic of the Old Believers. Instead of the diachrony "old, pagan" versus "new, Christian," a diachronic contrast of another type arises in their consciousness: "old, Christian" and "new, pagan," where "pagan" is equivalent to "Satanic." The reversal of time among the Old Believers was expressed in their placement of paganism *after* Christianity instead of *before*. This ordering undoubtedly derived from the general eschatological nature of their thought, which was oriented toward the end, rather than the beginning, of history.[44]

Insofar as evil was thought to have been brought to Russia from outside (the result of contact with heretics), paganism and heresy came to be united in a single image of the heretical West. Avvakum, for example, did not recognize any internal diversity in the Western

---

[41]*Pamiatniki istorii staroobriadchestva XVII v.*, book 1, no. 1 (Leningrad, 1927) = *Russkaia Istoricheskaia Biblioteka*, vol. 39, cols. 192-193. Cf. the same passage in other recensions of Avvakum's *Zhitie*: cols. 42 and 119.

[42]Ibid., col. 32; in other recensions, cols. 111 and 186.

[43]One manifestation of this is the fact that while cultures oriented toward "the new" created the ideal of refined and cultivated behavior, "the old" was always connected with "natural" behavior, with those who cultivated crudeness as a norm.

[44]Lotman, "Zvoniachi v pradedniuiu slavu," *Trudy po russkoi i slavianskoi filologii*, no. 28, *Uchenye zapiski Tartuskogo gosudarstvennogo universiteta* (Tartu, 1977).

world: "the people of Rome and the whole West fell into sin";[45] "we, the orthodox, pronounce triple anathema on the whore's wisdom of the Roman church and its bastards, the Poles and the Kievan Uniates, and also our own Nikonians, for all their new heretical sorceries";[46] "everything Frankish, that is to say German."[47] An analogous phenomenon occurs in Kirsha Danilov's collection, in the song "There in the hills the Bukharians attacked," where "nonsense" phrases such as "Vesur, vesur valakhtantar-ararakh-tarandarufu" are simultaneously interpreted as Polish, Hebrew, and "Bukharian" speech, all of which are apparently seen as a single "incorrect" (that is, occult) language.[48]

Thus the problem of "the old versus the new" is transformed into the antithesis "the Russian land versus the West." Since all that is right and divine is viewed as primeval, and everything sinful and diabolical is the result of corruption, that is, newness, the West is thought of as a "new" land. Positive ideas like piety and Orthodoxy receive the epithet "ancient," while everything sinful is perceived as "newly introduced." In the process, the polemic against pre-Christian ideas (ancient paganism) becomes less significant and completely disappears from the literature. It is replaced in one camp by attacks against the Nikonians and in the other by attacks against the Old Believers. At the same time, denouncing the West becomes especially important. The conception of the West not only as a "new" land, but as an "inside-out," "left handed" space, a diabolical space, becomes firmly fixed. We find striking evidence of such a conception in Gogol's "Terrible Vengeance": "An extraordinary wonder appeared outside Kiev. All the nobles and hetmen assembled to marvel at it: suddenly one could see far away to all the ends of the earth. Far off was the dark blue of the mouth of the Dnieper and beyond that the Black Sea. Seasoned travelers recognized the Crimea jutting like a mountain out of the sea and the marshy Sivash. *On the left* one could see the Galician land."[49] If the "seasoned travelers" saw the Crimea from Kiev, they must have stood facing south. Galicia must have been to their *right*. But for the West to be on the left in Russian medieval consciousness

---

[45]*Pamiatniki istorii staroobriadchestva*, col. 268.
[46]Ibid.
[47]Ibid., col. 283.
[48]*Drevnie rossiiskie stikhotvoreniia*, pp. 275 and 488-489.
[49]N. V. Gogol, *Polnoe sobranie sochinenii*, vol. 1 (Moscow/Leningrad, 1940), p. 275; emphasis added.

was a constant rather than a relative attribute. Gogol, with his keen historical-psychological intuition, felt this.

In order to understand the sharply negative reaction to Nikon's reforms on many levels of Russian society, one must keep in mind that in a large number of instances new rituals could be seen as a reversed representation of the old. For example, the clockwise circuit of the church was replaced with a counterclockwise one, the right and left sides changed places in the church service, and so on. Since, in view of the persistence of paganism within Russian Christianity, the "inside-out," "lefthanded" world was seen as anti-Christian, the cultural consciousness could associate Nikon's reforms with pagan or occult rituals. (Compare the counterclockwise circuit and the use of the left hand in various magical rituals.) Simultaneously, since Nikon's reforms were associated with "Latinism," Western culture itself could be perceived as occult.

At the same time, from the point of view of those upholding the new rites, such ideas, which were the result of "reading" the reforms in the light of earlier cultural experience, had to be interpreted as "ignorance." Thus, a link with the memory of earlier cultural development was called ignorance, while a break with that memory was perceived as "enlightenment." "To remember" meant being an ignoramus, and "to forget" was to be enlightened. It is interesting that a century and a half later Peter the Great performed many actions which he could not have failed to know would be perceived as signs of sacrilege or even as the mark of the Antichrist. But he intentionally disregarded such a "reading" as ignorant.[50] In this respect, the attitude toward beards, which for long years sharply divided Russia into two antagonistic groups, is quite significant. For one part of the population the beard was an essential attribute of Orthodoxy and even religiosity in general; for the other it became a symbol of backwardness. Just as the Old Believers did not allow the clean-shaven into their churches, so the practitioners of the new rites sometimes did not permit the bearded to join in triumphal religious ceremonies. It was for this reason that the famous Il'ia Baikov, the personal coachman of Alexander I, was not wanted in the Kremlin during the ceremony of parting with the body of the deceased emperor.[51] Likewise, the artist Aleksandr Ivanov was not

[50]Uspenskii, "Historia sub specie semioticae," in *Materialy Vsesoiuznogo simpoziuma po vtorichnym modeliruiushchim sistemam,* 1 (5) (Tartu, 1974); also in *Kul'turnoe nasledie Drevnei Rusi* (Moscow, 1976).

[51]N. K. Shil'der, *Imperator Aleksandr Pervyi, ego zhizn' i tsarstvovanie,* vol. 4 (St. Petersburg, 1898), p. 436.

welcome at the consecration of St. Isaac's cathedral; he felt himself to be an icon-painter and so wore a beard and Russian dress. Count Gur'ev declared to him: "So, you're Russian? I can't possibly let you into the ceremony in that costume, and with a beard. With a Frenchman it would be a different matter, but a Russian—impossible!"[52] At this stage, a beard on a Russian, though not on a foreigner, could be a hindrance to entering an Orthodox church!

At first, at the moment of ecclesiastical schism, the positions of the quarreling sides were rather similar. Both camps reproached each other with the same thing, offenses against orthodoxy. As a result, the standard of the old rites was borne by the emotional innovator Avvakum, while the views of the reformer Nikon could be seen as traditional enough, if viewed from the perspective of the Josephites. Each party saw the opposing group as pagan, in the broad sense of the word. In one case, however, "ignorance" was emphasized (compare the traditional appellation for pagans in polemical Christian literature: "ignoramuses" [neveglasi]), in the other, "demonism."

Subsequently, the Old Believer position froze into stable, traditional forms, while the new-rite ideology remained open to new cultural influences. The result was the ever-increasing penetration of the Renaissance and baroque world view into the new-rite ecclesiastical culture.[53] Such a process is quite noticeable in painting (cf. the famous tract by Iosif Vladimirov) and in architecture.[54] Most interesting is the mid-seventeenth-century polemic concerning singing, which covered two oppositions: "special pronunciation" (*khomovoi*) versus "speech pronunciation" (*narechnyi*) singing, and monophony versus polyphony.[55] It is characteristic that the supporters of "speech like" singing carried out their polemic both with "special pronunciation" singing and with polyphony: the new cultural consciousness viewed the two completely unrelated phenom-

---

[52]V. M. Zummer, "Problematika khudozhestvennogo stilia Al. Ivanova; stil' 'bibleiskikh eskizov,' " *Izvestiia Azerbaidzhanskogo gosudarstvennogo universiteta*, vols. 2-3, *Obshchestvennye nauki* (Baku, 1925), p. 94.

[53]Similar processes also occurred before the schism, and therefore touched the Old Believers as well. They could not, however, develop among the Old Believers, and left no significant traces.

[54]I. I. Ioffe, "Russkii Renessans," *Uchenye zapiski Leningradskogo gosudarstvennogo universiteta*, no. 72, *Seriia filologicheskhikh nauk*, no. 9 (Leningrad, 1944-1945).

[55]On the battle over monophony, see N. F. Kapterev, *Patriarkh Nikon i tsar' Aleksei Mikhailovich*, vol. 1 (Sergiev Posad, 1909), pp. 8-9 and 84-105. On *khomovoe* and *narechnoe* singing, see Uspenskii, *Arkhaicheskaia sistema tserkovnoslavianskogo proiznosheniia (Iz istorii liturgicheskogo proiznosheniia v Rossii)* (Moscow, 1968), pp. 39-40, 61-65.

ena as organically united. Simultaneously, a battle was waged against all kinds of glossolalic insertions, like *anenaek* and *khabuv*, which had been preserved in church singing. The reasons for this become clear if we keep in mind that both special pronunciation and polyphonic singing (and reading) are essentially not intended for understanding by the human audience. The verbal content of such singing may be incomprehensible, which is evidence of its orientation toward the Highest Addressee: the fact of pronunciation in the sacral language is of principal importance. The church service is understood as a communication with God, not with man. In consequence, the only important thing is the *objective* sense of the text pronounced, which is, in principle, separate from its *subjective* perception. The opposing method of performance may be compared with a tendency toward the translation of sacred texts into the language of the people; it is oriented toward making the words comprehensible to the human audience. From the viewpoint of the new Renaissance culture, both "special pronunciation" and polyphonic singing had to be perceived as unintelligible and ignorant. Looked at from the historical point of view, however, they are the fruit of a long, refined cultural tradition.

We may note in this regard that from the viewpoint of one of the conflicting sides, "knowledge" meant the mastery of a long and carefully worked out tradition, and "ignorance" was the rejection of that tradition. From the other position, "knowledge" meant forgetting the tradition in the name of a concise and rational consciousness "as clear as sunshine"; "ignorance" was seen as following all the twists of traditional thought. Again, both sides are in agreement in their underlying classification, differing only in their evaluations. We may compare the medieval method of training apprentices, in the course of which the future master had to repeat the twists and difficulties of his teacher's path, including his unproductive efforts; opposed to this is the rational training of the pupil in the results of knowledge by the shortest path. In the first case the *path* is taught, in the second, the *results*.

3. The eighteenth century marched in under a banner of novelty. "The new" was identified with what was good, valuable, and worthy of imitation; "the old" was thought of as bad, as something to be demolished and destroyed. The people of Peter's era viewed Russia either as a being "reborn in a new form" or as a newborn child. In his "Eulogy on the battle of Poltava," Feofan Prokopovich called for a "reborn, powerful, and completely matured Russia."[56]

[56]Feofan Prokopovich, *Slova i rechi pouchitel'nyia, pokhval'nyia i pozdravitel'nyia*, part 1 (St. Petersburg, 1760), p. 145.

He expressed the conception of Russia's full and profound transformation under the power of Peter in the famous words "When
he was dying, the Roman emperor Augustus said, in great praise
of himself, 'I found Rome a city of brick, and I leave it a city of
marble.' Were our Most Brilliant Monarch to say this it would be
to trifle, not to praise; verily it would become him to confess that
he found Russia a land of wood, and turned it into gold."[57] Peter
the Great, when he noted down the "idea" for a triumphal poem,
which poets "have only to expand," found another image, that of
blindness and the recovery of sight. In Peter's words, Russia's
opponents swore to hold her in blindness, "in order to keep us
from the light of reason in all our dealings, and most especially in
military matters." But God performed a miracle: they themselves
became blind and failed to note the miraculous transformation of
Russia, "as if this were hidden from their eyes."[58]

All of these images point to the same thing: the instantaneous,
miraculous, and complete transformation of Russia under the power
of the emperor Peter. Kantemir found a compound formula:

> He always holds in his hands the wise commands of Peter,
> Through which we have already become *in a moment's time*
> *a new people*. . . .[59]

The image of a "new Russia" and a "new people" became a
distinctive myth, which arose as early as the beginning of the
eighteenth century and was bequeathed to the subsequent cultural
consciousness. The idea that the eighteenth century constituted an
utterly new stage, separate from previous development, became
so deeply rooted that it has, in essence, never been subject to doubt.
Debates could rage about whether the break with the past occurred
at the middle or the end of the seventeenth century, whether it
was instantaneous or gradual, and finally, how one should view
it in the perspective of later Russian history: as a positive event,
ensuring Russia's rapid cultural progress, or as a negative phenomenon, leading to the loss of national individuality. The fact
itself, however, is accepted by everyone in almost the form in which
it was stated by the era in question. The culture of the eighteenth
century is considered to have had a consistently worldly, civil, and
anti-ecclesiastical character, and so to be in direct contrast with the

[57]Ibid., p. 113.
[58]S. M. Solov'ev, *Istoriia Rossii c drevneishikh vremen v piatnadtsati knigakh*, book 9
(Moscow, 1963), p. 553.
[59]Antiokh Kantemir, *Sobranie stikhotvorenii* (Leningrad, 1956), p. 75; emphasis added.

pre-Petrine period. At the same time this process of breaking with the past is viewed as a part of the consistent Europeanization of Russian culture.

A close examination reveals convincingly, however, that the new (post-Petrine) culture was significantly more traditional than is usually thought. The new culture was constructed not so much on models from "Western" culture (although it was subjectively experienced as "Western") as on an "inverted" structural plan of the old culture. It was here that a clear separation occurred between the more superficial level of culture, which was subject to change, and all the underlying forms. In the new categories of thinking, the underlying forms appeared even more vividly.

The new culture demonstrated its blasphemous, anti-ecclesiastical nature with emphatic zeal.[60] Thus it is all the more interesting that the growth of the new culture constantly reveals models of an ecclesiastical-medieval type. (The latter, in their turn, are merely a manifestation of the enduring models that have organized the entire stretch of Russian cultural history, including, one may suppose, both the pre-Christian and Christian periods.)

3.1. The crucial importance of the words "Enlightenment" and "enlightener" for eighteenth-century culture is well known. The words were fundamental to the most basic ideas of "the Age of Reason." They were not, however, neologisms: pre-Petrine Russia knew them too. " 'To enlighten' . . . means to baptize, to effect a holy Baptism."[61] It is in this sense that the word "enlightener" is used in a liturgical hymn, addressed to St. Vladimir: "Oh teacher of orthodoxy and enlightener of all Russia, you have enlightened us all with baptism."[62] In his first letter to Kurbskii, Ivan the Terrible speaks likewise: "the great tsar Vladimir, who enlightened the whole Russian land with holy baptism."[63] Iosif Volotskii called his composition against heretics "The Enlightener." This same expression, however, came to be used even in Peter's lifetime to describe him as the founder of a secular, Europeanized culture. In this sense, the foundation of a new culture, which demolished traditional Orthodoxy, was thought of as Russia's *second baptism*. Feofan Prokopovich's tragicomedy *Vladimir* is interesting in this regard. The

[60]On the conscious and semiotic nature of Peter the Great's "blasphemy," see Uspenskii, "Historia sub specie semioticae."
[61]Petr Alekseev, *Tserkovnyi slovar'*, part 3 (St. Petersburg, 1818), p. 348.
[62]V. I. Sreznevskii, ed., *Musin-Pushkinskii sbornik 1814 goda v kopii nachala XIX v* (St. Petersburg, 1893), p. 69.
[63]*Poslaniia Ivana Groznogo* (Moscow/Leningrad, 1951), p. 9.

juxtaposition of Peter's reforms and the apostolic enlightenment of Russia was not Prokopovich's own invention. In the "journal of daily notes" of Peter the Great, we read: "At the same time [1699] I instituted the Russian order of the holy apostle Andrew, because the Russian people received the first principles of Christian faith from him."[64]

In Prokopovich's play, Vladimir, the "enlightener" of Russia, is an obvious alter ego for Peter the Great. The reform of Christianization (read "Enlightenment") was supposed to remind the audience of the Petrine reform. Peter's opponents from the Orthodox hierarchy are represented in the comedy as pagan sorcerers who attempt to stop the enlightenment of Russia with the help of demons. This is an exceptionally revealing exchange of roles, carried out without altering the overall conceptual scenario. Direct textual parallels show that the pagan priests Zherivol, Piar, and Kuroiad are to be understood as Peter's ecclesiastical opponents. In the tragicomedy, when Vladimir declares his desire to "change the law," Zherivol declares that there is no need for that:

> A change is not needed, where there's not a bit
> Of evil to be found. What vice is there
> In our statutes?[65]

Compare the following, from Prokopovich's "address at the inauguration of the Holy Governing Synod, in the presence of his Imperial Majesty Peter I" (1721):

> But oh! our accursed times! There are those, and they are many, who with all-destructive insouciance blush not to reject Christian teaching, preaching, and instruction that is the only light to our paths; why, they say, do we need teachers, why do we need preachers? ... with us, thank God, everything is fine, and it is not the healthy who need a doctor, but the sick .... But what kind of world is around us? How is our health? It has come to this, that everyone, be he the most lawless, thinks himself honorable and holier than others, like a mad-

---

[64] *Zhurnal ili Podennaia zapiska, blazhennyia i vechnodostoinyia pamiati gosudaria imperatora Petra Velikago s 1698 goda, dazhe do zakliucheniia Neishtatskago mira*, part 1 (St. Petersburg, 1770), p. 7. The introduction of the epithet "first-called" into the name of the order is connected with this. In a statute of 1720 this tendency was somewhat masked, and the order was presented as a (purely fictional) continuation of the ancient Scottish order of St. Andrew. The post-factum attempt to present one's own invention, created according to Old Russian models, as a product of more prestigious Western influence, is extremely characteristic.

[65] Feofan Prokopovich, *Sochineniia* (Moscow/Leningrad, 1961), p. 178.

55

man: that is our health. . . . It has come to this, and such are the times in which we were born, that the blind lead the blind, that the most utter ignoramuses practice theology and write treatises worthy of laughter.[66]

A supporter of Orthodoxy is presented as superstitious; "like a madman," "in his tradition, he eagerly believes a woman's fable." Rationalism is thought of as "straight faith" (Orthodoxy) and the tsar, the champion of Western enlightenment, acquires the traits of Prince Vladimir, the equal of the Apostles.

3.2. It is no less revealing that free thinkers among the Russian nobility, whose free thinking bordered on that practical type of godlessness which was much more common than theoretical philosophical atheism, often not so much rejected faith as *converted to a new one*. Often it was not arguments, but the very fact of "receiving" unbelief and the person who "conveyed" it that held the center of attention. People did not become convinced of unbelief, but "joined" it. We recall Teplov's account of his debate with an atheist, made famous by Fonvizin, who recorded it: "The negator kept shouting, 'No need to talk nonsense; there is no God!' I entered the fray and asked him, 'But who told you that there is no God?'—'Petr Petrovich Chebyshev, yesterday at the Merchant's Court,' he answered. 'A fine place, indeed,' I said."[67] Fonvizin himself, in a conversation with the same Teplov, explained his method of answering the question of God's existence as follows: "I said in response, 'I begin by looking to see which people deny the existence of God and whether they are at all worthy of being trusted.' "[68] The central question is the source of the true faith: from whom it can be received, who communicates this conviction, and (which is very revealing) whether it was received in the proper place. At issue is not a transition from religious to philosophical views, but a replacement of one faith by another.

Cultural historians studying the consciousness of the average eighteenth-century Russian nobleman have seen a superficial European gloss, whose thin surface covers a powerful stratum of pre-Petrine daily life. This surface gloss may have another origin as well.

Pre-Petrine culture did not banish the world of pagan ideas from

[66]Feofan Prokopovich, *Slova i rechi*, part 2 (St. Petersburg, 1765), pp. 66-67.
[67]D. I. Fonvizin, *Sobranie sochinenii v dvukh tomakh*, vol. 2 (Moscow/Leningrad, 1959), p. 103.
[68]Ibid., p. 102.

the consciousness of the Orthodox Christian. They survived at the lower, demonic level of mythology, which was believed to exist, although limited and subordinated in importance. Thus, in certain solutions one was *required* to behave in a non-Christian way. Of course, Christian behavior was open and demonstrative, while pagan behavior, like the employment of a sorcerer or witch doctor, was secret, hidden, and seemingly nonexistent. Nonetheless, it was widely practiced not only among peasants, but among eighteenth-century nobles on their country estates.

"The Age of Enlightenment" did not abrogate this construction, but inverted it. The energetic struggle that the secular state and education waged against the ecclesiastical monopoly in the sphere of culture was interpreted in an unexpected way in the mass consciousness of the nobility, where it appeared as a regeneration of paganism. The cohabitation of Christianity and paganism continued, but in an inverted form. Public, official life, "fashionable" ethics, and everyday behavior in the social world soon evinced a multitude of reanimated pre-Christian or Oriental features (features that were "pagan" from an Orthodox viewpoint—thus, the same framework was maintained despite the substantive change in the way it was regarded). As for Orthodoxy, it survived in the "closed," hidden side of life—from penitential chains worn under the cambric shirts of public figures in Peter's era to confession and nighttime prayers after Potemkin's balls and masquerades. Moving into a deeply intimate and hidden sphere, Orthodoxy even gained. (It was not by chance that the periods of childhood and old age were left to Orthodoxy.[69])

3.3. The subjective "Europeanization" of everyday life had nothing in common with a genuine movement toward Western patterns of living. Moreover, it tended to take on the kind of anti-Christian forms that were quite impossible in the everyday life of the Christian West. Russians perceived the West as anti-Christian; therefore, they experienced an "infidelization" of life as Europeanization. Objectively, however, such "Europeanization" often made the real forms of European life more distant. This paradox is apparent, for example, in the phenomenon of harems made up of serfs. This institution had been absolutely impossible (in an unconcealed form) in pre-Petrine life, but it became commonplace in the eighteenth

[69]With respect to pre-Petrine norms and ideas "showing through" Europeanized everyday life, Labzina's memoirs are exceptionally interesting: *Vospominaniia Anny Evdokimovny Labzinoi* (St. Petersburg, 1914).

century. The serf harem was not an inheritance from the past; the eighteenth century engendered it, and the owner, as a rule, was an "enlightener" and Westernizer who battled against "ossified ignorance."

The memoirs of Ianuarii Neverov describe everyday life in the home of the landowner Petr Koshkarov. An old man by the time of the memoirs (the 1820s), Koshkarov had preserved in his household the forms of everyday life which had taken shape around the 1780s:

> ... Petr Alekseevich had a harem. In actual fact, the life of the female servants in his house was organized purely along the lines of a harem .... Twelve to fifteen young and pretty girls occupied a whole half of the house and were set aside solely for Koshkarov's service. [As Neverov notes, this was in addition to his common-law morganatic wife, a soldier's wife named Natal'ia Ivanovna, with whom he had a daughter and seven sons, and his permanent mistress Feoktista Semenovna, "a woman of middle years, beautiful, lively, and cultivated, whose mother was the head of Koshkarov's harem"—Iu. L., B. U.] These girls constituted what I have called a harem. The whole manor house was divided into two halves, men's and women's .... The women's half properly began with the drawing-room, which was in fact a neutral room, because Koshkarov was usually sitting there on his couch, with Natal'ia Ivanovna opposite him on another couch, and there was a place for Feoktista Semenovna too. All the other members of the family and guests would spend their time here, and the piano was here as well. A servant usually stood on duty by the doors of the drawing-room which led into the hall. A girl stood on duty at the doors opposite, which led to Koshkarov's bedroom. Just as the servant could not step over the threshold of the bedroom, so the girl could not step over the threshold of the hall .... Not only the servant on duty or the male servants, but even the male members of the family and guests could not pass beyond the doors guarded by the girl on duty .... Usually in the evening, after supper, the girl on duty, at his command, announced loudly to the manservant on duty, "The Master wishes to sleep." This was a sign for the whole family to go off to their rooms; Natal'ia Ivanovna would bow and leave, and all of us did likewise. The manservants at once brought a simple wooden bed into the drawing-room from the men's half of the house. They placed it in the center of the room and left at once. The door from the drawing-room was locked, and the girls brought a feather-bed, bed-clothes, and the other necessities for Koshkarov's bed. Koshkarov meanwhile said his evening prayers from a prayer-book, while the girl on duty held a candle. At the same time the other girls brought in their cots and placed them around Koshkarov's bed,

since all of them with the exception of Matrena Ivanovna, the head of the harem, absolutely had to sleep in the same room with Koshkarov . . . . Once a week Koshkarov went to the bathhouse; and all those who dwelled in the harem had to accompany him there. Often girls who had not yet managed to adopt all his views because they had not been in those surroundings very long would try to hide from him out of modesty; they often returned from the bathhouse beaten.[70]

We should emphasize that the life of the harem was perceived as Europeanized. This distinguished it from the peasant life the girls had been torn from, which preserved certain features of a pre-Petrine pattern of life.

All of the girls without exception were not only literate, but very cultivated and well-read. There was a rather large library at their disposal, consisting almost exclusively, of course, of belles-lettres. Literacy was compulsory for the girls, for otherwise they could not have fulfilled their duties as readers for Koshkarov, partners at whist, and so on. Therefore each new arrival began to learn to read and write at once.

One of the girls remembered that as a child, Neverov had learned Pushkin's "*Fountain of Bakhchisarai* by heart and later started a notebook of Pushkin's and Zhukovskii's verse." "Of course," writes Neverov, "everyone dressed not in national, but in European clothing." If a transgression occurred, the girl in question was sent back to her family, and "the prohibition of wearing so-called noble [European] clothing" served as punishment.[71] Thus, the entry of a girl into the harem signified her transition to "European" status; her expulsion meant a return to her original "uneducated" (peasant) existence and pre-Petrine dress.

Of course, the identification of secular ("European") and pagan (anything non-Christian) was unconscious and held sway primarily in poorly educated circles that lacked direct contact with Europe. This group was very large, however, and exerted an active influence on noble culture as a whole. The unconscious character of these ideas merely emphasized their connection with underlying models of culture formation, and not with an individual's level of education. Note the case of General Arakcheev: every morning before breakfast, he performed a libation with a cup of coffee in

[70]"Zapiski Ianuariia Mikhailovicha Neverova, 1810-1826 gg.," in N. N. Rusov, ed., *Pomeshchich'ia Rossiia po zapiskam sovremennikov* (Moscow, 1911), pp. 138-143.
[71]Ibid., pp. 147-148.

front of a bust of Paul that stood in his garden, and he always kept a place set for the deceased emperor at his dinner table. Nonetheless, he probably had no conception of the pagan rituals of which his actions were reminiscent. When he deified the Petersburg emperors, he had not, of course, heard of the Hellenistic idea of the epiphany of divinity in the earthly king. The situation was different: the mechanisms which produced both pagan and Christian texts lay deep in the system of Russian culture, with its double set of beliefs. A blow directed at one of the parts of this unified duality inevitably led to the vigorous development of the opposing tendency.

The binary structure of Russian culture was significantly more stable than any of its concrete realizations. A particular clear manifestation was the language situation in Russian.

3.4. One of the bases of Russian culture during the pre-Petrine period was the two-tiered relationship between Church Slavonic and spoken Russian. The secularization of language—the introduction of a secular alphabet, changes in the structure of the literary language, and so on—has been generally regarded as a characteristic mark of the new culture. Vinogradov writes (1938), "The reform of the alphabet delivered a sharp blow to medieval fetishism in the sphere of the Church Slavonic language (1708). This was a clear expression of the collapse of the hegemony of ecclesiastical ideology."[72]

Still, even in this instance, the two-tiered structure (the presence within a society of one language marked by high prestige and a second language deprived of that feature) had survived, although its elements changed. Let us cite just one example. The well-known censor and professor Aleksandr Nikitenko, during a tour of the Arkhangelsk region in 1834, saw "a cross, made by Peter the Great himself, and erected by him on the shore of the White Sea. There is a Dutch inscription on it, declaring that it was made by Captain Peter."[73] If for no other reason than its presence on the cross, it is obvious that the inscription should have been in Church Slavonic. From the point of view of medieval consciousness, the possibility of placing an inscription in a "heretical" language on a cross was completely unthinkable. However, Peter made such an inscription, demonstrating that to his mind the Dutch language had function-

---

[72]V. V. Vinogradov, *Ocherki po istorii russkogo literaturnogo iazyka XVII-XIX vv.* (Moscow, 1938), p. 79.
[73]A. V. Nikitenko, *Dnevnik v trekh tomakh*, vol. 1 (Moscow, 1955), p. 154.

ally replaced Church Slavonic. Later its place was taken by German and French.[74]

3.5. Although the continuity of traditional forms of pre-Petrine social thought in certain aspects of eighteenth-century consciousness was not manifested in the contrast between the "Europeanized" surface of life and its "Asiatic" depth, it is just this interpretation of the interrelationship between the old and the new in post-Petrine culture that has received much currency:

> Reading these regulations, instructions, and ukases, you cannot rid yourself of the impression that the form of Russian life has undergone profound changes, effected by the benevolent labors of a solicitous authority. It is as if all of Russian life is emerging from its foundations before your eyes, and a new, European Russia is growing from the debris of the devastated past. Under the influence of this impressive picture, you then begin a study of this Europeanized Russia, but now using documents that record not daydreams of transformation, but the everyday facts of current life. And soon not a trace of the mirage remains. From the half-faded pages of these documents, through the outer shell of the chancery jargon, old Muscovite Russia gazes upon you, having successfully stepped over the threshold of the eighteenth century and settled comfortably within the new framework of the Petersburg Empire.[75]

One may say, and by no means for the sake of paradox, that it was precisely the shift brought about by "Europeanization" (or what was subjectively perceived as Europeanization) that enhanced archaic traits in Russian culture. *Mutatis mutandis*, it laid bare several archaic semiotic models. Though these models were present in medieval Russian culture in the form it developed in the fourteenth to fifteenth centuries, they probably have their origins in a significantly older cultural stratum. In this regard, despite the widespread superficial impression to the contrary, the eighteenth century was deeply an organic part of Russian culture as a whole.

The way geographic space was experienced is an exceptionally revealing illustration of the connection between the culture of the eighteenth century and pre-Petrine culture. By the eighteenth century there was already a scientific-realistic conception of the earth's surface as a specific space divided into various latitudes and lon-

---

[74]Lotman and Uspenskii, "Spory o iazyke v nachale XIX v. kak fakt russkoi kul'tury," p. 200.

[75]A. A. Kizevetter, "Novizna i starina v Rossii XVIII stoletiia. Rech' pered magisterskim disputom," in Kizevetter, *Istoricheskie ocherki* (Moscow, 1912), pp. 268-269.

gitudes that were distinguished by the ethnic character of their inhabitants and the conditions in which they lived, as well as by natural features and objects of trade. This point of view did not separate geographical space into "infidel" sinful lands and "holy" good lands, the visiting of which either condemned one to damnation or brought one salvation.[76] But alongside this, another conception was active and enduring in the consciousness of eighteenth-century people, especially ordinary Russian nobles. Geographical knowledge per se, from this viewpoint, is technical and subordinate. Although section 43, on "geography, general and Russian," of the introduction to Tatishchev's history of Russia declares that "geography is necessary to the nobility,"[77] the more widespread opinion can be seen in the famous formulation of Fonvizin's Prostakova: "That, now, is not a science for gentlemen."[78] And a conception of the medieval type, which ascribed religious-ethical or other general evaluative features to geographical location, held on very stubbornly.

Not only the people, but also the mass of the nobility, clung to the conception that the West was a destructive, sinful land. Conceptions of the West as the kingdom of Enlightenment and the source whence the light of reason was to pour forth upon Russia are all the more striking against this ideological background. In medieval consciousness, the holy lands (the East) were the source from which "a spark of piety shall go even unto the kingdom of Russia."[79] The eighteenth century, on the other hand, began with the demonstrative assertion that the new "enlightener" of the Russian land must make a pilgrimage to the West: Peter's "Great Embassy." Later, a trip to Paris for the eighteenth-century Russian nobleman acquired the character of a pilgrimage to holy places. Correspondingly, the opponents of Westernization saw such journeys as the primary source of evil. Communion with the Enlightenment for some, or with the subculture of the *petits-maîtres* (Russian francophiles) for others, was accomplished by a simple movement

---

[76]Lotman, "O poniatii geograficheskogo prostranstva v russikikh srednevekovykh tekstakh," *Trudy po znakovym sistemam*, no. 2 (Tartu, 1965).

[77]V. N. Tatishchev, *Izbrannye trudy po geografii Rossii* (Moscow, 1950), p. 214.

[78]D. I. Fonvizin, *Sobranie sochinenii v dvukh tomakh*, vol. 1 (Moscow/Leningrad, 1959), p. 163.

[79]*Poslaniia Ivana Groznogo* (Moscow/Leningrad, 1951), p. 9.

in space, following the model of communion with a sacred place during a pilgrimage.[80]

The West was thought of as "new" in relation to "old" Russia. Note, though, that the "new Russia" founded by Peter was thought of as younger than the Western world as well as younger than Muscovite Russia (a reiteration of Hilarion's scheme, with Byzantium replaced by the West). Although in this case "youth" and "newness" signified association with Western civilization, archaists like Griboedov and the later Slavophiles thought of Russia's "youth" as a quality of freedom from spiritual commonality with the West. Griboedov, in a plan for a tragedy on the theme of 1812, intended to give Napoleon, the representative of the West, "a monologue about this young, newly formed people, about the distinctive traits of its dress, buildings, beliefs, and morals. Left to itself, what would it produce?"[81]

3.6. The second half of the eighteenth century developed under the banner of ideas that show parallels to the cultural models of the late Russian middle ages. Once more we come across the attempt to reject Culture in the name of Nature. Again a decisive break with the past was clothed in the form of a turn to primordial "natural" forms of social life. A fundamental antihistoricism was clothed in the form of a turn to an artificially constructed past utopia.

What might be called "memory-making"—the reconstruction of the utopia of the past—created possibilities for surprising identifications. Aleksandr Radishchev, for example, saw no difference between the classical pagan past, the Russian pagan past, and the past of Russian Orthodox Christianity. All had been blended into an ideal picture that combined primordial popular sovereignty with a world of heroes. Included there were chiefs of ancient Slavic tribes ("Songs Sung at Competitions in Honor of Ancient Slavic Divinities"), fighters against tyrants, classical Stoics (like Cato Uticensis, whose image runs through all of Radishchev's work) and Christian martyrs (the life of St. Filaret the Gracious). In describing a contemporary "man of firmness," Fedor Ushakov, Radishchev

---

[80]Lotman, and Uspenskii, "K semioticheskoi tipologii russkoi kul'tury XVIII veka," in *Khudozhestvennaia kultura XVIII veka, Gosudarstvennyi muzei izobrazitel'nykh iskusstv imeni A. S. Pushkina i Institut istorii iskusstv Ministerstva kul'tury SSSR: Materialy nauchnoi konferentsii 1973* (Moscow, 1974), pp. 275-278.

[81]A. S. Griboedov, *Sochineniia* (Moscow, 1956), p. 343.

was able to combine in him traits of both Cato and the Christian martyr; it is not accidental that he called his tale a "Vita."

Later, from an utterly different ideological position, Paul would mix the ideal knightly past of Catholicism with Russian Orthodoxy to create a single utopian picture. Paul freely united chapters of Catholic and Orthodox knighthood into his renewed order of the Knights of Malta (the renewal was interpreted as the reestablishment of the ancestral past). It is hard to imagine a more striking example of how historical nihilism can, from a subjective point of view, clothe itself in the garments of a reestablishment of the past.[82]

It is no less characteristic that some writers found it possible to identify Slavic and Scandinavian mythology, while others contrasted them sharply.[83] Especially revealing is the possibility of *choosing a suitable* past for oneself: consider the polemics between Derzhavin and Nikolai L'vov, in which L'vov argues against writing poetry using Scandinavian mythology in place of Greek; he prefers replacing Greek myths with Slavic ones because they are "primordially ours." At the same time, L'vov sees "Russian" and "Gypsy" songs as synonymous in a certain sense.[84]

If we add to this evidence the prevalence of the eschatological mood, from the social eschatology of the Russian admirers of Mably and Rousseau to the cosmic eschatology of Semen Bobrov, there is support for the idea that Russian medieval culture and the culture of the eighteenth century show a typological parallelism despite their different positions on the historical spiral.

The problem of finding the primary foundations of natural culture was an important one at the end of the eighteenth century. It

[82]There is a certain regularity in this: the proponents of the idea of historical progress and the irreversibility of the forward movement of history think historically and study the past as historians. (The appearance of such a conception was one of the principal innovations of post-Petrine culture, but does not come within the scope of our article. A strong proponent of this real, nonmythological Europeanization was Karamzin.) The proponents of "returning to the past" think along mythological lines and see the past as a beautiful fairy tale. The very idea of studying the past historically strikes them as offensive. Mikhail Orlov, for example, objected to Karamzin's monarchic conception of the origin of the Russian state, but instead of suggesting another interpretation of the sources, insisted that they be replaced by "a brilliant and probable hypothesis." Letter from M. F. Orlov to P. A. Viazemskii of 4 July 1818, in *Literaturnoe nasledstvo*, vol. 59, p. 567.

[83]Cf. Lotman, " 'Slovo o polku Igoreve i literaturnaia traditsiia XVIII-nachala XIX v.," in *Slovo o polku Igoreve—pamiatnik XII veka* (Moscow/Leningrad, 1962), pp. 362-374; see the letter from N. A. L'vov to G. R. Derzhavin of May 24, 1799, in *Poety XVIII veka*, vol. 2 (Leningrad, 1972), pp. 246-247.

[84]*Poety XVIII veka*, vol. 2; see also Z. Artamonova, "Neizdannye stikhi N. A. L'vova," *Literaturnoe nasledstvo*, vols. 9-10, p. 283.

was approached through the construction of various equivalencies, some of which were mutually exclusive from the point of view of preceding historical tradition. (Compare, at a somewhat later stage, the assertions of Galenkovskii and Gnedich on the primary identity of the ancient Greek and Russian national characters, with Shishkov's identification of Church Slavonic and Russian written culture.) All these identifications, however, were realized against the background of a sharp contrast between the reconstructed national culture and the actual everyday life of the nobility, the worldly *petit-maître* culture, which was perceived as a superficial and alien borrowing from the West. In addition, although the latter was clearly the creation of the eighteenth century, it was seen as "decrepit," while the national culture reconstructed in contrast to it was paradoxically understood to be at once "primordial" and "young," unspoiled by civilization. It is perfectly obvious that in this context, the ideas of "youth" and "old age" had a conventional meaning, rather than an actual chronological (historical) one.

There is no need to demonstrate that eighteenth-century Russian culture was not a trivial repetition of a medieval cycle: the difference in the very nature of these stages is too deep and too obvious. Genuine Europeanization did take place in the culture of the eighteenth century. It rarely coincided, however, with what the culture's "native speakers" themselves saw as Europeanization. Historical tradition, as we have seen, was often at work precisely where a break with tradition was subjectively understood, and innovation at times appeared as a fanatical devotion to artificially constructed "traditions." If we take into account that all of this conceptual work was based on a cultural deposit of historical experience, now in a direct, now in an "inverted" interpretation, the result is a complex and interesting picture.

The essence of culture is such that the past contained in it does not "depart into the past" as in the natural flow of time; it does not disappear. It becomes fixed in cultural memory, and acquires a permanent, if background, presence. The memory of a culture is constructed not only as a store of texts, but as a certain mechanism for their generation. Culture, united with the past through memory, generates not only its future, but also its past, presenting, in this sense, a mechanism that works against natural time.

A living culture cannot constitute a repetition of the past; it always gives rise to structurally and functionally new systems and texts. But it cannot fail to contain within itself a *memory* of the past.

Iurii M. Lotman and Boris A. Uspenskii

The relationship between images of past and future which are potentially present in every culture, and the degree of their influence on each other, constitute a fundamental typological characterization, which should be considered in comparing different cultures.

The specifics of Russian culture of the period examined here were such that the connection with the past was objectively strongest when an orientation toward a complete break with the past was subjectively dominant; in contrast, a subjective orientation toward the past brought about the exclusion from memory of actual tradition and a turn toward chimerical constructs of the past.

The Poetics of Everyday Behavior in Eighteenth-Century Russian Culture

IURII M. LOTMAN

The title of this essay needs explanation. Indeed, the very assumption that everyday behavior is a semiotic system may cause some controversy. To speak of the poetics of everyday behavior is to assert that eighteenth-century Russian culture patterned certain aspects of ordinary life on the norms and rules governing artistic texts and experienced them directly as aesthetic forms. If this hypothesis can be proved it will stand as a major typological characteristic of this cultural period.

Everyday behavior in itself is hardly an unusual subject for research: consider the field of ethnography, where it has been a traditional object of study. The topic is also a traditional one for students of such relatively distant cultural epochs as the classical period, the Renaissance, and the baroque. And historical studies of Russian culture also include a number of still significant works, from Nikolai Kostomarov's sketch of Russian domestic life and customs in the sixteenth and seventeenth centuries to Boris Rybakov's book on the people and customs of ancient Russia (second edition, 1966).

On this basis, one can make the following observation: the further removed a society is in time, place, or culture, the more its everyday behavior becomes a well-defined object of scholarly attention. Most documents recording norms of everyday behavior have been written by or for foreigners, presupposing an observer external to the social unit. An analogous situation exists in relation

Translated by Andrea Beesing from "Poetika bytovogo povedeniia v russkoi kul'ture XVIII veka," *Trudy po znakovym sistemam*, no.8 (Tartu, 1977), pp.65-89.

to everyday speech. When a language is first recorded and studied, descriptions of everyday speech are generally oriented toward the external observer. This correlation is not coincidental; like language, everyday behavior belongs to the sort of semiotic system that "native speakers" view as natural, a part of Nature and not Culture. Its semiotic and conventional character is apparent only to the external observer.

Since only an observer who perceives everyday behavior as a semiotic phenomenon can experience it aesthetically, thus far my exposition would seem to contradict the title of this essay. A foreigner, for whom the everyday life of another culture is an exotic experience, can perceive that life as an aesthetic fact. The direct participant in a culture, as a rule, is simply unaware of its distinguishing qualities. In the eighteenth century, however, the everyday behavior of the Russian nobility underwent such an elemental transformation that it acquired uncharacteristic features.

In every group with a relatively developed culture, human behavior is organized according to the following basic opposition: (1) The ordinary, everyday, customary social behavior which members of the group consider "natural"; the only possible, normal behavior; (2) All types of ceremonial, ritual, nonpragmatic behavior. This category includes state ceremonies, religious cults and rites, and all those activities that "native speakers" of a culture perceive as having an independent meaning.

People within a given culture learn the first type of conduct as they do their native language. They are directly immersed in it through direct use and do not notice when, where, and from whom they acquired it. Its mastery seems so natural to them that such questions are meaningless. No one would think of providing such an audience with a grammar of the language of social behavior, a metatext describing its "correct" norms. The second type of conduct is learned in the same way as a foreign language, with rules and grammar books. At first its norms are assimilated and then, on their foundation, "texts of behavior" are constructed. The first type of behavior is acquired naturally, unconsciously. The second is acquired consciously, with the aid of a teacher, and its mastery is usually celebrated in a special rite of initiation.

Starting with the reign of Peter the Great, the Russian nobility underwent a change far more profound than a simple shift in the customary social order. The area of subconscious, "natural" behavior became a sphere in which teaching was needed. Instructions were issued regarding the norms of social behavior, since the entire previously existing structure had been rejected as incorrect and replaced by "correct" European rules.

As a result, during and after the Petrine period, the Russian nobleman was like a foreigner in his own country. As an adult he had to learn through unnatural methods what is usually acquired through direct experience in early childhood. What was strange and foreign took on the character of a norm. To behave properly was to behave like a foreigner, that is, in a somewhat artificial manner, according to the norms of somebody else's way of life. Remembering these norms was just as crucial as knowing the rules of a foreign language in order to use it correctly. The book *Iunosti chestnoe zertsalo* (the mirror of honor for youth), desiring to illustrate the ideal of polite conduct, suggested that its reader imagine himself in the society of foreigners: "He should express his needs gracefully, using pleasant and courteous expressions as if he were speaking with a foreign person, so that he will become accustomed to behaving in this way."[1]

This kind of cultural inversion is not at all a "Europeanization" of everyday behavior in the straightforward sense of the term. When forms of social conduct and foreign languages were transplanted from the West and became the normal means of social interaction for the Russian nobility, their function was changed. In Europe they were natural native forms and consequently "native speakers" were not aware of them: in Holland, the ability to speak Dutch did not raise a person's standing in society. But once they were transferred to Russia, European social forms took on value; like the mastery of foreign languages they did raise an individual's social status. *Iunosti chestnoe zertsalo* further suggests:

> Young men who have traveled abroad and have learned foreign languages at great expense should imitate foreigners and take pains not to forget these languages. They should study them more thoroughly by reading useful books and by engaging in social intercourse and by occasionally writing and composing in these languages so as not to forget them.
>
> Those who have not visited foreign lands and have been received at court either from school or from some other place should be humble and restrained in the presence of others, desiring to learn from everyone; they should not, looking like idlers, keep their hats on their heads

---

[1] *Iunosti chestnoe zertsalo, ili pokazanie k zhiteiskomu obkhozhdeniiu, sobrannoe ot raznykh avtorov poveleniem ego imperatorskogo velichestva gosudaria Petra Velikogo . . . piatym tisneniem napechatannoe* (St. Petersburg, 1767), p. 29.

as though they were chained there, prancing about and boasting as if they had no respect for anyone.[2]

Thus, despite what is generally believed, Europeanization accentuated rather than obliterated the non-European aspects of daily life. In order to perceive one's own behavior as consistently foreign, it was essential *not to be* a foreigner: for a foreigner, foreign behavior is not foreign. What was needed was to assimilate forms of European daily life while retaining an external "alien" Russian attitude toward them. A Russian was not supposed to become a foreigner; he was merely supposed to act like one. Indeed, the assimilation of foreign customs had, at times, the paradoxical effect of intensifying the Russian antagonism toward foreigners.

A direct result of the change in everyday behavior was the ritualization and semiotization of those spheres of life that would be considered "natural" and nonsignifying in a culture that had not undergone an inversion. The effect was the opposite of that "privateness" which struck the Russian observer of European life. (Consider Petr Tolstoi's remarks about Venice: "Nobody reproaches anybody; nobody is afraid of anybody or of doing anything; everybody acts according to his will, each as he wishes."[3]) The image of European life was reduplicated in a ritualized play-acting of European life. Everyday behavior became a set of signs for everyday behavior. The semiotization of everyday life, the degree to which it was consciously perceived as a sign, increased sharply. Daily life acquired the characteristics of the theater.

Play-acting at everyday life, the feeling of being forever on the stage, is extremely characteristic of Russian gentry life in the eighteenth century. The common people were inclined to view the gentry as masqueraders; they observed their life as if watching a play. An interesting indication of this attitude is the use of European (gentry) attire for folk masquerades at Christmas. The memoirist Il'ia Selivanov recalls that at Christmastime in the early nineteenth century crowds of masked serfs—peasants as well as house servants—would stop at the manor house, which would be open to them at that season. For masquerade costumes most put on peasant sheepskin coats *turned inside out* or jester's garb made up of things not ordinarily in use (bast caps, and so forth). But it was also acceptable to wear the ordinary clothes of the nobility, obtained in

[2]Ibid., pp. 41-42.
[3]*Russkii arkhiv*, 1888, vol. 26, book 4, p. 547.

secret from the housekeeper: "old uniforms and other items of men's and women's apparel kept in the storerooms."[4]

It is revealing that in popular lithographs of the eighteenth century, with their clear theatrical orientation (their framing by curtains, marquees, footlights), the folk figures, *inasmuch as they are actors*, are depicted in gentry dress. In the well-known lithograph "Please Go Away From Me," the pancake vendor is drawn with beauty marks on her face while her admirer, decked out in braided wig and beauty marks, has on a nobleman's uniform and a three-cornered hat.

That noblemen's attire was perceived as theatrical is further illustrated by the fact that well into the twentieth century actors of the Russian folk theater would wear ordinary jackets with decorations, ribbons, and shoulder-pieces as signs of theatrical costume. In his description of folk-theater costumes, Petr Bogatyrev notes that not only Tsar Maximilian and King Mamai but also the warrior Anika, Zmeiulan, and others wear ribbons across their shoulders and epaulets so that the player "does not resemble the audience."[5] Compare this observation with Bogatyrev's assertion that in the Czech puppet theater "the puppet speech of the noblemen is intentionally incorrect."[6] Clearly theatrical clothing is also seen as "incorrect" compared to ordinary dress. It is made from materials that seem real but are not. In this sense theater clothing is like funeral clothing (for example, *bosovki*—shoes without soles) sewn especially for the deceased before a burial. Both *represent* clothing of good quality.

For the consciousness still closely bound to pre-Petrine tradition, the theater retained an aspect of pagan revelry. It was a type of masquerade and carnival with the indispensable feature of "dressing up." The folk imagination (the traditional pre-Petrine point of view) perceived the moment of costume-changing as diabolical, permissible only at certain times of the year (Christmas), and then exclusively as magical play with unclean spirits. Because of this belief, it was natural to see the theatricalized and carnival-like life at court—the eternal holiday and the eternal masquerade—in a specific religious-ethical way. Conversely, the aestheticized life of the nobility tried to incorporate rural life into its orbit, interpreting rural behavior through a prism of idyllic intermezzos. There were

[4]I. V. Selivanovskii, *Predaniia i vospominaniia* (St. Petersburg, 1881), p. 115.
[5]Petr Bogatyrev, "Narodnyi teatr. Cheshskii kukol'nyi i russkii narodnyi teatr," *Sborniki po teorii poeticheskogo iazyka*, no. 4 (Berlin/Petrograd, 1923), pp. 83-84.
[6]Ibid., p. 71.

numerous real-life attempts to construct theatricalized images of the Russian countryside, against the background of the real countryside and in contrast to it. Such attempts are exemplified by the peasant girls in silk pinafores who danced on the banks of the Volga during Catherine the Great's journey, by Sheremetev's theatrical villages, or by the Kleinmikhel family who came to a ball dressed up as Georgian peasants to thank Arakcheev for his solicitude.

At the coronation of Elizabeth, the erasure of the boundary between the stage and real life was reflected in costume changes, as well as transformations in age and sex roles. The coronation was marked by brilliant masquerades and performances. On May 29, 1742, the opera *La Clemenza di Tito* was performed at the Iauza palace. Since the role of Tito was meant to be an allusion to Elizabeth, the part was played by a woman, Madame George, dressed as a man. The audience appeared in costume for a later masquerade. If one keeps in mind that Elizabeth was wearing a guardsman's uniform on the day of her coup d'état and that the men at her court, particularly young cadets, came to masquerades dressed in women's costumes while women dressed as men, it is easy to imagine how this world was judged by the peasants, servants, and common people.[7]

The Russian nobleman of the post-Petrine period has assimilated this sort of everyday life, but at the same time felt it to be foreign. This dual perception made him treat his own life as highly semioticized, transforming it into a play.

The dual perception was sustained by the fact that many aspects of everyday life retained their common national character. No only the petty provincial landowner, but also the distinguished gentleman—and even Peter the Great and Elizabeth—could easily make the transition to the traditional norms of everyday Russian customs and behavior. It was possible to select either of two types of behavior: neutral, "natural," behavior, a behavior that was markedly aristocratic and at the same time consciously theatrical. Peter characteristically preferred the former. Even when participating in ritualized re-creations of everyday activities, he assigned himself the role of director, organizing the performance, imposing it on others, but not involving himself. This love of "simplicity" however, did not bring Peter's behavior closer to that of the people, but rather signified something directly opposite. For the peasant leisure and

[7]Cf. Pimen Arapov, *Letopis' russkogo teatra* (St. Petersburg, 1868), p. 44.

holidays were associated with a transition to a sphere of highly ritualized behavior. The church service (an immutable sign of the holiday), the wedding, and even a simple visit to a tavern signified inclusion in some established rite that determined what should be said and done, when, and by whom. For Peter leisure meant a transition to a deritualized "private" behavior. (Ritualized behavior had the quality of a public spectacle: an uninvited audience thronged about the house in which a wedding was taking place. "Natural" behavior took place behind closed doors within a close circle of "one's own.") The contradiction between ritualized and "natural" behavior was, however, canceled within the parodic ritual. As an antiritual it tended to be exclusive, accessible only to a small circle. But although inverted it was still a ritual, and therefore tended to be public. The Petrine period saw the intermingling of behavior codes that were semiotically extremely diverse: the official church ritual and the parodies of church ritual in the blasphemous ceremonies conducted by Peter and his entourage, "foreign" behavior practiced in everyday life, and the "private" behavior consciously opposed to ritual.

If neutral European or "middle-class" behavior became sharply semiotized when transferred to Russia, the behavioral transformations experienced by Russians visiting Europe are no less interesting. In some cases behavior was highly semioticized as a continuation of pre-Petrine tradition. It is easy to understand the concern of these Russian travelers with the meaning of gesture and ritual, their perception of every detail as a sign. The Russian in Europe saw himself as a *representative*, an accredited individual, and transferred the laws of diplomatic protocol to his everyday conduct. European observers assumed that this was normal everyday Russian behavior.

The opposing transformation was also possible: behavior could be sharply deritualized, making Russians appear more natural than Europeans. This was the case with Peter, who despite his excellent command of the constraining norms of diplomatic ritual, preferred to startle Europeans with the unexpected simplicity of his behavior. His conduct was not only more spontaneous than the norms of "royal" behavior dictated; it was even more spontaneous than "bourgeois" conduct. During his visit to Paris in 1716, Peter demonstrated an understanding of the norms of ritual. Though burning with impatience to see Paris, he did not go out until the king had called on him. During the regent's visit he invited him into his room, passed through the door first, and was the first to sit down in an armchair. The regent also sat in an armchair during the conversation, and Prince Kurakin interpreted standing up. But when Peter repaid the visit to the six-year-old Louis XV and saw the latter descending the staircase to meet the carriage, "he jumped out, ran toward the king, picked him up, and carried him up the stairs to the hall."[8]

Against the background of the traditional Russian way of life, the intermingling of behavior codes created a perceptible category of *behavioral style*. A similar process took place in early-eighteenth-century Russian language, in which the motley disorder of vocabulary intensified the feeling that not only modes of speech, but every isolated word had stylistic significance (not only behavior as a whole, but also every act). This development set the groundwork for the strict language classifications of the mid-eighteenth century.

Thus, after the first step—the semiotization of everyday behavior—there followed a second: the creation of styles within the framework of everyday norms. This process was expressed in part as the development of behavioral styles appropriate to specific geographical locations. When a nobleman traveled from St. Petersburg to Moscow, from an estate near Moscow to a provincial one, or from Russia to Europe, often unconsciously but always unerringly he changed the style of his behavior. Style formation also had a social as well as a geographical component. A difference in behavioral style was defined for the nobleman in state service and the one who had retired to his estate, for the military man and the civilian, for nobleman who lived in the capital (at court) and his counterpart in the provinces. A person's manner of speaking, walking, and dressing unmistakably indicated his position in the stylistic polyphony of everyday life. In private correspondence (and later in his *Gamblers*) Gogol used the expression "A losing streak, a definite losing streak! Nothing but spot cards!" He considered this phrase "a real army expression and in its way not without dignity." That is, he emphasized that neither a civilian bureaucrat nor an officer of the guard would express himself that way.

Stylistic coloration was emphasized because behavior was a matter of choice, a selection from several alternatives. The presence of choice, the possibility of changing from one type of behavior to another, was the basis of the aristocratic way of life. The life-style system of the Russian nobleman was constructed much like a tree.

[8]S. M. Solov'ev, *Istoriia Rossii s drevneishikh vremen*, book 9 (Moscow, 1963), p. 68.

In the second half of the eighteenth century, the nobility had attained the freedom to choose whether or not to serve the state, and whether to live in Russia or abroad, and from that point on it continued its efforts to multiply the tree's "branches." The government, however, especially during the reigns of Paul and Nicholas I, actively sought to eliminate the choices for individual behavior and style of life. The attempt was made to transform everyday life into state service and turn all clothing into a uniform.

The diagram below presents the basic possibilities for noble behavior.[9] The availability of *choice* sharply separated the nobleman's behavior from that of the peasant. Peasant behavior was regulated by the agricultural calendar and was invariable within the boundaries of each stage. It is curious that from this point of view the behavior of the noblewoman was much closer in principle to that of the peasant than to that of the nobleman. In her life there were no moments of individual choice, and her behavior was determined by her age.

Through the development of behavioral styles, behavior naturally acquired the quality of an aesthetically experienced phenomenon. This in turn initiated the search for behavioral models within the sphere of art. The man not yet acquainted with the Europeanized forms of art had only the familiar types of dramatic performance as models: church liturgy and popular farce. Of the two, however, church liturgy enjoyed such authority that its use in everyday life was viewed as a parodic, blasphemous act. But a remarkable example of folk theater as an organizer of everyday activity among the gentry appears in a rare book of 1847, *The Family History of the Golovins, owners of the village of Novospaskoe, collected by the Baccalaureate of the Moscow Spiritual Academy, Petr Kazanskii.*[10] This curious work, based on the domestic archive of the Golovin

[9]The diagram indicates the possibility of a clerical career, which, although not typical for a nobleman, was not unheard of. There were noblemen in both the monastic and nonmonastic clergy during the eighteenth and early nineteenth centuries. The diagram does not indicate an essential characteristic of the eighteenth century: the decisive change in the attitude toward suicide in post-Petrine Russia. Toward the end of the century the young portion of the aristocracy was literally gripped by a wave of suicide. Radishchev saw in man's freedom to choose life or death a guarantee of emancipation from political tyranny. This theme was actively debated in literature (Karamzin, Russian Wertheriana) and in publicistic writings. In this way yet another alternative was added, and the very fact of existence became the result of personal choice.

[10]*Rodoslovnaia Golovinykh, vladel'tsev sela Novospaskago, sobrannaia Bakkalavrom M. D. Akademii Petrom Kazanskim* (Moscow, 1847); hereafter cited as *Rodoslovnaia Golovinykh.*

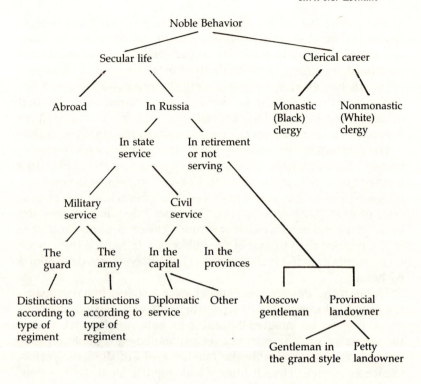

This chart shows only those basic types of noble behavior which could be chosen by the eighteenth-century Russian nobleman from among alternate possibilities. It does not take into account adjustments made according to the typology of behavior associated with age.

family, includes sources reminiscent of those used by Ivan Petrovich Belkin in his history of the village of Goriukhino. It includes among other things the life story of Vasilii Vasil'evich Golovin (1696-1781) based on the latter's own notes and on family legends. Golovin's life was turbulent: he studied in Holland, learned four European languages as well as Latin, acted as gentleman of the bedchamber at Catherine I's court, was implicated in the Mons affair, and wound up in Biron's torture chamber.[11] Having secured

---

[11]"He was imprisoned for about two years until March 3, 1738, subjected to horrible torture and inexpressible pain. Raising him on the rack, they twisted his shoulder blades out, they ran a hot iron down his back, stuck hot needles under his fingernails, beat him with a knout and finally returned him, broken by torture, to his family.... Unfortunately for posterity, the real nature of his offense is unknown," remarks Baccalaureate Petr Kazanskii mournfully (*Rodoslovnaia Golovinykh*, pp. 57-58).

his release with a huge bribe, he settled in the country. What is of interest here, however, is the theatrical aspect of his life. He transformed his everday life into a combination of marketplace theater, folk incantation, and Christian ritual. The following is an extensive passage:

Rising early in the morning, even before sunrise, he would read the midnight mass and matins together with his favorite deacon, Iakov Dmitriev. After the morning prayers, the butler, the steward, the guard, and the peasant elder would present him with reports and announcements. They usually entered and departed at the command of Pelegeia Petrovna Vorob'eva, a chambermaid of proven honesty. First she would intone, "In the name of the Father, the Son and the Holy Ghost," and those standing before her would answer "Amen." Then she would say, "Come in and watch out, be quiet and humble, careful and cautious, with purity and with prayer, and go to our lord and master with your reports and for your instructions. Bow low to his noble excellency and make sure you remember it well." They would all answer in chorus, "We understand, little mother!" Having entered the master's study, they would bow down to the ground and say, "My lord, we wish you good health!" The master would answer, "Greetings, my friends, my untortured and untormented, my untried and unpunished!" This was his customary saying. "So, my children, is all well and good with us?" The butler, bowing low, would be the first to answer this question. "My lord, everything is blessed by our Savior's grace, all is well and good and in God's keeping—in the holy church, in the divine sacristy, in your lordship's house, in the stable and the cattleyard, in the peacock and the crane cotes, in the gardens, in the bird ponds, and in all places." Following the butler, the steward would begin his report: "In your lordship's cellars, in your barns and pantries, in your sheds and drying rooms, in your hives and henhouses, your smokehouses and drying ovens, by the grace of our Lord, oh master, all is intact and in order. By your lordship's command fresh spring water from Grigorovo has been brought on the piebald horse. The water was poured into a glass bottle, placed in a wooden barrel and surrounded with ice. The barrel was covered on all sides and a stone was placed on top." The guard reported thusly: "All night, my lord, we walked around the manor house, we beat mallets, we shook rattles, sounded the alarm, pounded boards, took turns blowing the horn, and all four of us spoke loudly among ourselves. The night birds did not fly, they did not screech in strange voices, they did not frighten the young masters, and they did not peck at the lord's putty. They did not perch on the roof and they did not flutter about the attic." In conclusion the peasant elder would report: "In all four villages, by God's grace, all is well and good. Your lordship's serfs are growing wealthy, their livestock is growing fatter, the hoofed creatures are grazing, the domestic fowl are laying eggs, the earth didn't quake, nor were there any signs in the sky. The cat Van'ka,[12] the peasant woman Firebug[13] are living in Rtishchevo, and each month they receive their chaff by your lordship's command. Every day they lament their transgression and tearfully beg you, my lord, to have pity and set aside your anger and forgive them, your guilty slaves.

We will omit a description of the carefully organized daily ceremonial consisting of house prayer, church liturgy, and rituals associated with breakfast, dinner, and dessert. Each of these was a regularly repeated performance.

The preparation for bed began [at four o'clock in the afternoon—Iu. L.] with the order to close the shutters. Inside, they read the prayer to Jesus: "Lord Jesus Christ, Son of God, have mercy on us." From without, several voices would answer "Amen." On this word, they would close the shutters with a horrible bang and fasten them with iron bolts. At this time, the butler, the steward, the guard, and the peasant elder would appear. Only the butler was allowed into the master's study, and he would then give the others their orders. This was the guard's order: "Heed your master's command. See that you do not sleep all night, walk around the manor house, bang the mallets louder, blow the horn, pound the boards, shake the rattle, sound the alarm. Don't gape all around, and bear this firmly in mind: the birds must not fly, they must not screech in strange voices, they must not nibble at the lord's putty, they must not perch on the roof or flutter about in the attic. Watch out, my children, that you heed me well!" "We understand you," was the answer. The peasant elder's orders went like this: "Tell the sentries and sentinels to protect and watch over all the village inhabitants both great and small, and to keep an unremitting vigilance against fire. Watch carefully: Is there a disturbance anywhere in the villages of Tselevo, Medvedki, and Goliavino? Will the Iksha, Iakhroma, and Volgusha rivers be turbulent? Can you see any strange signs in the skies? Can you hear a fearful earthquake beneath the ground? If anything like this should happen, or if a miracle

[12]"This was the master's favorite cat. One day it crawled into the fishing creel, ate a live fish that had been prepared for the master's table, was trapped there, and suffocated. The servants did not report the cat's death, but only its crime, and the master exiled it" (Baccalaureate Kazanskii's notes).

[13]This was the nickname given to the woman whose carelessness was responsible for the fire that destroyed Novospaskoe in 1775. This fire frightened Vasilii Vasil'evich so much that he ordered the house serfs, numbering over three hundred, to cook only in one room specially set aside for the purpose. Naturally this order was never carried out. (Kazanskii's notes).

should occur, don't deliberate over it yourselves and form your own judgment, but come immediately to your lord and master and tell his noble excellency all. Heed me well!" The steward received his orders from the maid Vorob'eva. "His lordship commands you to watch over the supplies; send a horse to Grigorovo and fetch some holy water. Place it in a barrel, put ice around it, cover it up and put a stone on top. With purity and with prayer, care for people, watch over the animals, do not gape all around, and do not chatter nonsense. Heed this well!" Thus ended the commands. Usually it was Vorob'eva who locked and unlocked the doors of the rooms. She would take the keys to the master himself, and placing them at the head of the bed, she said, "Stay here, my lord, with Jesus Christ, and sleep under the cover of the Holy Mother of God. May a guardian angel watch over you, my lord." Then she would give an order to the girls on duty: "Watch the cats,[14] do not bang nor talk loudly, do not fall asleep, watch for eavesdroppers, and blow out the light. Heed this well!"

Having read the evening service, Vasilii Vasil'evich would lie down in bed, cross himself and intone: "God's servant is retiring; upon him are the seal and confirmation of Christ, the indestructible wall and protection of the Mother of God, the blessed right hand of John the Baptist, and omnipotent, life-giving cross of my guardian angel, the countenances of the incorporeal powers, and the prayers of all the saints. I hereby protect myself with the cross, cast out the demon and destroy his evil power now and forever and for ages unto ages. Amen!" At night at Novospaskoe a great noise ensued: ringing, knocking, whistling, shouting, rattling, and the scurrying of four servants and four watchmen. If anything prevented the master from falling asleep right away, he did not stay in bed and was restless for the entire night. In this case, he would either begin reading aloud his favorite book, *The Life of Alexander the Great* by Quintus Curtius, or he would sit in a large armchair . . . and intone the following words, now raising and now lowering his voice: "Satan, get thee to the barren places, to the thick woods and to the crevices of the earth, where the light of God's countenance shineth not. Satan, Enemy of Mankind, unhand me, get thee to the dark places, to the bottomless seas, to the shelterless uninhabited mountains of the wilderness where the light of God's countenance shineth not. Cursed wretch, be off to the Tartars! Be off, cursed wretch, to the inferno, to the eternal fire and appear to me no more. Thricedamned, thriceheathen and thricecursed! I blow on you and spit on you!" After finishing these exorcisms, he would rise from his chair and begin walking back and forth through all seven

---

[14]Vasilii Vasil'evich had seven cats around the house who walked about everywhere during the day and were tied to a seven-legged table at night. One girl was charged with watching after each cat. If one of the cats got loose and went into the master's room, both cats and girls were punished (Kazanskii's notes).

of his rooms shaking a rattle. These strange habits naturally provoked curiosity, and many of the servants peeked thrugh the cracks to see what the master was doing. But this too was taken into account. The housemaids would begin shouting, employing various witticisms and proverbs, and pour cold water on the eavesdroppers from an upper window. The master approved all these actions, saying, "It serves the culprits right. Suffering means nothing to them, thricedamned, thriceheathen and thricecursed, untortured, untormented and unpunished!" Stamping his feet, he would repeat the same thing over and over again.[15]

Before us is genuine theater, with unvarying, regularly repeated performances and texts. It is also *folk* theater with its rhymed monologues and its characteristic farcical finale when the audience is dowsed with water from the stage. On stage is the "nobleman," a figure quite familiar from folk theater and popular lithographs. He is also in part a "conjurer," chanting exorcisms and reading aloud in Latin interspersed with Russian folk-theater rhymes. The blending of the humorous and the frightful in this performance is very typical.

But the nobleman is not only an actor; he is also a spectator who in his turn watches the carnivalized ritual into which he has transformed the everyday flow of his life. He plays his frightful-humorous role with satisfaction and sees to it that others do not depart from the style of the performance. It is very doubtful that this man, an educated astronomer and geographer, European traveler, acquaintance of Peter the Great and grandson of Sophia's favorite, Golitsyn, really believes that his favorite cat Van'ka continues to live for decades in exile and every day laments his transgression. But he prefers to live in this world of convention and play rather than in the real one where, as he noted in his diary, "they cleaned off my disfigured fingernails, poor and sinful man that I am."[16]

We can see how, in later years, the system of genres which took shape in the aesthetic consciousness of eighteenth-century high

---

[15]*Rodoslovnaia Golovinykh*, pp. 60-70.

[16]Ibid., p. 58. Compare this account: "The famous wealthy count Skavronskii . . . surrounded himself with singers and musicians. He conversed with his servants in musical notes and in recitative. The butler would inform him in a rich baritone that dinner was being served. The coachman communicated with him in bass octaves, the postilions in soprano and alto, the footmen in tenor octaves, etc. During gala dinners and balls the servants would form trios, duets, and choruses while waiting on guests. The master himself would respond in musical form" (M. I. Pyliaev, *Staroe zhit'e, ocherki i rasskazy*, 2d ed. [St. Petersburg, 1897], p. 88).

culture began to influence the behavior of the Russian aristocrat, creating a complex system of *behavioral genres*. The tendency to divide the spaces of everyday life into units of performance is an illustration of this process. The transition from one unit to another was accompanied by a change in the genre of behavior. In pre-Petrine Russia there was a binary opposition between ritual space and nonritual space both in the universe at large and in the sphere of human habitation. This opposition was realized on various levels as "home" versus "church," "nonaltar space" versus "altar," "black (stove) corner" versus "red (icon) corner" of the peasant hut, and so forth. The division of the manor house into living quarters and reception rooms was a continuation of the opposition. Later a tendency developed both to turn reception rooms into living quarters and to introduce differentiation into the living space. The move from a winter residence to a summer one, the transition, in a few hours' time, from neoclassical or baroque palace halls to a rustic "cabin," a "medieval" ruin, a Chinese village, or a Turkish pavilion, even the walk from a "little Dutch house" to an "Italian" house in Kuskovo signified a change in type of behavior and speech. Not only royal palaces and noblemen's mansions, but even the far more modest estates of the petty gentry were filled with gazebos, grottos, chapels for solitary contemplation, sanctuaries for love, and so forth. Insofar as living space became scenery (another theatrical parallel was the tendency to accompany a change in space with a change in musical accompaniment), the spatial arrangement, if necessary, could be simplified and the cost lowered, reducing a construction of exceptional dimension (such as the most outstanding architectural ensembles) to a mere indication of such a construction, accessible even to the small landowner.

A poetics of behavior developed further with the appearance of the stock character. Like the theatrical stock character, this was one of a number of invariants within a group of typical roles. The eighteenth-century man would select a particular type of behavior for himself, which simplified and elevated his everyday existence according to some ideal. As a rule, he chose to model himself on a particular historical personage, a literary or government figure, or a character from a poem or a tragedy. The chosen figure became an idealized double of the real man, in a certain sense replacing the name-day saint. Patterning oneself after this figure became a program of behavior, and names such as "the Russian Pindar," "the Voltaire of the North," "our La Fontaine," "the new Sterne," or "Minerva," "Astraea," "the Russian Caesar," "the Fabius of our times" were used in addition to real names ("Minerva," for example, became the literary name for Catherine the Great).

This choice of a stock role structured self-evaluation and organized behavior. It also determined the way a man's contemporaries perceived his identity. It created an entire program of personal conduct, in a sense predetermining the character of future actions and the way they would be perceived. This situation stimulated the appearance of anecdotal epics structured according to a principle of accumulation. The mask-role was the thread upon which new episodes would be repeatedly strung to form an anecdotal life history. In principle such a text of behavior was open; it could be infinitely expanded since new "events" could always be added.

The number of stock roles to choose among was not unlimited and in fact, not even large. For the most part, the set of roles resembled a set of literary characters and theatrical heroes.

The first kind of stock character I shall discuss was derived from ordinary neutral behavior through quantitative exaggeration or inversion. An example of this type of the stock role is the *bogatyr*, or legendary hero, typical of the eighteenth century. This role was created through the purely quantitative expansion of certain normal, neutral human qualities. The eighteenth century abounded in giants. Pushkin's characterization of Peter as a "miracle-working giant" has a clear origin in the eighteenth-century imagination. Anecdotes about Lomonosov consistently emphasize his superlative physical strength and the heroic quality of his pastimes. Suvorov's term for his soldiers, "marvel-heroes," is related to this same perception (compare: "but you *doubled* [italics are mine—Iu. L] your *bogatyr's* stride," where *bogatyr* already signifies a doubling in relation to the ordinary[17]). A perfect manifestation of this tendency was the anecdotal epic about Potemkin, which created the image of a man whose every natural capability surpassed the norm.

[17]"Nastavlenie Suvorova Miloradovichu," in D. A. Miliutin, *Istoriia voiny Rossii s Frantsiei v tsarstvovanie imp. Pavla I v 1799 g*, vol. 1 (St. Petersburg, 1852), p. 588. Concerning the tendency in medieval texts to construct outstanding characters who possess ordinary human qualities but to an extraordinary degree, see Evelyn Birge Vitz, "Type et individu dans 'l'autobiographie' medievale," *Poetique: Revue de Théorie et d'Analyse Littéraires*, no. 24 (1975). Such a construction is based on a faith in the stability of the earthly role given to man from above. This construction created a tradition of "heroic" images (= models) which continued to affect people's behavior even when the role was actively chosen by the individual.

Here are stories of a monstrous appetite and digestion.[18] Consider examples like the following:

> Once in the last century Prince Potemkin was walking through a bathroom in the Tauride palace accompanied by Levashev and Prince Dolgorukov where they passed a magnificent silver bathtub.
> Levashev: What a splendid tub!
> Prince Potemkin: If you manage to fill it [this is the literary translation but in the oral text a different word is used] I will give it to you.[19]

Not only was the audience expected to appreciate the scope of Potemkin's imagination, it was also to suppose that, as the legitimate owner of the amazing bathtub, he was capable of accomplishing such a feat. There is yet another aspect of Potemkin's legendary heroism. It is no accident that Pushkin, hearing that Davydov's article had been given to the censor Mikhailov-Danilevskii for examination, said, "It's like sending Prince Potemkin to the eunuchs to learn about women."[20] Against this background appear the features of grandiose political designs, grandiose feasts and festivals, grandiose prodigality, thievery, bribe-taking, magnanimity, generosity, and patriotism. Essentially any anecdote that emphasizes the criminal or the heroic can become part of the biographical epic of Potemkin anecdotes, but these features must be highly exaggerated and carried to the extreme.

Another typical stock role that structures a group of biographical legends and real life stories is that of the wit, the jester, and the buffoon. This role is also connected with the marketplace theater and the popular lithograph. An example is the life history of Kop'ev, episodes of which were circulated widely among his contemporaries. For the most part, these episodes were simply rambling anecdotes about a wit who extricates himself from difficult situations with bold answers. Viazamskii, retelling episodes from the "biography" of Kop'ev, pointed out that these actions and rejoinders were also attributed to other persons (Aleksandr Golitsyn, for example) and that some were even known as French anecdotes. The stock role acted like a magnet for new material and the legendary

---

[18]The Potemkin stories are entirely in the spirit of Rabelais or the lithograph series "Great Glutton and Merry Drunkard." In its Russian variants, the series lost the feature of political caricature peculiar to the French original, and became closer to its true origin in the tradition of Rabelais and the marketplace carnival.

[19]P. A. Viazemskii, *Staraia zapisnaia knizhka* (Leningrad, 1929), p. 194.

[20]*Russkii arkhiv*, 1880, vol. 18, book 2, p. 228 n.

life history became a text that tended to grow by incorporating various anecdotes about wits.

Illustrative of this process is the fate of a certain Marin. Marin was a military man who received four grapeshot wounds at Austerlitz (in the head, the leg, and two in the chest), after which he was given a golden sword for bravery and raised to the rank of staff captain. At Friedland he received a shell fragment in the head and was awarded the St. Vladimir's cross and an adjutant's epaulets. In 1812 he was staff general under Bagration and died at the end of the campaign from wounds, disease, and exhaustion. He was an active politician (participating in the events of March 12, 1801), an interlocutor of Napoleon, to whom he delivered a letter from the Russian emperor, and finally, a poet-satirist. But in the eyes of his contemporaries all these accomplishments were eclipsed by the mask of the prankster and wit. It is this image of Marin that has impressed itself in the minds of historians of early-nineteenth-century Russian culture.

Another widespread type was the "Russian Diogenes," or "new cynic," a role that combined a philosophical contempt for wealth with poverty, a disregard for the norms of propriety, and obligatory incessant drinking. This stereotype, created by Barkov, later structured the image and behavior of Kostrov, Milonov, and a dozen other literary figures.

A man who patterns his conduct after a particular stock role transforms his life into a kind of improvised performance; the type of behavior for each character is prescribed, but not the situations that arise in the plot when characters confront one another. The action remains open-ended and can continue as an accumulation of episodes. Such a structuring of life inclined toward folk theater and was ill suited for comprehending tragic conflicts. Suvorov's mythologized life history is an example. In constructing an idealized myth about himself, Suvorov clearly focused on Plutarch's subjects, Caesar in particular. This lofty image could, however, be overlaid by that of the Russian *bogatyr* in his letters to his daughter or his addresses to his soldiers. (The stylized descriptions of military action in the letters to his daughter, the famous "Suvorochka," strikingly resemble Captain Tushin's transformation, in *War and Peace*, of military action into something like a fairy tale, suggesting that Tolstoi was familiar with the source.)

Suvorov's behavior was governed, however, by two sets of norms, not one. The second set was clearly patterned on the buffoon. An endless number of anecdotes about Suvorov's eccentricities, his rooster's crow, and his jester's pranks, are connected with this stock role. The combination of two mutually exclusive stock roles in the behavior of the same person was connected with the poetics of preromanticism,[21] where contrast was an element of great significance. The eccentric also plays a central role in the sketch "Kharakter moego diadi" (my uncle's character) by Griboedov.[22] The unpredictable quality of a man's behavior in this case arises from the fact that his interlocutors can never tell beforehand which of the two possible roles he will play. If the aesthetic effect of behavior patterned on a single stock role was a matter of the consistent projection of that role in different situations, here the audience was constantly surprised. For example, Prince Esterhazy, sent by the Viennese court to negotiate with Suvorov, complained to Komarovskii: "You can't get any sense out of this man; how can you talk to him?" All the greater was his astonishment at their next meeting: "C'est un diable d'homme. Il a autant d'esprit, que de connaissance."[23]

The next stage in the evolution of a poetics of behavior may be characterized as the transition from stock role to plot.

Plot is in no way a chance component of everyday behavior. Indeed, the appearance of plot as a definite category organizing narrative texts in literature may ultimately be explained by the need to select a behavioral strategy for activity outside it.

Everyday behavior acquires a full-fledged interpretation only when each separate chain of real-life actions can be related to a meaningful, fully realized sequence of activities that has a unified meaning. On the level of coded message, such a sequence serves as a generalized sign of situation, of the chain of actions and results: in other words, plot. The presence of a set of plots in the consciousness of a particular group makes it possible to encode real-life behavior, to separate the signifying from the nonsignifying and to ascribe meaning to the former. In such a system, the low-level units of semiotic behavior—the gesture and the act—receive semantic and stylistic meaning not in isolation but in relation to higher level categories: plot, style, and genre of behavior. The

[21]Consider this excerpt from Batiushkov's notebook: "Recently I made the acquaintance of an eccentric man, of which there are many!" K. N. Batiushkov, *Sochineniia* (Moscow, 1934), pp. 378-380. Or consider a note from Pushkin's diary for December 17, 1815 while he was a student at the lycée: "Would you like to see a strange man, an eccentric?" Pushkin, *Polnoe sobranie sochinenii*, vol. 12 (Moscow/ Leningrad, 1949), pp. 301-302.

[22]A. S. Griboedov, *Sochineniia* (Moscow, 1956), pp. 414-415.

[23]*Zapiski grafa E. F. Komarovskogo* (St. Petersburg, 1914), p. 90.

totality of plots that encode a person's behavior in a particular epoch can be defined as the mythology of everyday and social behavior.

In the last third of the eighteenth century, when a mythology of this kind was taking shape in Russian culture, the main source for behavioral plots was literature with few ties to the everyday: the ancient historians, neoclassical tragedies, and in isolated cases, saints' lives.

Perceiving one's own life as a text organized according to the laws of a particular plot sharply emphasized "unity of action," or life's movement toward an immutable goal. The theatrical category of the "finale," the fifth act, became particularly significant. Structuring life as an improvised performance in which the actor must remain within the boundaries of his role created an open-ended text. One new scene after another could contribute and add variation to the flow of events. The presence of plot immediately introduced the idea of conclusion and simultaneously endowed this conclusion with decisive significance. Death, particularly tragic death, became the object of constant reflection and life's climactic moment. Naturally this attitude brought a focus on the heroic and tragic models of behavior. Identifying oneself with the hero of a tragedy determined not only the type of behavior but also the type of death. Concern over the "fifth act" became a distinguishing feature of "heroic" behavior at the end of the eighteenth century and the beginning of the nineteenth.

> I have been born so that the entire world should be a spectator
> To my triumph or my ruin....[24]

In these lines Lermontov clearly expresses the concept of man as an actor playing out the drama of his life before an audience. (The romantic proclivity for overstatement is reflected in the fact that the audience is the "entire world.") The identification of life's culmination with the theatrical concept of the fifth act (triumph or ruin) is also expressed. Hence Lermontov's constant reflection on life's finale: "The end. How resounding is the word."

> And I will not die forgotten. My death
> Will be terrible: foreign lands

[24]M. Iu. Lermontov, *Sochineniia v shesti tomakh*, vol. 2 (Moscow/Leningrad, 1954), p. 38.

Will marvel at it, but in my native country
Everyone will curse even the memory of
me.[25]

Early on the morning of December 14, 1825, when the Decembrists
came out onto Senate square, Aleksandr Odoevskii cried out: "We
are going to die, brothers, oh, how gloriously we are going to die!"
The uprising had not yet begun, and it was still entirely possible
that the affair would be a success. But the idea of heroic ruin was
what gave the event the character of high tragedy, elevating the
participants in their own eyes and in the eyes of their descendants
to the level of characters in a theatrical plot.

The fate of Aleksandr Radishchev is an exceptionally clear example of fascination with tragic death. The circumstances surrounding his death remain unclear to this day. The stories often
repeated in scholarly literature concerning threats supposedly addressed to Radischev by Zavadovskii or even by Vorontsov cannot
be credited. Of course Radishchev may have incurred displeasure
by a careless word or action. But to anyone in the least bit familiar
with the political climate of the "splendid beginning of Alexander's
reign," it is obvious that it was not the time when a bold project,
solicited by the government, could cause any serious repression
(and no other "dangerous" actions are attributed to Radishchev
during these months!). The version Pushkin offers is clearly ten-
dentious. Unconcealed irony is apparent, arising from the dispro-
portion between Zavadovskii's reprimand ("he told him in friendly
reproach") and Radishchev's reaction ("Radishchev *perceived* a threat
[italics are mine—Iu. L.]. Hurt and frightened he returned
home . . ."). There is as yet no scholarly consensus on how to
interpret Pushkin's article, and until its purpose is duly explained,
drawing conclusions from it is extremely risky. But one thing is
clear: Radishchev was a courageous man, and he could not be
frightened by the shadow of danger or by an ambiguous threat.
He did not commit suicide out of fear. It is hardly worthwhile to
refute Georgii Shtorm's anecdotal musings in connection with Radishchev's suicide: "Everything was significant, even the gradual
worsening of the weather which was noted by the meteorological

[25]Ibid., vol. 1, p. 185.

bulletin in *The St. Petersburg News* on September 11 and 12."[26] According to Shtorm, it was not only the weather, or even his disillusionment with his hopes to improve the peasants' lot, that played a fateful role in Radishchev's life, but also "personal" circumstances. One of these circumstances, Shtorm says, was "undoubtedly" the conviction of a distant relative who had been caught swindling.[27]

All attempts to find a concrete motive for Radishchev's tragic act in the events of his life during the fall of 1802 lead to nothing. Yet this act, though unmotivated by the biographical circumstances of his last months, is a logical end to the long chain of his endless deliberations on this theme. In his life of Fedor Vasilevich Ushakov, in *A Journey from St. Petersburg to Moscow*, in his treatise "concerning man, his mortality, and immortality," and in other works Radishchev persistently returns to the problem of suicide. His thinking on this theme is connected with the eighteenth-century materialist ethic and directly opposes the moral teachings of the church. He affirms man's right to dispose of his life as he wishes. On the other hand, he emphasizes not only the philosophical but also the political aspect of the issue. The right to commit suicide, to liberate oneself from the fear of death, places a limit on man's submissiveness and circumscribes the power of tryants. Delivering himself from the obligation to live no matter what the circumstances, man becomes absolutely free and negates the powers of despotism. This idea played an extremely important role in Radishchev's political thought, and he often returned to it: "Oh, my beloved fellow men! Rejoice over my death! It will be an end to torment and suffering. You who have been delivered from the yoke of superstition, remember that misery is no longer the lot of the deceased."[28]

This idea did not belong exclusively to Radishchev. In Kniazhnin's

---

[26]Georgii Shtorm, *Potaennyi Radishchev. Vtoraia zhizn' Puteshestviia iz Peterburga v Moskvu*, 2d ed. (Moscow, 1968), p. 439. See my review of the first edition: "V tolpe rodstvennikov," *Uchenye zapiski Gorkovskogo gosudarstvennogo universiteta*, no. 78 (Gorki, 1966). The "second, revised edition" did not benefit from the criticism of the first but piled on more blunders. Let us note only that the author considered it appropriate to conclude the book with "unpublished lines in the spirit of the Radishchev tradition," hinting that the unknown author might have been Pushkin. Unfortunately these lines are a familiar text frequently published in anthologies, an excerpt from Viazemskii's poem "Negodovanie." They can be considered "unpublished" only in the sense that their author can be considered "unknown." This is not simply a random error but a glaring display of dilettantism, a fitting conclusion to Shtorm's book.

[27]Shtorm, p. 383.

[28]A. N. Radishchev, *Polnoe sobranie sochinenii*, vol. 2 (Moscow/Leningrad, 1941), p. 101. Compare Montesquieu, *The Spirit of Laws*, book 1, chapter 8.

Vadim Novogorodskii (Vadim of Novgorod) this is Vadim's final line, addressed to Riurik:

> In the midst of your triumphant troops
> Crowned, seeing everything at your feet,
> What are you next to him who dares to die?[29]

Consider also the ending of Ivanov's *Marfa Posadnitsa*:

> Marfa: . . . Recognize in the tsar a monster
> In myself an example for you.
> Live your life without dishonor
> And without dishonor die. (*stabs herself*)[30]

Being prepared to die, Radishchev believed, distinguishes the man from the slave. In the chapter entitled "Mednoe" of *A Journey from St. Petersburg to Moscow*, the author addresses a serf footman, the accomplice and victim of a depraved master: "Noble ideas are alien to your mind. *You do not know how to die* [italics are mine—Iu. L.]. You will bow down and you will be a slave in spirit as you are on your estate."[31] The image of Fedor Ushakov's courageous death reminded Radishchev of "people who bravely take their own lives." And the final teaching he placed in Ushakov's mouth reminds the reader that "one must be firm of mind in order to die without trepidation."[32]

Radishchev attached great importance to the heroic conduct of a single individual as an instructive spectacle for his fellow citizens since, as he often repeated, man is an imitative animal. The demonstrational nature of personal behavior brought to the fore the theatrical component in the life of a person aspiring to the role of "teacher . . . in firmness," who provides an "example of courage."[33] "A man who is born with sensitivity, who is gifted with a powerful imagination and moved by a love of honor, is expelled from the midst of the crowd. He ascends the scaffold. All eyes are upon him; everyone impatiently awaits his pronouncement. He

---

[29]"*Vadim Novogorodskii.*" *Tragediia Ia. Kniazhnina s predisloviiem V. Sadovnika* (Moscow, 1914), p. 63.
[30]*Sochineniia i perevody F. F. Ivanova*, part 2 (Moscow, 1824), p. 89.
[31]Radishchev, vol. 1 (1938), p. 351.
[32]Ibid., p. 184.
[33]Ibid., p. 155.

himself awaits either applause or mockery more bitter than death itself."[34]

Radishchev found Addison's *Cato* particularly significant because it combined theatrical qualities with this concept of heroic death. The hero of Addison's tragedy became a kind of code for Radishchev's own behavior. In the chapter entitled "Krest'tsy" from *Journey from St. Petersburg to Moscow*, Radishchev placed the following words in the mouth of a virtuous father: "This is my testament to you. If misfortune exhausts its arrows on you, if your virtue finds no earthly refuge, if you are driven to extremes, and can find no protection from oppression, remember that you are a man. Remember your greatness and grasp the crown of bliss which they try to take away from you. Die. I bequeath to you the words of the dying Cato."[35]

Which words of the "dying Cato" does Radishchev mean? The commentator for the academy edition (Barskov) proposed that "Radishchev had in mind Plutarch's account of Cato's death speech."[36] The most recent commentators also support this view.[37] It is obvious, however, that Radishchev was thinking of the concluding monologue of Addison's tragedy. He wrote of this same monologue later while in Siberia: "I always read with the greatest pleasure the reflections of those who stand at the edge of the grave, at the threshold of eternity. When I consider the reasons for their death, and the motives inspiring these men, I learn much more than I could find anywhere else . . . You know the soliloquy or monologue of Shakespeare's Hamlet and the soliloquy of Addison's Cato Uticensis."[38]

Radishchev includes his own translation of this monologue at the end of his chapter entitled "Bronnitsy": "Some secret voice tells me that something will be forever alive."

> The stars shall fade away, the sun himself
> Grow dim with age and nature sink in years,
> But thou shalt flourish in immortal youth,
> Unhurt amidst the war of elements,
> The wrecks of matter, and the crush of worlds.

[34]Ibid., p. 387.
[35]Ibid., p. 295.
[36]Ibid., p. 485.
[37]A. N. Radishchev, *Puteshestvie iz Peterburga v Moskvu*, ed. L. I. Kulakova and V. A. Zapadov, (Leningrad, 1974), p. 157.
[38]Radishchev, *Polnoe sobranie sochinenii*, vol. 2, pp. 97-98.

He added this note to his translation: "The Death of Cato, Addison's tragedy. Act V, Scene I."[39]

The connection between the words of the nobleman from Krest'tsy and this excerpt is obvious. It is an unvarying element in Radishchev's philosophy: the idea of being prepared to commit suicide is merely a variant on the theme of the glorious deed. The concept of the glorious deed is connected with belief in the immortality of the soul: "It happens—and we see many examples of it in literature—that the man who is told he must die beholds his approaching death with contempt and without trepidation. We have seen and do see people who courageously take their own lives. And in truth one must be fearless and possess great spiritual strength to behold one's own destruction with a steady eye.... Often such a man sees beyond the boundaries of the grave and trusts in his own resurrection."[40]

Thus Radishchev's suicide was not an act of despair, an acceptance of defeat. It was a deliberate act of struggle he had contemplated for a long time, a lesson in patriotic resolution and in the unyielding love of freedom. It is difficult for us now to reconstruct in detail Radishchev's attitude to the political situation at the beginning of Alexander I's reign. Toward the autumn of 1802 he apparently came to the conclusion that it was necessary to perform some glorious deed to arouse and mobilize Russian patriots. His children write in their memoirs that during his final days he was agitated and one day even said to them, "Well, my dear children, what if I am sent to Siberia again?" The nature of Radishchev's activities at the beginning of Alexander I's reign make such a concern seem so unfounded that his son Pavel's conclusion is a natural one: "His mental infirmity continued to grow."[41] Pavel Radishchev was young when his father died and by the time he wrote his memoirs, though he had an unconditional and touching admiration for his father's memory, he was quite far from understanding the essence of Radishchev's views. The words recorded in the memoirs were not the result of mental illness. It is most likely that Radishchev was agitated because he had decided that the time had come

[39]Ibid., vol. 1, p. 269.

[40]Ibid., pp. 183-184.

[41]See *Biografiia A. N. Radishcheva, napisannaia ego synov'iami* (Moscow/Leningrad, 1959), p. 95. Radishchev was really ill in August 1802 (see his letter to his parents written August 18 [*Polnoe sobranie sochinenii*, vol. 3 (1952) p. 535]). There is no basis, however, for surmising that he is speaking of mental illness. Such a conclusion is no more accurate than the official reason given in government documents for his death: "consumption."

for the final heroic deed: "life's fifth act." Nevertheless, there must have been a moment when he had still not decided what the act of protest would be or if it would involve his destruction. Apparently the momentum of long consideration took the upper hand. Pushkin had reason to insist that even from the time of Ushakov's conversations with Radishchev before his death "suicide had become one of his favorite topics of deliberation."[42]

One can suppose that Radishchev's estimation of himself as the "Russian Cato" determined not only his own behavior but also the way his contemporaries perceived his action. The Russian reader was very familiar with Addison's tragedy. The eighth issue of the journal *Ippokrena* for 1801, for example, included a characteristic assortment of materials. In addition to Gart's complete prose translation entitled "The Death of Cato or the Birth of the Roman Dictatorship, a tragedy composed by the great Addison," there appeared the excerpts "Brutus" and "Hamlet's Reflections on Death." It is interesting that Cato's and Hamlet's monologues were brought together here just as in Radishchev's text. One writer addressed Brutus: "Some people, judging by your own strict rules, believe that you have sinned in spilling Caesar's blood but these honorable men are mistaken. *What mercy should be shown to the usurper of excessive power from one who thought it better to die by his own hand than to agree to servility?* [italics are mine—Iu. L.]"[43] The hero of Sushkov's tale "The Russian Werther" commits suicide, leaving behind on the table a copy of Addison's "Cato" open to the same passage Radishchev quoted in the "Bronnitsa" chapter. Sergei Glinka was one of Radishchev's admirers (Radishchev's son, a friend of Glinka's, called him "one of Radishchev's greatest followers"). When Glinka was a cadet, his entire estate consisted of three books: *A Journey from St. Petersburg to Moscow, Vadim Novgorodskii,* and *A Sentimental Journey.* On one occasion he ended up in the guardhouse, and wrote of it in his memoirs: "Cato's act of stabbing himself with a dagger after Julius Caesar had locked him in chains spun around in my head and I was ready to smash it against the wall."[44]

Both Cato's image and Addison's interpretation of it continually attracted the attention of Karamzin. In his 1791 review of *Emilia Galotti* Karamzin called Emilia, "a heroine who speaks of human

[42]Pushkin, vol. 12 , p. 31.
[43]*Ippokrena*, vol. 8 (1801), pp. 52-53.
[44]*Zapiski S. N. Glinki* (St. Petersburg, 1895), p. 103.

freedom in Cato's language." (Later he called Marfa Posadnitsa "the Cato of her republic."—Iu. L.) "At this point," he wrote, "Emilia demands a dagger in her fanaticism viewing her suicide as a sacred deed."[45]

In his *Letters of a Russian Traveler*, Karamzin quotes the same verses by Voltaire that Radishchev's son was later to recall when explaining the motives for his father's death: "Quand on n'est rien et qu'on est sans espoir / La vie est un opprobre et la morte un devoir . . . " Elsewhere he writes: "Addison's wonderful tragedy is especially good where Cato speaks and acts."[46] In his historical eulogy to Catherine the Great,[47] Karamzin included "Cato the suicide" among the classical heroes. In 1811 he wrote in the album of Paul's daughter, Princess Catherine, a quotation from Rousseau in which Cato is called "a god among mortals."[48]

In 1802 Karamzin published an article in *Vestnik Evropy* (the European messenger) which presents a coded response to Radishchev's death.[49] The extensive polemic is directed not at Radishchev but at the false interpretation of the ideas and images in Addison's tragedy, *Cato*.

Budgell, a clever English writer, was a kinsman of the great Addison. Together with him he published *The Spectator* and other journals. All the pieces in *The Spectator* signed with the letter X are his compositions. Addison tried to make Budgell wealthy, but he squandered everything and went to ruin after Addison's death. Finally he threw himself into the Thames, leaving the following note in his room: 'What Cato did and Addison approv'd cannot be wrong!' Everyone knows that Addison wrote *The Death of Cato*. So moral an author would not have justified suicide for a Christian but he allowed himself to praise it for Cato. His splendid monologue, 'It must be so . . . Plato, thou reasonst well,' rid the unfortunate Budgell of the gnawings of his conscience, which could have saved him from suicide. Good authors! Think on the consequences of what you write.[50]

In this article Karamzin condemned the principle of structuring one's own life as if it were a theatrical plot. At the same time he

[45]*Moskovskii zhurnal*, 1791, part 1, p. 67.
[46]N. M. Karamzin, *Izbrannye sochineniia*, vol. 1 (Moscow/Leningrad, 1964), p. 573.
[47]*Sochineniia Karamzina*, vol. 1 (St. Petersburg, 1848), p. 312.
[48]*Letopis' russkoi literatury i drevnosti* (Moscow, 1859), book 2, p. 167.
[49]For a substantiation of this hypothesis and a text of the note see Iu. M. Lotman, "Istochniki svedenii Pushkina o Radishcheve (1819-1822)," *Pushkin i ego vremia*, no. 1 (Leningrad, 1962), pp. 53-60.
[50]*Vestnik Evropy*, No. 19 (1802) p. 209.

clearly showed that deciphering Radishchev's action presented no difficulty to him.

The approach to personal life as plot signaled the transformation of the poetics of behavior from spontaneous improvisation to a consciously regulated activity. The next step in this development was the tendency, characteristic of the romantic era, to merge the life-text with the artistic text. Poetry began to form into lyrical cycles, forming "poetic diaries" and "romances of personal life." The biographical legend became an indispensable condition for perceiving any work as an artistic text. The fragmented quality of the romantic text has long been noted. It must be emphasized, however, that this fragmentation was redeemed by the immersion of the recorded (either printed or handwritten) text in the context of the oral legend surrounding the author's personality. This legend was the strongest factor regulating the poet's real behavior as well as the audience's perception of his behavior and his works.

The extreme development of the poetics of behavior in the romantic era made it natural that the realists should demonstratively exclude this category. The poet's life left the realm of artistically significant facts (the best evidence of this is the appearance of the parodic pseudobiographies of the type written by Koz'ma Prutkov). Art, having partly lost its play-acting element, no longer leapt over the footlights or descended from the pages of the novel into the sphere of the author's and the reader's real-life behavior.

But the eclipse of the poetics of behavior would not last long. Disappearing with the last romantics of the 1840s, it would rise again in the years 1890-1900 in the lives of the symbolists, in the concept of "life-building," the "theater for one actor," the "theater of life," and other cultural phenomena of the twentieth century.[51]

[51]This essay is related to a number of earlier publications devoted to the study of behavior as a cultural category from the viewpoint of historical semiotics: "Teatr i teatral'nost' v stroe kul'tury nachala XIX v."; "Stsena i zhivopis' kak kodiruiushchie ustroistva kul'turnogo povedeniia cheloveka nachala XIX stoletiia" in the collection Lotman, *Stat'i po tipologii kul'tury* (Tartu, 1973), as well as to the following essays in this book.

The Decembrist in Daily Life (Everyday Behavior as a Historical-Psychological Category)

IURII M. LOTMAN

Historical laws do not work mechanically. Within the complex and contradictory movement of history, various processes intersect and conflict. In some of these human beings are passive agents, while in others their activity takes a direct and spontaneous form. To understand humans as active agents (often defined as the subjective aspect of the historical process) one must examine not only the sociohistorical aspects of a situation but also the special nature of the human actor. Studying history from the point of view of human activity requires an understanding of the psychological premises of human behavior.

Even the psychological aspect has several levels, however. Certainly some behavioral traits and reactions to external situations are characteristic of humans as such. This level interests the psychologist who consults historical material only to find illustrations of psychological laws. But human psychology in general also provides a foundation for specific types of social and historical behavior. Under the influence of complex sociohistorical processes, ways of reacting arise that are peculiar to specific periods and social settings, along with conceptions of what actions are correct or incorrect, permissible or prohibited, significant or nonsignificant. Such regulators of behavior as shame, fear, and honor are brought into play. Complex ethical, religious, aesthetic, and other semiotic

Translated by Andrea Beesing from "Dekabrist v povsednevnoi zhizni," *Literaturnoe nasledie dekabristov* (Leningrad, 1975) pp. 25-74.

norms come to influence human consciousness, serving as a background for the psychology of group behavior.

In fact, in real life there is no such thing as group behavior. Just as language norms are realized and simultaneously violated in thousands of idiolects, so group behavior is the sum total of the realization and violation of behavioral norms within the individual systems of innumerable group members. But "incorrect" behavior that violates the behavioral norms of a given social group is by no means accidental. Violations of commonly accepted behavioral norms—eccentricities or "improprieties"—took very different forms in the Russia of the pre-Petrine and that of the post-Petrine period. Moreover, the nobleman's differed from the merchant's, and the peasant's from the monk's (of course some violations were "national" in character and therefore common to all). A norm and its violations are not locked into a static state of contradiction; they are continually changing places. Rules arise for violating rules and violations appear that are essential to norms. A person's actual behavior will vacillate between these poles, depending on the type of culture. A higher value may be assigned to following the norm: "the correct life," "life according to tradition," "the way it's done," "according to regulations." Or a higher value may be assigned to the violation of the norm, leading to an emphasis on originality, oddity, eccentricity, playing the holy fool, and the devaluation of the norm through the ambivalent union of extremes.

Human behavior is always variegated, and this point should not be forgotten. Elegant abstractions like "romantic behavior" or "the psychological type of young Russian nobleman of the early nineteenth century" will always remain highly theoretical constructs, not to mention the fact that every sociopsychological stereotype implies the existence of variants according to sex, age ("childlike," "adolescent," "both the frivolous old man and the staid youth are comical"), and so on.

The individual psyche represents such a complex structure with so many levels and such a variety of specific arrangements that the appearance of two identical individuals is a virtual impossibility. Despite the wealth of individual psychological variants and the variety of possible behaviors, however, it is important to remember that in practice not all of an individual's actions are relevant to society. The only acts considered relevant are those that have been assigned some kind of social significance. By interpreting an individual's behavior, society simplifies and typifies it in accordance with its own social codes. The individual completes this process of organization by assimilating society's view and becoming "more typical" not only to observers but also to himself.

Thus, as one analyzes the structure of human behavior in a specific historical period and works with various theoretical constructs, one must keep their links to numerous variants constantly in mind. Without an account of the dialectics of regularity and chance the mechanisms of social psychology cannot be understood.

Was there a specific pattern of everyday behavior that distinguished the Decembrist not only from reactionaries and like minded "stiflers" (*gasil'niki*) but also from contemporary liberal and educated noblemen? A study of historical materials permits a positive answer to this question. Indeed, Russians, as the cultural heirs of the same historical tradition, can sense it directly. Even without reading the commentators we perceive Chatskii, the hero of Griboedov's *Woe from Wit*, as a Decembrist. But we do not see Chatskii at a "secret society" meeting; we see him rather in the everyday surroundings of a Moscow mansion. Several phrases in Chatskii's monologues, characterizing him as an enemy of servitude and ignorance, are essential to this interpretation. But his manner of speaking and conducting himself are no less important. It is Chatskii's *behavior* at Famusov's, his rejection of a particular type of behavior:

> To come for a visit and just be silent, bow
>   and scrape, eat dinner,
> Offer a chair, pick up a handkerchief.
>   [*Woe from Wit*, act 3, scene 1]

that impels Famusov to identify him quite accurately as a "dangerous man." Elements of the everyday behavior of the nobleman-revolutionary can be found in numerous period sources, allowing us to speak of the Decembrist not only as the advocate of a particular political program but also as a distinct cultural-historical and psychological type.

The behavior of any individual is not the carrying out of a single program of action. It represents the continual exercise of choice, the actualization of one strategy from a wide selection of possibilities. A Decembrist by no means always acted like a Decembrist. He could act like a nobleman or an officer (more narrowly a guardsman, hussar, staff theoretician), like an aristocrat, a male, a Russian, a European, a young man and so forth. But within this complex selection of possibilities there was a special kind of behavior, a particular type of speech, action, and reaction that characterized the member of a great society.

Naturally each Decembrist was an individual and in a certain sense conducted himself in a unique way. In his everyday life Ryleev was not like Pestel'; Orlov was not like either Nikolai Turgenev or Chaadaev. But this casts no doubt on the appropriateness of my task as I have posed it. The fact that human behavior is individual does not preclude the study of "adolescent psychology" (or the psychology of any other age group), "the psychology of women" (or of men) and ultimately, "human psychology." History is not only the playing-field of various social and historical laws it is also the result of *human activity*. Without studying the historical-psychological mechanisms of human actions, we will inevitably remain tied to highly schematic representations. Historical laws do not work directly. They work through the mechanisms of human psychology, which become in turn important mechanisms of history. Without them, historical laws would operate with fatal predictability and the entire historical process would be redundant.

The Decembrists were first and foremost men of action. This characteristic is understandable, given their sociopolitical orientation toward change in Russian political life as well as their previous experience as military officers who came of age during the Napoleonic wars. They valued courage, energy, an enterprising spirit, firmness, and tenacity as much as the ability to compose a programmatic statement or conduct a theoretical debate. Political doctrines interested them not in themselves, but as criteria for judging and choosing certain courses of action. (Of course there were exceptions—for example, Nikolai Turgenev.) Their orientation toward action can be felt in Lunin's jibe that Pestel' proposed "first to write the Encyclopedia and then proceed to the Revolution."[1] Even those members of secret societies who were most accustomed to staff work emphasized, as Sergei Trubetskoi put it, that "order and procedure" were subsidiary to "the utmost success of an action."[2] We may therefore feel justified in our choice of the Decembrist's *behavior* and not his inner emotions, as the object of our necessarily limited analysis.

One final qualification is essential. The Decembrists were members of the nobility in addition to being revolutionaries. The es-

---

[1]*Vosstanie dekabristov*, vol. 4 (Moscow/Leningrad, 1927), p. 179.
[2]*Ibid.*, vol. 1 (1925), p. 23.

sential aspects of their behavior followed the norms that had become established within the Russian nobility between the Petrine period and the war of 1812. Even while rejecting class distinctions in behavior, consciously struggling with them, and refuting them in theoretical treatises, the Decembrists were organically tied to these forms in their own daily lives. To understand and describe Decembrist behavior in full, one would have to treat it as part of a larger question—the behavior of the Russian nobility during the 1810s and 1820s. This question cannot be dealt with within the bounds of the present essay, and we will therefore skip over all the details of ordinary life that linked the Decembrists with other Russian noblemen of their age.

The Decembrists' significance in the history of Russian society is not exhausted by the aspects of their activity that have most attracted the attention of researchers: social and political programs, ideas on revolutionary tactics, participation in literary disputes, creative and critical writings. It is time to add to this list (which includes many other problems examined in the extensive literature) one question not yet raised. The Decembrists expended significant creative energy on the shaping of a particular type of Russian whose behavior made him different from anything previous history had known. In this they were genuine innovators. Theirs was the behavior of a sizable group of young men, who because of their talents, personalities, backgrounds, individual and family connections, and prospects for future careers, were at the center of society's attention. (The majority of the Decembrists did not hold high government posts and could not have held them because of their youth, but a significant number belonged to the circle which opened the door to brilliant government careers.) Their behavior therefore exercised a strong influence on an entire generation of Russians, becoming a unique civic school. The ideological-political movement of the revolutionary-minded nobility generated certain psychological traits, creating a specific behavioral type. The aim of this essay is to characterize some of its essential components.

It would be difficult to cite another period in Russian life when the various forms of spoken language—conversations, friendly discourse, discussions, sermons, diatribes—played such a central role. From the birth of the movement, which Pushkin accurately defined as "friendly disputes" "over Laffitte and Clicquot" until its tragic end before the Commission of Inquiry, the Decembrists were strikingly "talkative," constantly striving to register their feelings and ideas through the spoken word. Pushkin was justified in his description of a meeting of the Union of Welfare:

> Famous for their cutting eloquence,
> The members of that family gather . . .
> [*Eugene Onegin*, 10, xiv]

This centrality of the word made it possible, from the viewpoint of later norms and concepts, to accuse the Decembrists of phrasemongering and substituting words for deeds. Not only the nihilists of the 1860s but also close contemporaries who often shared the Decembrists' ideas were inclined to this opinion. Nechkina has pointed out that although Griboedov's Chatskii, as a Decembrist, reproaches Repetilov for empty talk and phrasemongering, he himself did not escape a similar reproach from Pushkin: "Everything that he says is very intelligent. But to whom does he say all this? To Famusov? To Skalozub? To the grandmothers at Moscow balls? To Molchalin? It is unforgivable. The first mark of an intelligent man is to know at first glance with whom he is dealing."[3]

When, in 1826, Viazemskii contested the accusation that the Decembrists had contemplated regicide, he emphasized that regicide is a deed and in his opinion the conspirators had made no attempt to proceed from words to deeds. He defined their behavior as "heinous chatter" ("bavardage atroce")[4] and forcefully argued against giving words the same weight as accomplished acts. In his judicial arguments in defense of the victims of injustice we can also see indications that in his opinion the conspirators' "chatter" overshadowed their "deeds." There are many other testimonies of this type.

It would be an error, however, to view the Decembrists through the norms of other historical periods, taking their "cutting eloquence" as a weakness and judging them as Chernyshevskii judged the heroes of Turgenev. My task is not to "exonerate" or "condemn" the men whose names belong to history, but to try to explain this characteristic of their behavior.

Contemporaries emphasize not only the Decembrists' talkativeness, but also the harshness and frankness of their opinions. They

---

[3]A letter to A. Bestuzhev before the end of January 1825, in Pushkin, *Polnoe sobranie sochinenii*, vol. 13 (Moscow/Leningrad, 1937), p. 138.

[4]Lotman, "P. A. Viazemskii i dvizhenie dekabristov," *Uchenye zapiski Tartuskogo gosudarstvennogo universiteta*, no. 98 (1960) p. 134.

cite the finality of their judgments, their "rude" tendency to call things by their real names without recourse to socially acceptable euphemisms, and their penchant for speaking their minds plainly in disregard of time-honored rituals and the hierarchies of verbal behavior in high society. Nikolai Turgenev was famous for his abruptness and deliberate disregard of "verbal propriety." The circles close to the Decembrists defined tactlessness and the absence of good manners in one's speech as "Spartan" or "Roman" behavior as opposed to "French" behavior, which was assigned a negative value.

Subjects that polite conversation either avoided altogether or masked with euphemisms, such as the question of landowners' power or bureaucratic patronage, became objects of open discussion. This openness was important because during the Alexandrine period educated, Europeanized noble society led a dual existence. In the sphere of ideas and "philosophical speech," society had assimilated the norms of European culture that had grown out of the eighteenth-century Enlightenment. The sphere of ordinary behavior—of everything related to everyday preoccupations, custom, the real conditions of estate management, and the real circumstances of the civil service—was not open to "philosophical" interpretation. From the point of view of ideas, it was as good as nonexistent. In terms of language, ordinary behavior was associated with the oral, colloquial sphere and was reflected only minimally in texts of high culture. This dichotomy resulted in a behavioral hierarchy structured on the principle of increasing cultural value (the level of semiosis increased accordingly). At its bottom was a purely practical stratum which, for the theorizing mind, was as good as nonexistent.

This pluralism of behavior—the ability to choose behavioral style according to situation and the duality arising from the division between "practical" and "philosophical"—characterized the progressive Russian nobleman of the early nineteenth century. It also distinguished him from the nobleman-revolutionary. This point is essential, for although it is easy to separate the behavioral types represented by Fonvizin's boorish provincial Skotinin and the Decembrist Ryleev, it is far more meaningful to compare Ryleev to a progressive nobleman like Del'vig or Nikolai Turgenev to his brother Aleksandr.

The Decembrists did away with the hierarchical nature and stylistic diversity of the behavioral act. First of all, they eliminated the difference between spoken and written language. The extreme orderliness, political terminology and syntactic roundedness of written language were transferred to oral usage. Griboedov's Famusov was justified in saying that Chatskii "speaks as he writes." In this case it is not just a saying: the bookishness of Chatskii's speech is what distinguishes it from the speech of the other characters. He speaks as he writes since he sees the world in its ideological rather than its everyday manifestations.

Not only did purely practical behavior become the object of ideological-philosophical interpretation, but it also acquired a semiotic character, crossing over from a group of activities carrying no value to a group of actions interpreted—to use the terminology of Nikolai Turgenev—as "noble" and "dignified" or "base," "boorish," and "vile."[5]

A particularly illustrative example of the semiotization of ordinary behavior comes in the following conversation, recorded by Pushkin: "One day Del'vig invited Ryleev to go out whoring. 'I am married,' answered Ryleev. 'So?' said Del'vig. 'Are you unable to eat at a restaurant simply because you have a kitchen at home?' "[6] This conversation is interesting not so much for the reconstruction of biographical details (both Del'vig and Ryleev were living men whose everyday actions could appear in multiple variants, determined by innumerable factors) as for an understanding of their relationship to the very principle of behavior. Here is a confrontation between a "playful" and a "serious" relationship to life. Ryleev was a man of serious conduct. Not only on the level of abstract ideological structures but also in everyday life this approach assumes that for every signifying situation there is one single norm for correct behavior. Del'vig, like the members of the Arzamas or the Green Lamp societies, behaved in a playful, ambivalent manner. The play situation could be transferred to real life, permitting the conditional exchange of "correct" behavior for its opposite in certain circumstances.

The Decembrists cultivated seriousness as a behavioral norm. Dmitri Zavalishin characteristically emphasized that he "was al-

---

[5]In the political lexicon of Nikolai Turgenev, boor (*kham*) denoted "reactionary," "supporter of serfdom," "enemy of education." Consider, for example, his statements of this sort: "Darkness and boorishness are everywhere and have possessed everyone," in a letter to his brother Sergei dated May 10, 1817 from St. Petersburg. *Dekabrist N. I. Turgenev: Pis'ma k bratu S. I. Turgenevu* (Moscow/Leningrad, 1936), p. 222; (hereafter cited as *N. Turgenev*).
[6]Pushkin, vol. 12 (1949), p. 159.

ways serious" and had "never played" even as a child.[7] Equally negative was the Decembrists' attitude toward word play as a form of verbal behavior. In the exchange cited above the speakers are in effect using different languages. Del'vig does not seriously propose that his words be taken as a declaration of moral principles. He is interested in the witticism, the *bon mot*. But Ryleev cannot enjoy a paradox when ethical principles are at stake. His every statement is a program.

In a verse epistle to Zhukovskii, Milonov expressed the antithesis of play versus civic responsibility with extreme accuracy, showing the extent to which this was felt in progressive literary circles.

> . . . we each remain with our own
> You with your nonsense, and I with my Parnassian sting;
> Let your name be Schiller; mine shall be Juvenal;
> Posterity will judge us, not your friends,
> As for Bludov, he is no judge for us.[8]

An entire paradigm of contrasts is given here: nonsense (the play on words, the joke as an end in itself) versus dignified, civil, and serious satire; Schiller (here as the author of ballads translated by Zhukovskii[9]—Schiller's name was associated with balladlike fantasies) versus Juvenal, perceived as the poet-citizen; the judgment of a literary elite, a closed circle of friends,[10] versus the opinion of posterity. To indicate the sweep of the antitheses outlined by Milonov, it is enough to note their similarity, down to the attack on Bludov, to Pushkin's criticism of Zhukovskii. (See his letter to Zhukovskii during the last ten days of April 1825.)

From Del'vig's point of view, "going whoring" belonged to the sphere of everyday behavior and had no relation to the ideological sphere. The possibility of being one person in poetry and another

---

[7]*Zapiski dekabrista D. I. Zavalishina* (St. Petersburg, 1908) (hereafter cited as *Zavalishin*), p. 10.

[8]*Poety 1790-1810-kh godov* (Leningrad, 1971), p. 537.

[9]Compare Kiukhel'beker's scornful reference to Schiller as the author of ballads and his image of Zhukovskii as an "immature Schiller" in his article "O napravlenii nashei poèzii, osobenno liricheskoi, v poslednee desiatiletie," in *Dekabristy: Poèziia, dramaturgiia, proza, publitsistika, literaturnaia kritika,* comp. V. N. Orlov (Moscow/Leningrad, 1951), p. 552.

[10]Nikolai Polevoi wrote quite openly about how the Karamzinists' habit of invoking the opinions of "famous friends" irritated those outside their camp. "The words 'famous friends' or simply 'the famous' had a special meaning in the conventional language of the time." Nikolai Polevoi, *Materialy po istorii russkoi literatury i zhurnalistiki tridtsatikh godov* (Leningrad, 1934), p. 153.

person in life did not appear to him as a duality that cast shadows on his character. But Ryleev's behavior was in principle undivided, and for him such an action would have been equivalent to admitting that in theory man has a right to be immoral. What Del'vig saw as devoid of meaning, Ryleev perceived as bearing ideological content. The difference between the freedom-lover Del'vig and the revolutionary Ryleev appears not only on the level of ideas and theoretical concepts, but also in the nature of their everyday behavior. Karamzin had affirmed the multiplicity of behavioral styles and the possibility of changing them as the norm for a poetic attitude toward life. He wrote:

> Is it not natural for the tender soul to change?
> It is supple as wax, clear as a mirror: . . .
> . . . It cannot be constant to you.[11]

In contrast, romanticism saw as poetic the unity of behavior and the independence of actions from circumstances. "He was the same everywhere, cold, unchanging," wrote Lermontov about Napoleon.[12] "Be yourself," Aleksandr Bestuzhev wrote to Pushkin.[13] In characterizing Pestel's behavior during the inquiry the priest Myslovskii noted: "He was always and everywhere true to himself. Nothing shook his firmness."[14]

The romantic ideal of the unity of behavior did not contradict the neoclassical concept of heroism. The two ideals coincided with the principle of "unity of action." In this respect Karamzin's "proteanism" is closer to the multifacetedness of realism. Pushkin, contrasting the uniform behavior of Molière's heroes with the multifaceted nature of Shakespeare's, wrote in a well-known sketch, "The characters created by Shakespeare are not at all like the schematic types of Molière, who represent a certain passion or vice; they are living beings filled with many passions and many vices. As events unfold, their diverse and complex characters develop before the spectator."[15]

In moving from observations about life to the poetic text, the

---

[11]N. M. Karamzin, *Polnoe sobranie stikhotvorenii* (Moscow/Leningrad, 1966), pp. 242-243.
[12]M. Iu. Lermontov, *Sochineniia v seshti tomakh*, vol. 2 (Moscow/Leningrad, 1954),p. 183.
[13]Pushkin, vol. 13, p. 142.
[14]From the notebook of P. N. Myslovskii, in *Shchukinskii sbornik*, no. 4 (Moscow, 1905), p. 39 (hereafter cited as Myslovskii notebook).
[15]Pushkin, vol. 12, p. 159.

classical or romantic artist consciously chose a particular plane that he considered the only one worthy of literary representation. In the reverse movement, from the reader's perception of the text to the reader's behavior, a transformation took place. Perceiving the text as a program for everyday behavior, the reader assumed that certain aspects of everyday activity should ideally be absent. That something was not mentioned in the text was understood as requiring that certain types of actions be excluded from real-life behavior. So, for example, a rejection of the love elegy as a poetic genre could be taken as a call for rejecting love in real life. One should emphasize the "literariness" of the romantics' behavior, their tendency to view *all* actions as signifying.

One result of this propensity was the exaggerated role of the gesture in everyday behavior. A gesture is an action which is not so much practical as meaning-bearing. It is always a sign and a symbol. For this reason every act on the stage is a gesture, even those that pretend to complete freedom from theatrical teleology. Its meaning is the author's intention.

The contemporary observer would see the everyday behavior of the Decembrists as theatrical, that is to say, directed toward a spectator. But to say that behavior is "theatrical" does not imply that it is insincere or reprehensible in any way. It simply indicates that behavior has a meaning that extends beyond the everyday. It is the object of attention, valued not for itself but for its symbolic significance.

The everyday behavior of the Decembrists reversed the customary correlations between words and acts. In the typical verbal behavior of the period, the relationship between words and acts was structured according to the following scheme:

| expression | → | content |
| word | → | action |

Words that designated acts had a tendency to shift into euphemism, paraphrase, or metaphor. The result of this shift can be seen in the everyday language of high society, whose upper reaches used French terms for "Russian" activities, while the lower ranks resorted to such locutions as "I availed myself of a handkerchief." Contemporaries accurately grasped the organic and typological connection between this language and the "reformed" speech of the Karamzinians, charging both with affectation. The tendency of polite society to weaken or "loosen" the connection between a word and its meaning provoked Tolstoi to persistent exposure of the hypocrisy of its speech.

The language of the lowly government clerk was structured according to the same idea of "ennobling" the unseemly. In this language "a sheep in a sheet" designated a bribe, and the euphemistic "an adjustment should be made" meant "increase the amount." The verbs "give" and "take" acquired specific meanings. The clerks' chorus in Kapnist's *Chicane* is illustrative:

> Take, there's no great learning to it.
> Take some more, you'll never rue it.
> For why should shoulders end in hands
> If not to take all that we can?[16]
>
> [Act 3, scene 6]

Commenting on these lines Viazemskii wrote: "No further explanations are necessary: the kind of taking involved here is obvious. In the same way the verb 'to drink' with no further explanation means 'to drink vodka.' . . . Another official said that when he had to sign service records and write the words *worthy* and *capable* in the appropriate columns he often wanted to add 'capable of every villainy, worthy of all contempt.' "[17]

On this basis, functional office speech could become a secret tongue reminiscent of the sacerdotal language of priests. The patron was required not only to perform certain acts (the giving of a bribe) but also to decipher the riddles upon which the speech of officials was constructed. A good example is the conversation between Varravin and Muromskii in Sukhovo-Kobylin's play *The Affair*. A sample of the same kind of chancery speech occurs in Chekhov:

"Brother, give us a half a marvel and twenty-four miseries." In a few minutes, the waiter appeared with a half-bottle of vodka and several plates of hors d'oeuvres."So, my dear man," Pochatkin said to him, "give us a portion of the master of slander and calumny with mashed potatoes."[18]

[*Three Years*, ch. 17]

[16]V. V. Kapnist, *Sobranie sochinenii v dvukh tomakh*, vol. 1 (Moscow/Leningrad, 1960), p. 358.

[17]P. A. Viazemskii, *Staraia zapisnaia knizhka* (Leningrad, 1929), p. 105.

[18]A. P. Chekhov, *Sobranie sochinenii v dvenadtsati tomakh*, vol. 7 (Moscow, 1962), p. 506.

The verbal behavior of the Decembrists was sharply distinctive. I have already mentioned their insistence on naming those everyday phenomena that the language of society surrounded with taboos. But this practice did not entail the rehabilitation of a low, vulgar, or even everyday lexicon. The Decembrist mentality was characterized by a sharp polarization of moral and political judgment, which placed every act into one of two categories: that of "boorishness," "baseness," and "tyranny," or "liberalism" "enlightenment," and "heroism." Neutral or nonsignifying acts did not exist, and the possiblity of their existence was not presumed.

Decembrist speech gave unambiguous verbal labels to acts that previously did not have names or were designated through euphemism and metaphor. The set of labels was relatively small and coincided with the ethical and political lexicon of Decembrism. As a result, everyday behavior ceased to be merely everyday behavior. It acquired an elevated ethical and political meaning. There was also a reversal in the usual relationship between expression and content in behavior. For the Decembrists, the word did not signify the act; it was the act that signified the word:

| expression | → | content |
| act | → | word |

It must be emphasized that it was the word publicly spoken that became the content and not the idea or the evaluation of an act. The Decembrist was not satisfied to disapprove silently of a manifestation of the "bygone age." He publicly called things by their names, "thundering" at balls and in society, for it was precisely in this condemnation that he saw human liberation and the beginning of social transformation. For this reason, a certain rigidity and naivete, and an aptitude for falling into ridiculous (from the viewpoint of society) situations are as typical of Decembrist behavior as brusqueness, pride, and even haughtiness. The one thing absolutely excluded was compliancy, the toying with judgments or ability to "strike the right tone" in the spirit of Griboedov's Molchalin or even Dostoevskii's Petr Verkhovenskii.

It may seem as though this characteristic is true of Decembrism only in the period of the Union of Welfare, when "eloquence at balls" was part of the society's general plan. That later tactical evolution shifted the accent of the secret societies to conspiracy, with the conspirator replacing the ballroom propagandist, is well known.

But this change in the tactics of struggle did not lead to a fundamental shift in the style of behavior. Having become a conspirator, the Decembrist did not begin to act "like everyone else" in the drawing-room. No conspiratorial goals could impel him to act like a Molchalin. Though he forswore his passionate tirades for the contemptuous word or look, he remained a "carbonaro" in everyday life. Since everyday behavior could not be the target of direct political accusations, the Decembrists did not modify it but, on the contrary, emphasized it, thereby transforming it into a distinctive sign.

Dmitrii Zavalishin, arriving in St. Petersburg from a voyage around the world, behaved in such a defiant manner that Arakcheev said to Baten'kov, "That Zavalishin! Mark my words, Gavrila Stepanovich, he's either insufferably proud like his father, or else he's a liberal."[19] The cause of this remark was a matter entirely within the sphere of everyday behavior: Zavalishin had refused to use a letter of introduction to Arakcheev. It is characteristic that Arakcheev expected a "proud" person and "a liberal" to act alike. It is also curious that Zavalishin unmasked himself in such a way before even starting his political activity. None of his fellow Decembrists thought of criticizing his behavior, although they were no longer the ecstatic propagandists of the Union of Welfare period but conspirators preparing for decisive action. On the contrary, had Zavalishin been able to mask his attitude and pay homage to Arakcheev, his behavior would have aroused disapproval and mistrust. Indeed, Baten'kov's close relations with Arakcheev met with disapproval within conspirators' circles.

The following example is also illustrative. In 1824, Katenin disapproved of Chatskii because of his "propagandizing at balls." As Nechkina has observed, such propagandizing was a tactic employed by the Union of Welfare. Thus Katenin writes, "This Chatskii is the main character. The author presents him *con amore* and in his opinion Chatskii possesses all the merits and none of the vices. But in my opinion he talks too much, abuses everything, and preaches at the wrong times."[20] Yet only a few months before this statement—and we have no reason to believe that his views changed—Katenin had tried to persuade his friend Bakhtin to engage in literary politics without using a pseudonym. In the course

---

[19]*Zavalishin*, p. 86.
[20]"Pis'ma P. A. Katenina k N. I. Bakhtinu," *Materialy dlia istorii russkoi literatury 20-kh i 30-kh godov XIX veka* (St. Petersburg, 1911), p. 77.

of this argument he stated unequivocally that it was imperative to demonstrate one's convictions not only with words but also with one's entire behavior. "We are obliged now to stand up for ourselves and for what is right, to speak the truth without stammering, to boldly praise the good and expose the bad not only in books *but also in deeds*. We must repeat what we have said to them without fail so that scoundrels cannot pretend they have not heard. We must force them to cast off their disguises, to face us in a duel, and when they have done so we must beat them into oblivion."[21]

It does not matter if Katenin took his own literary program or services to the cause of literature to be "what is right." For him to be able to put his own ideas in these terms, the expressions themselves, in their most general meaning, must have already been the watchwords of a generation.

In a multitude of instances, everyday behavior gave young liberals the means of distinguishing "their own kind" from the "stiflers." That everyday behavior could play such a role was characteristic of the culture of the Russian nobility, with its complex and diverse system of behavioral signs. Within this system specific qualities came into being, distinguishing the Decembrist as a *revolutionary*. Everyday behavior became one of the criteria for selecting candidates for membership in the secret society and gave rise to the characteristic Decembrist chivalry. This chivalry lay behind the oral fascination that the Decembrist tradition had for Russian culture. But it also proved detrimental to the Decembrists in the tragic circumstances surrounding the investigation, where it unexpectedly turned into fragility. The Decembrists were not psychologically prepared to perform under the conditions of legitimized baseness.

The hierarchy of signifying elements in behavior is composed of three sequential parts: the gesture, the act, and the behavioral text. The last of these should be understood as a completed chain of conscious actions located between intention and result. Since real human behavior is complex and motivated by a multitude of factors, behavioral texts can remain incomplete, change into new texts, or interweave with parallel ones. But on the level of an individual's idealized interpretation of his own behavior, behavioral texts are always complete and meaningful plots. Otherwise, goal-directed activity would be impossible. Therefore, for each behavioral text

[21]Ibid., p. 31 (italics mine—Iu. L.).

on the level of action there is a corresponding program of behavior on the level of intention. The relationship between these categories can be very complex, depending, in the final analysis, on the type of culture under consideration. The categories can converge when reality and its interpretation strive to "speak a common language." Or they can consciously or unconsciously diverge. The latter situation is exemplified by what Gogol called the "split between dream and reality": the romantic discrepancy between the "behavioral texts" and dreams—programs for behavior—experienced by the artist Piskarev in "Nevskii Prospect." Divergence is no less apparent in a character's attempt to shore up his unfortunate behavior with alluring programs that are presented as reality: the lying of Gogol's Khlestakov or the memoirs of General Ivolgin in Dostoevskii's *Idiot*. A tragic variant of this situation is the memoirs of Dmitrii Zavalishin. (See the detailed discussion in "On Khlestakov," below.) It is worth remembering that Prince Myshkin did not expose or mock General Ivolgin, as Gogol did with Khlestakov; instead he seriously accepted the general's reminiscences as "*acts, accomplished in intent.*" Evaluating the general's ecstatic lies about his influence on Napoleon, Myshkin says: "You did wonderfully . . . from evil thoughts you led him to kindness."[22] Zavalishin's memoirs deserve precisely this kind of treatment.

The everyday behavior of the Decembrist cannot be understood without examining not only gestures and actions but also separate and discrete units of a higher order: behavioral texts.

The gesture or act of a nobleman-revolutionary was meaningful for all concerned because it signified a *word*. Similarly, any chain of acts could become a text (acquire a meaning) if it could be illuminated through its connection with a particular literary plot. The kinds of plots that gave meaning to such chains of everyday activities were Caesar's death, Cato's glorious deed, the prophet's accusatory sermon, Hector leaving for battle or parting with Andromache; Tyrtaeus, Ossian, or Baian singing for the troops on the eve of battle (the latter plot created by the early novelist Vasilii Narezhnyi).

Such an approach entailed the "blocking out" of all behavior. Literary masks were asigned to real acquaintances, and the location and space in which actions occurred were idealized (real space was interpreted through literary space). Thus in Pushkin's verse epistle

---

[22]F. M. Dostoevskii, *Polnoe sobranie sochinenii v tridtsati tomakh*, vol. 8 (Leningrad, 1973), p. 417 (italics mine—Iu. L.).

to Fedor Glinka, St. Petersburg is Athens and Glinka himself is Aristides. This is not merely the result of the literary transformation of a real-life situation. The reverse process is also actively taking place: those aspects of real-life situations that can be related to a literary plot become meaningful (and therefore noticeable to the people involved).

In a letter to his friend Bakhtin in 1821, Katenin described himself as in exile "not far from Siberia."[23] This is a geographical absurdity: Kostromskii province, where Katenin was exiled, is closer not only to Moscow but also to St. Petersburg than it is to Siberia, and both men knew this. But by the time of their correspondence, Siberia had already become the place of exile in literary plots and the oral mythology of Russian culture. In this capacity it was associated with dozens of historical names: Ryleev placed his Voinarovskii in Siberia, and Pushkin put himself there in his "Imagined Conversation with Alexander I." But Kostromskii province had no such associations. Consequently, just as Athens denoted St. Petersburg, Kostroma denoted Siberia—that is, exile.

Different artistic styles have different relationships to human behavior. If the realistic plot is justified by the assertion that it describes the way people really behave, and classicism shows how people should behave in an ideal world, romanticism prescribes behavior for the reader, including everyday behavior. Although neoclassicism and romanticism seem similar in this respect, there is an essential difference between them. The ideal behavior of a neoclassicial hero is realized within the ideal space of the literary text. Only the exceptional human being, someone who has attained the ideal, could attempt to transfer it to real life. For the majority of readers and spectators the behavior of neoclassical literary figures was an elevated ideal meant to ennoble ordinary behavior rather than be embodied in it.

Romantic behavior was more accessible, since it included not only literary virtues but also literary vices, like the exaggerated egoism that became the norm of "everyday Byronism":

> Lord Byron with bold fancy
> Dressed even hopeless egoism
> In melancholy romanticism.
> [*Eugene Onegin*, 3, xii]

[23]"Pis'ma P. A. Katenina k N. I. Bakhtinu," p. 22.

The fact that the hero of romantic literature was a contemporary substantially helped the reader to approach the text as a program for his own behavior. The heroes of Byron, Marlinskii, Lermontov, and Pushkin in his romantic period generated an entire phalanx of imitators among young officers and officials, who aped the gestures, facial expressions, and manners of literary characters. If the realistic text imitates reality, in the case of romanticism reality rushed to imitate literature. With realism, it is characteristic for a type of behavior to arise first in real life and then appear on the pages of the literary text. (Turgenev, for example, was known for his ability to spot new modes of thought and behavior in real life.) In the romantic work, the new type of human behavior is conceived in the pages of the text and then transferred to life.

Decembrist behavior bore the stamp of romanticism. Actions and behavioral texts were determined by literary plots, by stock literary situations like "the parting of Hector and Andromache," "Horace's pledge," or even by names that condensed entire plots. Thus Pushkin's exclamation "Here is Caesar; where then is Brutus?" can easily be deciphered as a program for a future act.

By recalling certain literary images we can easily decipher a number of otherwise puzzling actions performed by individuals during this period. An example is Petr Chaadaev's retirement at the very height of his success after his meeting with the tsar in Troppau in 1820—an event that perplexed both contemporaries and historians. Chaadaev had been adjutant to Vasil'chikov, the commander of the guards and staff general to the emperor. After the Semenovskii regiment uprising, he volunteered to deliver a report about it to Alexander I. His contemporaries saw this act as a desire to turn the misfortune of his comrades to his own advantage. (In 1812 Chaadaev had served in the Semenovskii regiment.)

It was hard to understand why Chaadaev, whose integrity was well known, would do something like this. Then his unexpected resignation soon after his meeting with the emperor threw everyone into confusion. Chaadaev himself, in a letter to his Aunt Shcherbatova dated January 2, 1821, offered the following explanation:

This time I am writing to you, dear Aunt, to inform you in a positive way that I have handed in my resignation.... My request has caused a genuine sensation among some people. At first they didn't want to believe that my request was serious. Then they had to believe it, but even now they can't understand how I could decide to resign at the very moment that I was about to receive something I seemed to desire, something the entire world desires, something everyone considers extraordinarily flattering for a young man of my rank. And indeed I was to be designated adjutant to the emperor upon his return, at least according to Vasil'chikov. I found it more amusing to scorn this favor than to receive it. It amused me to show my contempt for people who have contempt for everyone.[24]

Lebedev sees Chaadaev's letter as an attempt "to reassure his aunt"[25] who was supposedly much interested in her nephew's success at court. This interpretation is extremely doubtful.[26] It was hardly necessary to explain to the sister of the well-known malcontent, Prince Shcherbatov, the meaning of aristocratic disdain for careerism at court. If Chaadaev had retired to the life of a Moscow grandee, showing off his malcontentedness at the English club, his behavior would not have seemed mysterious to his contemporaries nor scandalous to his aunt. But, in fact, his interest in the service was well known. He had openly pushed for a personal meeting with the emperor, forging ahead with his career. He had invited conflict with society's opinion and aroused the envy and ill will of his fellow officers, whom he had outstripped in spite of their seniority. (The order of promotion according to seniority was not a written law, but it strictly governed advancement through the ranks. Circumventing it contradicted the codex of social relations and was perceived by the officers as a violation of the rules of honor.) The riddle of Chaadaev's act lies in the combination of his open, even conspicuous interest in the quick advancement of his career with his voluntary retirement just *before* his efforts were to be brilliantly crowned.[27]

[24]*Sochineniia i pis'ma P. Ia. Chaadaeva*, vol. 1 (Moscow, 1913), pp. 3-4 (original in French).

[25]A. A. Lebedev, *Chaadaev* (Moscow, 1965), p. 54.

[26]Lebedev's book is very interesting but unfortunately it is not free from arbitrary interpretation of documents and a certain modernization.

[27]Chaadaev's nephew Zhikharev later recalled: "Vasil'chikov sent Chaadaev to the emperor . . . with the report, although Chaadaev was a junior adjutant and a senior adjutant should have gone." Further on he writes: "Upon his return to Petersburg almost the entire guard felt a general instantaneous outburst of dissatisfaction with him. The reason was his acceptance of the mission to Troppau with the report to the emperor about the Semenovskii affair. The general opinion was that he should not have gone, that he should not have pushed for the trip, but (that) he should have avoided it in every way." Zhikharev continues: "I do not doubt that he sought the assignment instead of refusing it. In this unfortunate

According to Tynianov, the Troppau meeting was Chaadaev's attempt to explain to the emperor the connection between the "Semenovskii affair" and serfdom, and to persuade him to undertake reforms. Tynianov hypothesizes that the tsar did not sympathize with Chaadaev's ideas and this created a breach. "It was all too evident that the meeting with the tsar and the report delivered to him were unpleasant." Further on Tynianov calls the meeting a "catastrophe."[28] Lebedev concurs with this opinion.[29]

Although Tynianov's conjecture is more convincing than all the other explanations thus far proposed, it has one weak point. The break between the emperor and Chaadaev did not immediately follow the meeting and report at Troppau. On the contrary, the significant promotion that would have resulted from the meeting and the fact it would have brought Chaadaev into the tsar's retinue indicate that their conversation was not the cause for the break and the resulting coldness. Chaadaev's report at Troppau is hard to interpret as a catastrophe for his career. It is far more likely that his "fall" began later. The tsar, unpleasantly surprised by Chaadaev's unexpected request to resign his position, was further irritated by the letter to his aunt which had been opened and inspected in the mails. Although Chaadaev's words describing his contempt for those who have contempt for everyone were aimed at his commander Vasil'chikov, the emperor could have interpreted them as applying to himself. Indeed, the entire tone of the letter must have struck him as impossibly disrespectful. This was apparently the "extremely disadvantageous" information about Chaadaev that Prince Volkonskii mentioned in a letter to Vasil'chikov on February 4, 1821. It resulted in Alexander I's decision to retire Chaadaev without advancement to the next rank. It was at this point that the emperor "spoke of this officer very unfavorably" as the Grand Duke Constantine later reported to Nicholas I. Thus, Chaadaev's

---

situation he gave in to his innate weakness of excessive vanity. I do not think that as he departed from St. Petersburg, the epaulets of adjutant shone in his imagination as much as the enchantment of a close relationship, an intimate conversation with the emperor." M. Zhikharev, "K biografii P. Ia. Chaadaeva," *Vestnik Evropy*, no. 7 (1871), p. 203. Of course Chaadaev's inner world was inaccessible to Zhikharev but he was often better informed than Chaadaev's other contemporaries and his words deserve attention.

[28]Iu. N. Tynianov, "Siuzhet *Goria ot uma*," *Literaturnoe nasledstvo*, vol. 47-48 (Moscow, 1946), pp. 168-171.

[29]Lebedev, pp. 68-69.

resignation cannot be viewed as resulting from a conflict with the emperor, since the conflict itself resulted from his resignation.

The riddle of Chaadaev's behavior can be better explained through a comparison with certain literary plots. The dedication of Herzen's article on the emperor Alexander I and V. N. Karazin was to N. A. Serno-Solov'evich, "our last Marquis of Posa." Thus, for Herzen, the hero of Schiller's *Don Carlos* was a definite type in Russian life. A comparison with Schiller's plot may throw much light on the puzzling episode in Chaadaev's biography. There is no doubt that Chaadaev was familiar with Schiller's tragedy. Karamzin saw *Don Carlos* performed during his visit to Berlin in 1789. In his *Letters of a Russian Traveler* he made a brief but sympathetic reference to it, emphasizing the role of the Marquis of Posa. At the beginning of the nineteenth century, a veritable cult of Schiller reigned at Moscow University, where Chaadaev enrolled in 1808.[30] Chaadaev's university professor Merzliakov and his close friend Nikolai Turgenev paid passionate homage to Schiller. Another of Chaadaev's friends, Griboedov, freely quoted the Marquis of Posa's famous monologue in his sketch for the tragedy *Radamist i Zenobiia*. Speaking of the participation of one of his characters, a republican, in "an autocratic empire," he wrote: "He is a danger to the government and a burden to himself for he is *the citizen of another age*."[31] The italicized words paraphrase Posa's self-characterization: "I am the citizen of a coming age" (*Don Carlos*, act 3, scene 9).

The hypothesis that Chaadaev wanted to act out another "Russian variant of the Marquis of Posa" (just as in his conversations with Pushkin he tried on the roles of the "Russian Brutus" and the "Russian Pericles") clarifies the "enigmatic" aspects of his behavior. First of all, it allows us to challenge Lebedev's assertion that Chaadaev in 1820 was counting on the government's liberalism. Lebedev writes that "hopes of the tsar's 'good intentions' were generally very high among the Decembrists and the pro-Decembrist

---

[30]See: M.-V. Harder, *Schiller in Russland: Materialien zu einer Wirkungsgeschichte. 1789–1814* (Berlin-Zurich, 1968); Lotman, "Neue Materialien über die Anfänge der Beschäftigung mit Schiller in der russichen Literatur," *Wissenschaftliche Zeitschrift der Ernst-Moritz-Arndt-Universität Greifswald Gesellschafts- und sprachwissenschaftliche Reihe*, no. 5/6 (1958/59); Iu. M. Lotman, *Andrei Sergeevich Kaisarov i literaturno-obshchestvennaia bor'ba ego vremeni, Uchenye zapiski Tartuskogo gosudarstvennogo universiteta*, no. 63 (1958).

[31]A. S. Griboedov, *Polnoe sobranie sochinenii*, vol. 1 (St. Petersburg, 1911), p. 256.

nobility at that time."[32] It is inaccurate and risky to speak of a consistent attitude on the part of the Decembrists toward Alexander I without referring to specific dates and statements. By 1820, as is well known, no one retained a modicum of faith in the tsar's promises. More important, according to the highly convincing hypothesis proposed by Tsiavlovskii[33] and supported by other noted scholars, Chaadaev had been discussing the possibility of assassination with Pushkin before his journey to Troppau. This hypothesis is hard to reconcile with the notion that Chaadaev's faith in the tsar's "good intentions" impelled him to race to their meeting.

Schiller's Philip is not a liberal tsar. He is a tyrant. Posa's speech is addressed to a despot, and not to "virtue on the throne." The suspicious, hypocritical tyrant relies on the bloody Alba, who could recall Arakcheev.[34] But the tyrant is the one who needs friendship because he is infinitely alone. Posa's first words to Philip concern the latter's loneliness, and these are the words that shake Schiller's despot.

Alexander's contemporaries—at least those who could, like Chaadaev, converse with Karamzin—were aware that he suffered from loneliness within the vacuum created by political autocracy and his own suspicion. His contemporaries also knew that just like Schiller's Philip, Alexander harbored a deep contempt for people and suffered greatly from it. Alexander did not hesitate to exclaim aloud, "People are wretches . . . Oh, scoundrels! These are the people who surround us unfortunate rulers."[35]

Chaadaev seized an opportune moment. Choosing a time when the tsar would be experiencing a terrible shock,[36] he appeared to

---

[32]He does say right after this that Chaadaev "hardly placed great hopes on the emperor's good intentions." In this case the author sees the purpose of the conversation as a final and irrevocable elucidation of Alexander I's true intentions and plans (Lebedev, pp. 67-69). This last statement is entirely incomprehensible. There is no reason that a conversation with Chaadaev should result in such clarity when the tsar's conversations with dozens of others and his many declarations never achieved this.

[33]M. A. Tsiavlovskii, *Stat'i o Pushkine* (Moscow, 1962), pp. 28-58.

[34]The image of Alba covered with the blood of Flanders gained special meaning after the bloody suppression of the Chuguev rebellion. Concerning the rebellion see Tsiavlovskii, pp. 33 ff.

[35]N. K. Shil'der, *Imperator Aleksandr Pervyi, ego zhizn' i tsarstvovanie*, vol. 3 (St. Petersburg, 1897), p. 48.

[36]During this time Viazemskii wrote: "I cannot think without horror and dejection of the sovereign's loneliness at such an important moment. Who will answer to his voice? Wounded pride, a pernicious advisor, insignificant lackies, or something even more shameless." *Uchenye zapiski Tartuskogo gosudarstvennogo universiteta*, no. 98 (1960), p. 78.

inform him of the sufferings of the Russian people, just as Posa appeared to tell of the misfortunes in Flanders. If you can imagine Alexander, shaken by the rebellion in the first regiment of the guards, exclaiming as Philip did:

> Good Providence, give me a human being.
> Much hast thou given me. But send me now
> A human being.[37]
>
> [Act 3, scene 1]

then Posa's words "Give us freedom of thought!" come naturally to the tongue. It is conceivable that on the road to Troppau Chaadaev more than once recalled Posa's monologue.

But Posa's speech in praise of freedom could captivate Philip only if the king were certain of his friend's personal disinterestedness. It is no accident that Posa refuses every reward and does not want to serve the king. The most insignificant reward would transform him from a selfless advocate of truth into a hireling of autocracy.

Attaining an audience and explaining his credo to the tsar was only part of Chaadaev's task. After that he had to demonstrate his personal selflessness by refusing the rewards he deserved. Posa's words, "Ich kann nicht Fürstendiener sein" (I cannot be a courtier), became a literal program for Chaadaev. Following this program, he refused the title of adjutant to the emperor. Thus there is no contradiction between his desire to speak with the tsar and his need to resign. They are components of the same plan.

What was Alexander I's reaction? First of all, did he comprehend the meaning of Chaadaev's behavior? In answering this question it is appropriate to recall an episode that is perhaps legendary but very characteristic. Herzen reports:

> During the first years of Alexander I's reign . . . literary evenings were often held at court. On one of these evenings the reading continued for a long time. They were reading Schiller's new tragedy.
> The reader finished and stopped. The tsar was silent and his eyes were cast down. Maybe he was thinking about his own fate which so nearly approached Don Carlos's destiny. Or perhaps he was thinking about the fate of his own Philip. Perfect silence continued for several minutes. Prince Alexandr Golitsyn was the first to break it.

---

[37]Friedrich Schiller, *Don Carlos*, trans. Charles Passage (New York: Frederick Ungar, 1959), p. 107.

Turning to Count Victor Kochubei he said in a low voice but loud enough for everyone to hear, "We have our own Marquis of Posa."[38]

Golitsyn had in mind Karamzin.

The importance of this anecdote goes beyond the evidence of Alexander's interest in Schiller's tragedy. According to Herzen, Golitsyn's reference to Karamzin as Posa was a clever move aimed at doing in a court rival. Golitsyn knew that the emperor would not tolerate anyone aspiring to the role of leader.

Alexander I was a despot, but not the type portrayed by Schiller. Kind by nature, educated as a gentleman, he was a Russian autocrat and consequently a man who could not give up any of his prerogatives. He was in great need of a friend, a friend who was absolutely selfless. Even the faintest suspicion that the reigning favorite had "private interests" would cause his removal from the rank of Alexander's friends to the despised category of courtier. Schiller's tyrant had been won over by selflessness combined with nobility of mind and personal independence. Alexander's friend was required to combine selflessness with an endless personal devotion equivalent to servility. The emperor endured Arakcheev's refusal to accept a decoration and his audacious return of the medals which Alexander in a special decree had commanded him to wear. Demonstrating that his servility could not be bought, Arakcheev had refused to carry out the tsar's will, and in answer to Alexander's persistent pleas, agreed only to accept the tsar's portrait, not as the emperor's reward but as a gift from a friend.

If, however, a sincere love for the emperor was combined with independent opinions, the friendship would be over—and it was the fact of independence rather than the political nature of the opinion that counted. This explains the cooling of Alexander's relationship with Karamzin, a political conservative who had a personal affection for him, was absolutely selfless, and never asked

---

[38] A. I. Herzen, *Sobranie sochinenii v tridstati tomakh*, vol. 2 (Moscow, 1959), pp. 38-39. The reading evidently took place in 1803 when Schiller sent *Don Carlos* with Vol'tsogen to Mariia Fedorovna, widow of Paul, in St. Petersburg. On September 27, 1803, Vol'tsogen confirmed that he had passed on the play. See *Charlotte von Schiller und ihre Freunde* vol. 2 (Stuttgart, 1862), p. 125; Harder, *Schiller in Russland*, pp. 15-16.

for anything for himself.[39] Even less was Alexander able to tolerate a gesture of independence from Chaadaev, a man with whom he had only begun to establish a relationship. The gesture which sealed the love of Philip for the Marquis of Posa just as irrevocably repelled the tsar from Chaadaev. Chaadaev was not destined to be the Russian Posa, or the Russian Brutus or Pericles.

Thus, Chaadaev's story illustrates how the behavior of a man close to the Decembrists could be an encoded text with a literary plot as its code. Discovering the plot enables us to penetrate the hidden meaning of the behavioral text.

Let me give another illustration. The heroic sacrifice of the Decembrist wives is well known, as is its significance for the spiritual history of Russian society. But if the content of their act was spontaneous and sincere, its expression nonetheless conformed to certain rules, just as the most passionate appeal in a language is subject to the same grammatical rules that govern all other expressions. The act of the Decembrist wives was one of protest and challenge. But in the sphere of expression it made inevitable use of a particular psychological stereotype. Behavior also has its norms and rules, although the more complex the semiotic system, the more complex the relationship between regulation and freedom. Did Russian noble society *before the act of the Decembrist wives* have any behavioral

[39]Karamzin's example is very notable. The tsar became cool toward him following the presentation in Tver' in 1811 of his "Zapiska o drevnei i novoi Rossii" (Note on ancient and modern Russia). A second, more serious episode occurred in 1819 when Karamzin read the tsar his "Mnenie russkogo grazhdanina" (Opinion of a Russian citizen). Later he recorded what he said to Alexander on that occasion: "Your highness, your pride is too easily wounded.... I fear nothing. We are all equal before God. I would also have told your father what I have told you. Your excellency, I despise ephemeral liberals. I cherish only that freedom which no tyrant can take from me.... I will no longer ask for your good will. Perhaps I am speaking to you for the last time." *Neizdannye sochineniia i perepiska N. M. Karamzina*, part 1 (St. Petersburg, 1862), p. 9 (original in French). This criticism is voiced from a position more conservative than the tsar's and thus clearly illustrates that it was not the progressive or reactionary nature of the ideas expressed but rather the independence of thought that was odious to the tsar. Under these circumstances any Russian who aspired to the role of Marquis of Posa was doomed to failure. After Alexander's death, Karamzin, in a note addressed to posterity, again emphasized his love for the emperor and admitted the complete failure of his mission as counsel to the throne: "I loved him sincerely and fondly. Sometimes I was indignant and annoyed with the monarch, but still I loved the man.... I was always sincere. He was always inexplicably patient, humble, and kind; he did not ask for my advice but he listened to it, although he rarely followed it. In mourning his death today together with Russia, I cannot comfort myself with the thought of his ten years of kindness and trust in me, for this kindness and trust remained unfruitful for my country." Ibid., pp. 11-12.

precedents that might have given the women's sacrificial impulse a form? Indeed it did.

To begin with, for a wife to follow an exiled husband to Siberia was an entirely traditional behavioral norm among the common people. Prisoners' parties were accompanied by carts carrying their families into voluntary exile. This was not viewed as a heroic sacrifice, or even as a matter of personal choice. It was the norm. Furthermore, in pre-Petrine society the same norm applied to the family of an exiled boyar, unless special punitive measures had been taken against his wife and children. It is thus the behavior of the common people (or native Russian, pre-Petrine behavior) that was behind the decision of Radishchev's sister-in-law, Elizaveta Rubanovskaia, to accompany him to Siberia. She did not think of herself as performing a heroic sacrifice; in fact, she took with her only Radishchev's younger children and not the older ones who had to complete their education. The reaction to what she did was different from what it would be in 1826. No one thought to restrain her or talk her out of going. Her contemporaries, it seems, did not even notice her great sacrifice. The entire episode remained part of Radishchev's family affairs and left no imprint on society. Radishchev's parents were even scandalized that Elizaveta had followed him to Siberia without being betrothed to him and there, ignoring the close family relationship, had become his wife. For this reason Radishchev's blind father refused to give the writer his blessing when he returned from Siberia, even though Elizaveta had died there from the hardships of exile. Her great sacrifice was neither understood nor valued by her contemporaries.

There was yet another ready-made behavioral norm that could have prompted the Decembrist wives in their decision. The majority of them were officers' wives. In the Russian army during the eighteenth and early nineteenth century it was possible to take one's family along on campaigns in an army wagon. The custom had already been forbidden to common soldiers, but it was still practiced by officers, primarily those who were senior in age and rank. Kutuzov's daughter Elizaveta Tizengauzen (later Khitrovo), the wife of his favorite adjutant, Ferdinand Tizengauzen ("Fedia" in Kutuzov's letters), was in his camp at Austerlitz. After the battle, when the dead had been exchanged, she placed her husband's body in a cart and drove him to Revel' by herself (the army had set out on other roads to the east) in order to bury him in a cathedral chapel. At that time she was twenty-one.

General Nikolai Raevskii also took his family with him on cam-

paigns. In a conversation with Batiushkov, he denied that his sons
had taken part in the battle near Dashkova, saying, "My younger
son was gathering berries in the forest (at that time he was just a
child) and a bullet pierced his breeches."[40] A wife following her
husband into exile or into a dangerous and oppressive campaign
was not something new and unheard-of in the life of a Russian
noblewoman. But for an act of this type to acquire the character
of a political deed, one further condition was necessary. Let us
recall a passage from the writings of Nikolai Basargin, whom Shchegolev characterized as a typical Decembrist:[41] "I remember, one
day I was reading my wife Ryleev's poem, 'Voinarovskii' which
had just appeared, and couldn't help thinking of my future. 'What
are you thinking of?' she asked me. 'Perhaps exile awaits me also,'
I said. 'Well, I will go too to comfort you and to share your fate.
Indeed it cannot part us, so why think about it?' "[42] Basargin's wife
(née Princess Meshcherskaia) did not have the opportunity to con-
firm her words; she died suddenly in August 1825 without living
to see her husband's arrest.

What is important here is not Basargina's personal fate but the
fact that through Ryleev's poetry the act of following a husband
into exile became a manifestation of civic virtue on a par with all
others. The behavioral stereotype for such a heroine was created
in the poems "Nataliia Dolgorukova" and "Voinarovskii":

> I have forgotton my native city,
> Wealth, honors, and family name
> To share with him Siberia's cold
> And endure the inconstancy of fate.[43]
> ["Nataliia Dolgorukova"]

> Suddenly I see a woman coming,
> Covered with a wretched sheepskin
> And hardly able to carry her firewood,
> Beaten down by work and sorrow.
> I come to her and then I see
> That this poor woman in the cold and snow
> Is my own Cossack girl
> My beautiful companion! . . .

[40]K. N. Batiushkov, *Sochineniia* (Moscow/Leningrad, 1934), p. 373.
[41]N. V. Basargin, *Zapiski* (Petrograd, 1917), p. xi.
[42]Ibid., p. 35.
[43]K. F. Ryleev, *Polnoe sobranie stikhotvorenii* (Leningrad, 1971), p. 168.

Learning of my fate,
She came to search for me in exile
Forsaking her native land.
Oh wanderer! It was painful for her
Not to share my suffering.[44]

["Voinarovskii"]

Even before Ryleev's poem, Nataliia Dolgorukova's life had been
the object of literary adaptation in a short story by Sergei Glinka
called "a model of love and conjugal fidelity or the trials and virtues
of Nataliia Borisovna Dolgorukova, the daughter of field marshal
Sheremetev" (1815). But for Glinka this plot was an example of
conjugal loyalty meant to contrast with the behavior of "stylish
wives." Ryleev placed his poem about her in a series of "life stories
of Russia's great men,"[45] and by so doing established an entirely
new way of decoding the behavior of women. Thus, it was literature, along with the religious norms that had become a part of
the Russian woman's national-ethical consciousness, that gave the
early-nineteenth-century noblewoman a program of behavior consciously interpreted as heroic. The author of the poems also saw
them as a program of action and a model of heroic behavior which
should directly influence the actions of his readers.

One can assume that the poem "Nataliia Dolgorukova" had a
direct influence on the behavior of Mariia Volkonskaia. Both her
own contemporaries—starting with her father, Nikolai Raevskii—
and later researchers have observed that she could not have experienced deep personal feelings for her husband. She did not
know him at all before their wedding and had spent only three
months with him out of the year that separated their marriage and
his arrest. Her father bitterly repeated her confessions that "she
sometimes found her husband unbearable," adding that he would
not have opposed her journey to Siberia if he could have been sure
that "a wife's heart drew her to her husband."[46]

These circumstances confounded her relatives no less than certain historians. But for Mariia Volkonskaia herself, they only intensified the heroic nature of her act, making the journey to Siberia
all the more obligatory. She certainly recalled that only three days
had passed between Nataliia Sheremetova's marriage to Prince
Dolgorukii and his arrest, which was followed by her heroic deed.

---

[44]Ibid., p. 214.
[45]V. G. Bazanov, *Uchenaia respublika* (Moscow/Leningrad, 1964), p. 267.
[46]M. O. Gershenzon, *Istoriia molodoi Rossii* (Moscow/Petrograd, 1923) p. 70.

In Ryleev's words, a husband "had been given her like a phantom, for a moment." Mariia Volkonskaia's father had an accurate sense that his daughter was not motivated by love, but rather by a conscious aspiration to accomplish a heroic act. "She did not need her emotions when she went to her husband but rather the influence of the Volkonskii women who, by praising her heroism, convinced her that she was a heroine."[47]

Raevskii was mistaken on one point only: "the Volkonskii women" were not guilty of anything. Volkonskii's mother, a lady-in-waiting, was cold toward her daughter-in-law and indifferent to her son's fate: "My mother-in-law asked about her son and among other things said that she could not resolve to visit him for the meeting would kill her. The next day she left with the empress-mother for Moscow, where preparations for the coronation had already begun."[48] As for her husband's sister, Princess Sofiia Volkonskaia, Mariia had never even met her. The "guilty parties" were Russian literature for creating a feminine counterpart to the heroic citizen, and the moral norms of the Decembrist circle for demanding that the behavior of literary heroes be transposed directly to life.

In this respect the Decembrists' complete bewilderment during the investigation is characteristic. They found themselves in the tragic situation of having to behave without witnesses, people who would have understood them and to whom they could have addressed their heroic deeds. They had no literary models, since a death without monologues, in the vacuum of a military bureaucracy, had not yet become a subject for art. These circumstances fostered the vivid emergence of other stereotypes which, though they had been pushed aside, were well known to all the Decembrists: an officer's duty to those of higher rank, loyalty to oaths, a nobleman's honor. These norms suddenly intruded into revolutionary behavior, and the Decembrists were tossed from one of them to the other. Not all of them could, like Pestel', accept posterity as the interlocutor and carry on a dialogue with it, ignoring the eavesdropping commission of inquiry and in the process, mercilessly destroying both himself and his friends.

It is indicative that the theme of a closed investigation without witnesses and the tactics it required of the accused clearly emerged in literature after 1826, from Griboedov's *Radamist i Zenobiia* to Lermontov and Polezhaev. The comical testimony in Nekrasov's

---

[47]Ibid, p. 70.
[48]*Zapiski kniagini Marii Nikolaevny Volkonskoi*, 2d ed. (St. Petersburg, 1914), p. 57.

poem "Sud" (the trial) clearly shows that for readers of the 1830s, Zhukovskii's "Sud v podzemel'e" (trial in a dungeon) was not about a nun victimized by the Inquisition. They read something else into that poem, measuring themselves against the situation of a "dungeon trial."

The powerful effect of the word on behavior, of sign systems on everyday life, is clearly revealed in those aspects of life that by their very nature are furthest removed from semiosis. One of these spheres is leisure.

Because of its social and psychophysiological function, leisure must be structured in direct opposition to the ordinary flow of life. Only then can it fulfill its function of psychophysiological variation and relaxation. In a society with a complex system of social se-miotics, leisure will inevitably be oriented toward spontaneity, naturalness, and the absence of signification. Thus, in urban cultures leisure will invariably include "getting back to nature." For the nineteenth-century Russian nobleman, and, by the second half of the century, for the civil servant as well, life was strictly regulated by norms of societal decorum and hierarchical rank. As a result, leisure became associated with the backstage life of the theater and the gypsy camp. In the merchant class, the strict observance of orderliness in everyday life was juxtaposed to the "binge" that knew no bounds. There was an obligatory exchange of social masks. If in everyday life, a member of a group belonged to the class of the downtrodden and the humiliated, then when he made merry he had to perform the role of someone to whom the sky is the limit. If in ordinary life he had been delegated great authority, at least from the perspective of his group, then his role in the mirror-world of the holiday would often include playing at being downtrodden.

The holiday is usually characterized by its marked separation from the "nonholiday" rest of the world. It often requires a change of scene, to either the more solemn (the parade hall, the temple) or the less solemn (going on a picnic or slumming). It also has a specially allotted time (calendar holidays, or the night hours during a nonholiday when one would usually sleep).

The holiday as observed by the Russian nobility of the early nineteenth century was a fairly complex and heterogeneous phenomenon. On the one hand, particularly in the provinces and villages, it was still closely tied to the peasant ritual calendar. On the other, the young post-Petrine culture, less than a hundred years old, was not yet suffering from the rigid ritualization of ordinary nonholiday life. At times, indeed, its lack of order was more prominent. The ball (or the parade in the army) became an occasion for sharply increasing the degree of ritualization rather than lowering it. Leisure was not a matter of removing restrictions on behavior. Diversified nonritualized activity was exchanged for an extremely limited number of behavioral patterns that were purely formal and ritualistic: dancing, whist, or in Pushkin's words, "the elegant order of oligarchic conversations."

The young men who served in the military presented a different case. Beginning during Paul's reign, a severe regime of depersonalizing discipline was established among the troops, particularly in the guards. Its fullest manifestation was the military parade. A contemporary of the Decembrists, von Bok, wrote in an epistle to Alexander I: "The parade is the triumph of nonentities. A warrior whom one would be afraid to look at on a day of battle becomes a mannequin at the parade, while the emperor looks like a god who alone thinks and commands."[49]

When everyday life was the drill and the parade, leisure naturally took the form of the spree or orgy. In this sense, sprees and orgies were an entirely predictable part of "normal" behavior for young men in the military. It can even be said that in certain circumstances in a certain age group they were an obligatory component of an officer's "good" behavior. Of course there were quantitative and qualitative differences, not only along the lines of the antithesis "guards versus army" but also in relation to the branch of service and even to the regiment. Each unit created its own obligatory tradition.

Against this background, a particular type of carousing began to emerge in the early nineteenth century. It was not perceived as a norm for leisure behavior in the army, but rather as a variant of free thinking. The element of freedom appeared here as a kind of everyday romanticism characterized by the tendency to act in an absolutely impetuous manner that swept away with all restrictions on behavior. Typically, such behavior was modeled as a victory over an acknowledged master of a given type of carousing. The meaning of the act was to accomplish something unheard of, to outdo the person whom no one could defeat. Pushkin characterized this type of behavior with the greatest accuracy in Silvio's mono-

[49]A. V. Predtechenskii, "Zapiska T. E. Boka," in *Dekabristy i ikh vremia* (Moscow/Leningrad, 1951), p. 198.

logue from "The Shot": "I served in the *** hussar regiment. My character is familiar to you: I am accustomed to being the first in everything, but in my youth it was a passion. In those years revelry was in fashion, and I was the biggest reveler in the army. We bragged about how much we could drink. I outdrank the renowned B[urtsov] immortalized by D[enis] D[avydov]."[50] The expression "to outdrink" is typical of the competition and passion to be first which was central to this kind of "revelry." Fashionable during the late 1810s, it bordered on "everyday free thinking."

Let us look at a characteristic example. The literature devoted to the Decembrist Mikhail Lunin invariably cites the following episode, recorded by Belogolovyi from the words of Ivan Iakushin:

> Lunin was an officer in the guards and was stationed in summer with his regiment near Peterhof. It was a hot summer, and both the officers and the soldiers would take pleasure in refreshing themselves by swimming in the gulf. The German general in command unexpectedly prohibited the swimming under threat of strict punishment. He gave the order on the basis that the bathing took place near a road and therefore offended propriety. Lunin, knowing when the general would be riding by along the road, several minutes beforehand waded into the water in full dress, with shako, uniform, and jackboots so that the general could see from a distance the strange spectacle of an officer floundering in the water. When he approached, Lunin quickly leapt to his feet, stood at attention in the water and saluted him. The puzzled general called the officer to him and recognized Lunin, the favorite of the grand dukes and one of the most brilliant officers in the guards. The general asked him in amazement, "What are you doing here?" "I am swimming," Lunin replied, "and so as not to disobey your excellency's order, I am trying to do it in the most proper possible form."[51]

Belogolovyi was entirely just in interpreting this as a display of "unrestrained protest." But the full meaning of Lunin's action remains unclear unless it is compared with other testimony that has gone unnoticed by historians. In the memoirs of Platon Zubov's dwarf Ivan Iakubovskii, there is a story abut Valerian Zubov's illegitimate son, Korocharov, who was a cadet in the Uhlan guards:

> Listen to what happened to him there! They were stationed in Strel'na, and he went with several officers to take a swim. But the Grand Duke

[50]Pushkin, vol. 8, book 1 (Moscow/Leningrad, 1948), p. 69.
[51]N. A. Belogolovyi, *Vospominaniia i drugie stat'i* (Moscow, 1898), p. 70.

Constantine, their commander, had gone for a walk along the shore and came upon them swimming. They were frightened and jumped from the boat into the water. Only Korocharov stood at attention, naked as the day he was born, and cried: "Good morning your excellency!" From that time on the grand duke was very fond of him! "He'll make a brave officer," he said.[52]

These two episodes correspond chronologically.

The entire story can be reconstructed as follows: a cadet from the Uhlan guards with extraordinary presence of mind performed a daring act that aroused the admiration of the guards and simultaneously resulted in the order prohibiting swimming. Lunin, as the "biggest reveler in the army" had to outdo Korocharov. (The desire to maintain the honor of the cavalier guards by "outdoing" the Uhlans no doubt played a role here too.) The value of the unconstrained act lies in *crossing a line* no one has yet crossed. Tolstoi captured this very perceptively in his description of the drinking bouts of Pierre and Dolokhov.

Another sign of the transformation of "ordinary" carousing into "free-thinking" carousing was the tendency to view it not as leisure, which is a necessary complement to military service, but rather as the antithesis of service. The world of carousing became an independent sphere, and immersion in it *excluded service*. It came to be associated with private life and with poetry, both of which had attained the status of an antipode to government service back in the eighteenth century.

This process was furthered when carousing, which had once belonged entirely within the sphere of practical everyday activity, became associated with theoretical, ideological concepts. Carousing was turned into a category of socially significant behavior. At the same time it underwent ritualization, which brought the friendly drinking bout close to a travesty of church liturgy or a parody of Masonic meetings.

When thinkers of the early nineteenth century attempted to find a place for passion and the pursuit of happiness within a system of ideas, they were obliged to choose between two possibilities, each of which was seen as linked to a particular direction of pro-

[52]*Karlik favorita, istoriia zhizni Ivana Andreevicha Iakubovskogo, karlika svetleishego kniazia Platona Aleksandrovicha Zubova, pisannaia im samim* (Munich, 1968), p. 68. Korocharov was promoted to the rank of cavalry commander, having been awarded three crosses and recommended for a St. Gregory's cross. He was fatally wounded at the siege of Paris during a bold attack on Polish uhlans.

gressive thought. One tradition, originating with eighteenth-century philosophers, starts from the premise that the right to happiness is part of human nature and the common good of all assumes the maximum good of each individual. Humanity, in its pursuit of happiness, fulfills the mandate of Nature and Morality. From this position, any appeal to self-denial was perceived as a teaching advantageous to despotism. Indeed the eighteenth-century materialists viewed their characteristic hedonist ethic as a demonstration of their love of freedom. Passion was equated with the thrust for freedom. Only the man of passion, craving happiness and ready for love, would never be a slave. The freedom-loving ideal appeared in two equivalent forms: the citizen filled with hatred of despotism and the passionate woman filled with desire for happiness. Pushkin juxtaposed these two images in his poem of 1817:

> . . . in my native land
> Where will we find the true mind, the true spirit?
> Where is the citizen with noble soul
> Elevated and flamingly free?
> Where is the woman whose beauty is not cold
> But flaming, captivating, alive?[53]
> ["An inexperienced admirer of foreign
> lands . . .,"1817]

If communion with freedom was perceived as a festival, the feast and even the orgy became in some respects manifestations of the freedom-loving ideal. However, another variety of the freedom-loving ethic was also possible. It was based on the complex of progressive ethical ideas that revised the philosophical heritage of the eighteenth-century materialists. Its contradictory sources range from Robespierre's interpretation of Rousseau to Schiller. It is the ideal of political stoicism, Roman virtue, and heroic asceticism. Love and happiness were banned from this world as feelings that were degrading, egotistical, and unworthy of the citizen. In place of "the woman whose beauty is not cold, but flaming, captivating, alive" were the austere Brutus and Marfa Posadnitsa ("the Cato of her republic" in the words of Karamzin). The goddess of love was rejected for the muse of "liberalism."

Flee, conceal yourself

[53]Pushkin, vol. 2, book 1, (Moscow/Leningrad, 1947), p. 43.

Frail tsarina of Cythera
Where are you, where are you, the terror of tsars,
The proud singer of freedom?[54]

["Liberty: An Ode"]

In the light of these possibilities, carousing could acquire either of two contrasting meanings. The only ground common to both interpretations was that this behavior was perceived as *having meaning*. It was transferred from the sphere of routine behavior to that of signifying activity. The difference is essential: individuals do not select routine behavior but rather acquire it from their society, from the historical period in which they live or from their own psychological or physiological makeup; there is no alternative to it. Signifying behavior, on the contrary, is always the result of choice. It always involves individuals' free activity, their choice of the language they will use in their relations with society. (In this context, it is interesting to observe how nonsignifying behavior can become signifying for the outside observer, for example the foreigner, who involuntarily contrasts it with his own ability to act differently in the same situations.)

This question has a direct bearing on our understanding of such essential phenomena of Russian social life of the 1810s as the Green Lamp society, Arzamas, and the Society of Loud Laughter. Let us take as an illustration the history of research on the Green Lamp.

Rumors concerning the orgies that supposedly took place in the Green Lamp society circulated among the younger generation of Pushkin's contemporaries, who knew the circumstances of the 1810s and early 1820s only through hearsay. These rumors were adopted by those who wrote the early biographical literature, and thus the foundation was laid for the tradition leading to the work of Bartenev and Annenkov, who saw the Green Lamp as an apolitical society, a place for orgies. In an article written in 1907 as a polemic attacking this tradition, Shchegolev raised the question of the society's links with the Union of Welfare.[55] With Modzalevskii's publication of part of the Green Lamp archives, this conjecture was supported by documents,[56] allowing several researchers to demonstrate its

---

[54]Ibid., p. 45.
[55]See P. E. Shchegolev, "Zelenaia lampa" in *Pushkin: Ocherki* (St. Petersburg, 1912); see also Shchegolev, *Iz zhizni i tvorchestva Pushkina* (Moscow/Leningrad, 1931).
[56]B. K. Modzalevskii, "K istorii 'Zelenoi lampy,' " in *Dekabristy i ikh vremia*, vol. 1 (Moscow, 1928).

accuracy.[57] This is the interpretation presented in Nechkina's conclusive study.[58] Finally, in his book *Pushkin*, where a forty-page section is devoted to the Green Lamp, Tomashevskii pursues this idea with extreme thoroughness and his usual critical acumen. There is no reason to revise these conclusions.

Nonetheless, the very thoroughness and detail employed in explaining the Green Lamp as an auxiliary of the Union of Welfare reveal a certain one-sidedness in the approach. Legends and scandals aside, let us look at Pushkin's cylce of poetry on the theme of the society and the letters he wrote to its members. There is something in these writings that unites them with the poetry of Iakov Tolstoi, whom Tomashevskii, with justification, called the "official poet" of the Green Lamp. This feature is the union of an obvious and unequivocal love of freedom with the cult of happiness, sensual love, blasphemy, and a certain defiant libertinism. It is not by chance that in these texts the reader often comes upon a series of dots—an indication of unprintable words—which would never be found in works addressed to Nikolai Turgenev, Chaadaev, or Fedor Glinka. Quoting an excerpt from Pushkin's epistle to Iur'ev, Tomashevskii compares it with Ryleev's dedication of "Voinarovskii": "The word 'hope' had a civic interpretation. Pushkin wrote to Iur'ev one of the members of the Green Lamp:

> Greetings, daring knights
> Of love, freedom and wine!
> For us, young comrades
> The lamp of hope has been lit.[59]
> ["To Iur'ev"]

"The civic interpretation of the word 'hope' is apparent in Ryleev's 'Voinarovskii' dedication:

> And once again in heaven's heights
> The star of hope began to shine."[60]

But in emphasizing the similar imagery of the two texts, let us not forget the lines that follow those of Pushkin cited above. Though

---

[57]See K. F. Ryleev, *Polnoe sobranie stikhotvorenii* (Leningrad, 1934) (commentaries); V. G. Bazanov, *Vol'noe obshchestvo liubitelei rossiiskoi slovesnosti* (Petrozavodsk, 1949).
[58]M. V. Nechkina, *Dvizhenie dekabristov*, vol. 1 (Moscow, 1955), pp. 239-246.
[59]B. Tomashevskii, *Pushkin*, Book 1 (1813-1824) (Moscow/Leningrad, 1956), p. 212.
[60]Ibid., p. 197.

entirely unimaginable for Ryleev, they are completely characteristic of this particular cycle of Pushkin's.

> Greetings, youth and happiness,
> The drinking goblet and the bordello
> Where sensuality with laughter loud
> Leads us drunken into bed.[61]

If one believes that the *entire* essence of the Green Lamp was expressed in its auxiliary role to the Union of Welfare, then it is impossible to reconcile such verses—and there are many—with the instructions in the Union of Welfare's "Green Book." There we read that "the goal of the Union is to spread the principles of morality and virtue" and the duty of members is "to extol virtue, denigrate vice, and show contempt for weakness in all conversation." It is worth recalling Nikolai Turgenev's fastidious attitude toward "feasts," which he saw as an activity worthy of "boors": "Moscow is the abyss of sensual pleasure. People eat, drink, sleep, play cards, and all this at the expense of the peasants who are overburdened with work."[62] (This note is dated 1821, the same year in which Baratynskii's poem "Piry" [feasts] was published.)

The first researchers to study the Green Lamp emphasized its "orgiastic" character, denying it any political significance. Contemporary researchers, having discovered the depth of real political interests among the society's members, have simply ignored any difference between the moral atmosphere of the Union of Welfare and that of the Green Lamp. Nechkina is completely silent on this aspect of the question. Tomashevskii evades it by separating the serious meetings of the Green Lamp, which fully correspond to the spirit of the Union of Welfare, from the more unconstrained evenings at the home of Nikita Vsevolozhskii. "It is time," he writes, "to separate the evenings at Vsevolozhskii's from the meetings of the Green Lamp."[63] But two lines down, he considerably softens his statement by adding that "for Pushkin, of course, the evenings at Vsevolozhskii's home were as inseparable from the meetings of the Green Lamp as the meetings of Arzamas were inseparable from the traditional goose dinners." It remains unclear why we have to separate what Pushkin saw as inseparable. Does

---

[61]Pushkin, vol. 2, book 1, p. 95.
[62]"Dnevniki N. Turgeneva," vol. 3, in *Arkhiv brat'ev Turgenevykh*, no. 5 (Petrograd, 1921), p. 259.
[63]Tomashevskii, p. 206.

it follow that we must separate the "serious" meetings of Arzamas from the "jocular" dinners? This hardly seems possible.

The Green Lamp was irrefutably a literary society dedicated to the cause of freedom and not a crowd of debauchers. It is unnecessary to belabor this point further.[64] That the Union of Welfare endeavored to exert an influence on it is no less evident. (The participation of Glinka and Trubetskoi in the society eliminates all doubt on this point.) But does this mean that the society was a mere offshoot of the Union and that no difference between them can be found? What was different was not the ideals and the programmatic aims but the type of behavior.

The Masons called their lodge meetings "work." To a member of the Union of Welfare, what he did in the society was also "work" or, even more solemnly, "service." This is the word that Pushkin was wont to use: "I am not the only one who has entered this new service to the fatherland."[65] The dominant mood of the political conspirator was serious and solemn. But for the member of the Green Lamp, love of freedom was couched in a tone of gaiety. The realization of its ideals was the transformation of life into an unending holiday. Grossman has made the accurate observation that Pushkin during this period "did not see political struggle as renunciation and sacrifice but as a joyful holiday."[66]

This "holiday" was linked with the idea that life, in overflowing its boundaries, made mockery of restrictions. Daring (as in Pushkin's "daring knights") distinguished the ideals of the Green Lamp from the harmonious hedonism of Batiushkov and the measured merrymaking of Arzamas, bringing it closer to Davydov's "hussar stance" and the student carousing of Iazykov.

---

[64]It is impossible to agree with either Annenkov or Tomashevskii. Annenkov writes that investigations into the Decembrist affair revealed the "innocent, i.e., orgiastic character of the 'Green Lamp,' " P. V. Annenkov, *A. S. Pushkin v Aleksandrovskuiu epokhu* (St. Petersburg, 1874), p. 63. Tomashevskii hypothesizes that "the rumours concerning orgies were perhaps circulated in order to put an end to curiosity and divert attention." Tomashevskii, p. 206. However, at the beginning of the nineteenth century the police prosecuted immorality no less actively than freedom of thought. Annenkov unwittingly transferred the mores of the last seven years of Nicholas's reign to the Alexandrine period. Tomashevskii writes that the "conspiratorial meetings could not have taken place on the weekly invitational evenings," using this to support his separation of "evenings" and "meetings." In refutation it is sufficient to recall "the secret meetings / On Thursdays. A most secret alliance . . . " in the words of Griboedov's Repetilov. The idea of secrecy conceived in the years 1819–1820 was far removed from the meaning it had acquired by 1824.
[65]I. I. Pushchin, *Zapiski o Pushkine: Pis'ma* (Moscow, 1956), p. 81.
[66]Leonid Grossman, *Pushkin* (Moscow, 1958), p. 143.

The rejection of the Karamzinian cult of "propriety" emerged in the speech behavior of society members. It was not simply a matter of using unprintable words; in that way the Lamp was no different from any army banquet. There is something comical in the proposition that young officers and poets, drinking at a bachelor dinner, would adhere to the lexicon of the Academic Dictionary, or that their notorious Kalmyk greetings indicate only the insufficient refinement of witticisms. That such assertions have been made shows the extent to which contemporary historical thought has been hypnotized by written sources: a document is equated with reality and the language of the document is taken for language of real life. The special nature of Green Lamp speech was its mixing of a crude vocabulary with the language of lofty political and philosophical thought or refined poetic imagery. This blending created a special, very intimate style, characteristic of Pushkin's letters to the members of the Green Lamp. Rich in unexpected combinations and in the mixture of styles, this language became a kind of password by which the members recognized their own. The use of a linguistic password, a distinct jargon accessible to a small circle, is characteristic of both the Lamp and Arzamas. Pushkin singled it out when in his imagination he returned from exile to the Green Lamp:

> Once again, faithful poets, I hear
> Your enchanted language . . . [67]
> [From a letter to Ia. N. Tolstoi, 1822]

Speech behavior had its correspondence in everyday behavior based on the same mixture. As early as 1817, in a verse addressed to Kaverin (the atmosphere of the hussars prepared for that of the Lamp), Pushkin wrote:

> . . . one can live in friendship
> With verses, with cards, with Plato and with wine,
> And hide beneath the gentle cover of playful pranks
> A noble mind and heart. [68]
> ["To Kaverin"]

Recall that the moralist and proselytizer Chatskii spoke sharply against precisely such a mixture (the Decembrist attitude toward cards will be taken up further on):

[67]Pushkin, vol. 2, book 1, p. 264.
[68]Ibid., vol. 1 (Moscow/Leningrad, 1937), p. 238.

When it's time for business, I hide from merriment,
When it's time to play the fool, I do that too.
But there are many who love to mix
These two trades. I am not one of them.
[*Woe from Wit*, act 3, scene 3]

Intimacy, elevated to a cult, resulted in a ritualization of the everyday life peculiar to this milieu. It was a ritualization "turned inside out," recalling the comic rituals of the carnival. It resulted in blasphemous substitutions such as "the holy bible of the Charites" for Voltaire's "Virgin." A rendezvous with "Lais" could be named outright, emphasizing a disregard for the language taboos of polite society:

When we four will again sit together
With w. . ., wine and long-stemed pipes.[69]
["May 27, 1819"]

Alternatively, it could be translated into the language of blasphemous ritual:

He passes the pious night
With a young nun of Cythera.[70]
["To Shcherbinin"]

This can be compared with the carnivalization of Masonic ritual in Arzamas. The antiritualism of the comic ritual is evident in both situations. But just as the "liberal" did not spend his leisure in the same way as Molchalin, the amusements of the Russian "carbonaro" did not correspond to those of the "liberal."

Everyday behavior, no less than the formal entry into a secret society, set the Decembrist apart not only from people of "bygone years" but also from a wide circle of malcontents, free thinkers and "liberals." The fact that such an emphasis on special behavior ("There is no end to your peculiarities," Sof'ia says to Chatskii) undercut the idea of conspiracy did not perturb the young conspirators. When the youngest of the Turgenev brothers, Sergei, was strongly attracted to Decembrist norms and ideals, it was not the Decembrist Nikolai but his more cautious older brother Aleksandr who felt called upon to convice Sergei to conceal his views

[69]Ibid., vol. 2, book 1 (Moscow/Leningard, 1947), p. 77.
[70]Ibid., p. 87.

in everyday life. Nikolai taught his brother the opposite: "We do not accept liberal principles to please the boors. They won't like us anyway. We will always despise them."[71]

The "severe look and sharp tone" that Sof'ia observes in Chatskii could not lend itself to the carefree joke without becoming accusatory satire. Decembrists were not merrymakers. When they joined societies devoted to the carnivalistic reveling of young liberals, they tried to direct them along a path of "noble" and "serious" activity. In doing so they destroyed the very basis of these organizations. It is hard to imagine what Fedor Glinka did at the meetings of the Green Lamp and even harder to picture him at Vsevolozhskii's dinners. But we are well aware of what happened to Arzamas after the Decembrists joined it. The speeches of Nikolai Turgenev and Mikhail Orlov were "passionate" and "intelligent" but could hardly be described as carelessly witty. Orlov understood this very well: "Can the hand accustomed to carrying the heavy steel sword of battle master Apollo's light weapon? And is it seemly for the voice roughened by yelling out commands to speak in the divine language of inspiration or the refined dialect of mockery?"[72]

The speeches given by Decembrists in the Society of Loud Laughter were also far removed from humor. Dmitriev describes one of them in his memoirs: "Shakhovskoi invited two guests, not members, to the second meeting—Fonvizin and Murav'ev.... During the meeting the guests smoked pipes, then went into the next room, and for some reason had a whispered conversation. Upon returning they started to say that work of this kind was too serious and so on, and began to give advice. Shakhovskoi turned red. The members were offended."[73] There was no loud laughter at this meeting.

By erasing the nobility's division of everyday life into spheres of work and leisure, the "liberals" wanted to transform life into a holiday the conspirators into "service."

All forms of social entertainment—dancing, cards, pursuing women—were severely condemned as signs of spiritual emptiness. In a letter to Iakushkin, Matvei Murav'ev-Apostol unequivocally connected the passion for cards with the general decline of public

---

[71]N. Turgenev, p. 208.
[72]*Arzamas i arzamasskie protokoly*, ed. M. S. Borovkova-Maikova (Leningrad, 1933), p. 206.
[73]A. G. Grumm-Grzhimailo and V. V. Sorokin, " 'Obshchestvo gromkogo smekha.' K istorii 'Vol'nykh obshchestv' Soiuza Blagodenstviia," in *Dekabristy v Moskve* (Moscow, 1963), p. 148.

morals in a reactionary period: "After the campaign of 1814 the passion for cards, it seems to me, disappeared among youth. To what can we ascribe the return of such a despicable activity?"[74] His question clearly rejected the possibility of a symbiotic relationship between cards and Plato.

Cards were equated with dancing, as a "trivial" pastime. Both these activities were banished from evening parties where the "cream of intelligent youth" gathered. At evening parties given by Liprandi there was neither "cards or dancing."[75] Griboedov, wishing to emphasize the gulf between Chatskii and his milieu, concluded his hero's monologue with the following stage direction: *"He looks around. Everyone is waltzing with great ardour. The old men have dispersed to the card table."* A letter that Nikolai Turgenev wrote to his brother Sergei is very characteristic. Nikolai is amazed that in France, where political life is intense, time is wasted on dancing: "I hear that you have been dancing. Count Golovin's daughter wrote him that she danced with you. And I was rather surprised to learn that in France, in addition to everything else, they also dance. Une écossaise constitutionelle, indépendante, ou une contredanse monarchique ou une danse contremonarchique?"[76]

We can see that at issue was not simply a lack of interest in dancing, because serious young men in 1818-1819 went to balls *in order not to dance there.* (Under the influence of the Decembrists, "seriousness" had become fashionable and affected a wider circle than just those who belonged to secret societies.) Pushkin's words from his "Novel in Letters" are well known: "Your speculative and important deliberations belong to the year 1818. At that time, austere mores and political economy were in fashion. We appeared at balls with our swords on. [An officer who intended to dance would unfasten his sword and give it to the doorman even before entering

[74]*Dekabrist M. I. Murav'ev-Apostol: Vospominaniia i pis'ma* (Petrograd, 1922), p. 85.

[75]*Russkii arkhiv*, 1866, vol. 4, 7, col. 1255.

[76]N. Turgenev, p. 280. Translation: An independent, constitutional ecossaise or a monarchical counterdance or a counter-monarchical dance? Olenina's memoirs provide extremely interesting evidence of the negative assessment of dancing as an activity incompatible with "Roman virtues" and of the belief in structuring behavior on the basis of texts that describe "heroic" behavior. In describing an episode from Nikita Murav'ev's childhood she writes: "During a children's party at the Derzhavins', Ekaterina Fedorovna [Murav'ev's mother—Iu. L.] noticed that Nikitushka was not dancing. She approached him to persuade him to dance. He asked her quietly: 'Maman, est-ce qu'Aristide et Caton ont dansé?' His mother answered him: 'Il faut supposer qu'oui, à votre age.' He immediately got up and went to dance." *Dekabristy: Letopisi*, State Literary Museum, book 3 (Moscow, 1938), p. 484.

the ballroom.—Iu. L.] It was improper for us to dance and we had no time for women."[77] Consider the remark of the old Princess in *Woe from Wit*: "Dancers have become frightfully rare."

The "Russian lunches" given by Ryleev, Spartan in spirit and markedly Russian in the choice of dishes, were demonstratively opposed to the "feast." Mikhail Bestuzhev writes: "They always took place around two or three o'clock in the afternoon and usually many literary men and members of our Society gathered there. The lunch invariably consisted of a carafe of pure Russian vodka, several heads of sour cabbage and rye bread. Do not consider such a Spartan luncheon to be strange." It "harmonized with Ryleev's constant inclination to Russianize his life."[78] Bestuzhev is far from ironic when he describes men of letters "pacing up and down with their cigars, eating sliced cabbage"[79] while criticizing Zhukovskii's obscure romanticism. But the combination is a characteristic one. The cigar is strictly a matter of habit, testifying to the profound Europeanization of everyday life, while the cabbage is an ideologically weighted sign. Bestuzhev does not see a contradiction here. That the cigar belongs to a different level from the cabbage is perceptible only to the outside observer—that is, to us.

The young man who divided his time between balls and drinking with his friends was contrasted to the hermit who passed his days in his study. The retreat into the study was joined even by the young men of the military, who began to resemble young scholars more than army revelers. Nikita Murav'ev, Pestel', Iakushkin, Zavalishin, Batenkov and scores of other young men of their circle studied, attended private lectures, ordered books and journals and shirked feminine society:

> . . . the fashionable circle is no longer in fashion.
> You know, my dear, we're all free men now.
> We stay out of society; don't know the ladies.
> We've left them to the mercies of [old men],
> The dear pets of the eighteenth century.
> [Pushkin, "To Chaadaev," 1821]

> Those professors! A relative of ours studied from them,
> And graduated! Would make a fine apothecary or apprentice

[77]Pushkin, vol. 8, book 1, p. 55.
[78]*Vospominaniia Bestuzhevykh* (Moscow/Leningrad, 1951), p. 53.
[79]Ibid., p. 54.

137

And hides from women. . . .

> [*Woe from Wit*, act 3, scene 21]

Dmitrii Zavalishin, who at the age of sixteen was appointed instructor of astronomy and higher mathematics at the naval academy which he had just brilliantly completed, and who at eighteen set out on a scientific voyage around the world, complained that in Petersburg there were "endless guests, endless cards, and the bustle of society life . . . often I would have no time for my serious and beloved studies."[80]

The nongentry intellectual (*raznochinets-intelligent*) of the late eighteenth and early nineteenth centuries could take an evasive position on the gulf between theory and reality: "Wear a mask in society / But be a philosopher when locked in your study,"[81] wrote P. A. Slovtsov in an epistle to Speransky.

But the Decembrist's reclusiveness was accompanied by the unequivocal and open expression of contempt for the common pastimes of the nobility. A special paragraph of the "Green Book" prescribed: "Don't waste time in the illusory pleasures of high society but devote leisure time to useful activities or to conversations with right-thinking men."[82] The type of the hussar-sage (both hermit and scholar) came into being. Such a man was Chaadaev,

> . . . I will see the study
> Where you are forever the sage and sometimes the dreamer,
> The dispassionate observer of the frivolous crowd.
>
> ["To Chaadaev," 1821]

Pushkin and Chaadaev spent time together *reading* ("I caroused with Kaverin,[83] denounced Russia with Molostvov, and read with

---

[80]*Zavalishin*, p. 39.

[81]P. A. Slovtsov, "Poslanie k M. M. Speranskomu," in *Poety 1790-1810-kh godov* (Leningrad, 1971), p. 209.

[82]A. N. Pypin, *Obshchestvennoe dvizhenie v Rossii pri Aleksandre I* (St. Petersburg, 1908), p. 567.

[83]An entry in Raevskii's diary describing a conversation with the Grand Duke Constantine when Raevskii was in the guardhouse reveals the semantics of the word "carouse" (*guliat'*). In answer to Raevskii's request to take walks (also *guliat'*), Constantine replied, "No, major, that is entirely impossible! When you have been acquitted, you will have plenty of time for carousing." Later it became clear that they had misunderstood one another. "Yes! yes! the Grand Duke added quickly. You want to stroll in the fresh air for your health and I thought you wanted to carouse. That's another matter." *Literaturnoe nasledstvo*, vol. 60, book 1 (Moscow, 1956), pp. 100-101. Constantine regarded carousing as a norm of military behavior (it was no accident that Pushkin called him a "romantic") impermissible as long as one is locked up in the guardhouse. For the "Spartan" Raevskii the verb *guliat'* would only signify a walk.

my Chaadaev"). Pushkin gives an extremely accurate picture of the way that nonconformist dispositions were manifested in everyday behavior. This scale, which ranged from feasts to "conversations about freedom" to reading not only aroused the suspicion of the government but also irritated those who continued to see revelry and independence as synonymous: "Jomini and again Jomini. But of vodka, not a word!"[84] wrote Denis Davydov in "Song of an Old Hussar."

But it would be most erroneous to imagine the member of a secret society as a solitary person who remained at home. The qualities just discussed signify only the rejection of older forms of everyday socializing. The idea of "collective effort" became central for the Decembrists, permeating not only their theories but also their everyday behavior. In a number of instances this concept preceded the idea of political conspiracy and psychologically facilitated the movement toward it. Zavalishin recalled: "When I was a cadet at the Academy [Zavalishin was at the Academy 1816–1819; he entered the Northern Society in 1824—Iu. L.], I not only very closely observed all the inadequacies, disorders, and abuses but always offered them as topics of debate to the more sensible of my comrades so that by combining our efforts we could elucidate their causes and devise means of avoiding them."[85]

The cult of brotherhood, based on the unity of spiritual ideals, and the exaltation of friendship were highly characteristic of the Decembrist, often at the expense of other ties. Ryleev was passionate in friendship, yet in the impartial recollection of his serf Agap Ivanov (whom Ryleev paid for his work) he "seemed cold toward his family and did not like it when they distracted him from his studies."[86]

Pushkin's words concerning the Decembrists—"Brothers, friends, comrades"—are exceptionally precise in characterizing the hierarchy of intimacy existing in the human relationships within the Decembrist camp. If the circle of "brothers" tended to contract into "conspirators," then at the opposite pole stood "comrades," a concept easily expanded to mean "young people" or "enlightened people." Even this broad concept, however, the Decembrists subsumed under an even broader cultural "we" as opposed to "they." "From us, from the young people," Chatskii says. Zavalishin

[84]Denis Davydov, *Sochinenii* (Moscow, 1962), p. 102.
[85]*Zavalishin*, p. 41.
[86]"Rasskazy o Ryleeve rassyl'nogo *Poliarnoi zvezdy*," in *Literaturnoe nasledstvo*, vol. 59 (Moscow, 1954), p. 254.

writes, "The positions of highest command [in the navy—Iu. L.] were occupied at that time by nonentities (particularly Englishmen) or crooks, which was especially apparent in comparison to the talent, education, and absolute honesty of *our generation.*"[87]

Just as the world of politics penetrated the fabric of personal relationships, so family and personal ties became part of the Decembrists' political organizations. In the later history of the social movement, love, friendships, and long-term attachments would be ended because of ideology and politics. But for the Decembrists the political organization itself was a form of direct human intimacy; it embodied friendship and devotion to the whole individual, not only to his convictions. All those participating in political life had connections to each other outside of politics. They were relatives, or members of the same regiment, or had been fellow students; they had fought in the same battles or simply turned out to be social acquaintances. These connections embraced the entire circle, from the tsar and the grand dukes, whom one could meet and talk with at a ball, down to the young conspirators. The existence of such connections gave the period its special stamp.

In no other Russian political movement are there so many blood ties. Within the Murav'ev and Lunin families and surrounding the Raevskii household there were numerous interconnections (Mikhail Orlov and Sergei Volkonskii were married to General Raevskii's daughters; Vasilii Davydov, the poet's cousin who was condemned to life imprisonment, was the general's half-brother). Consider the four Bestuzhev brothers, and the brothers Vadkovskii, Bobrishchev-Pushkin, Bodisko, Borisov, Kiukhel'beker, and so forth. If we take into account connections formed by marriage, first- and second-cousin relationships, and residence on neighboring estates (which involved common childhood recollections and sometimes bound people more tightly than family relationships), a picture is formed that was never to recur in the subsequent history of the liberation movement in Russia.

No less significant is the fact that these family and friendly relationships—social acquaintanceships from clubs and balls, military ones from regiments and campaigns—connected the Decembrists with adversaries as well as allies. However, ideological differences never disrupted these relationships.

The fate of the brothers Mikhail and Aleksei Orlov is perhaps

---

[87] *Zavalishin*, p. 39 (italics mine—Iu. L.).

the most striking, but it is hardly unique. Take the case of Mikhail Murav'ev, who participated in the Union of Salvation, coauthored the statutes of the Union of Welfare and then presided over the bloody suppression of the Polish insurrection. But the uncertainty that friendships and social ties introduced into the personal relationships of political enemies is revealed more clearly in more ordinary examples. On December 14, 1825, an adjutant by the name of N. D. Durnovo turned up next to Nicholas I on Senate Square. Late that night this same Durnovo was sent to arrest Ryleev and did so. At that time he was already enjoying the complete trust of the new emperor who on the day before had assigned to him the dangerous (and never fulfilled) mission of negotiating with the rebellious troops. Sometime later it was none other than Durnovo who escorted Mikhail Orlov to the fortress.

The matter would seem to be clear. Durnovo was a reactionary servant of the tsar, from the Decembrists' point of view—an enemy. But let us become better acquainted with this man.[88]

N. D. Durnovo was born in 1792. In 1810 he entered the military academy for staff officers. In 1811 he was promoted to staff lieutenant and served under the staff commander Prince Volkonskii. At this time Durnovo joined a secret society which until recently we knew about only through a brief note in the memoirs of Nikita Murav'ev: "The other members of the society [besides the column commander Ramburg—Iu. L.] were the officers Durnovo, Alexandr Shcherbinin, Vil'deman, and Dellingsgauzen. Although I had heard about the existence of this society, I did not know its goals in detail since the members, gathering at Durnovo's, kept it secret from their other comrades."[89] Durnovo's diary adds new information. On January 25, 1812, he noted: "A year has passed since the founding of our society, called 'Knighthood' (Chevalerie). After dining at Demidov's I went to our meeting at 9:00 at the 'hermit's' (Soli-

<hr/>

[88] Durnovo's voluminous diary is the primary source for information about him. Excerpts from it have been published in *Vestnik obshchestva revnitelei istorii*, no. 1 (1914), and in the book *Dekabristy: Zapiski otdela rukopisei Vsesoiuznoi biblioteki im. V. I. Lenina*, no. 3 (Moscow, 1939) (see the pages that directly concern the uprising of December 14, 1825). However, the part that has been published is only a small portion of a large multivolume diary written in French (in the collection of the Lenin State Library).

[89] "Zapiski N. N. Murav'eva," in *Russkii arkhiv*, 1885, book 9, p. 26. See: S. N. Chernov, *U istokov russkogo osvoboditel'nogo dvizheniia* (Saratov, 1960), pp. 24-25; Lotman, "Tarutinskii period Otechestvennoi voiny 1812 goda i razvitie russkoi osvoboditel'noi mysli," *Uchenye zapiski Tartuskogo gosudartsvennogo universiteta*, no. 139 (1963) pp. 15-17.

taire). It lasted until three o'clock in the morning. Four of the original knights presided at this meeting."[90]

From this entry we first learn the exact date of the society's founding, its name (curiously reminiscent of the "Russian Knights" of Mamonov and Orlov), and some aspects of its internal ritual. The society had written statutes, as the entry for January 25, 1813 indicates: "Today is the second anniversary of the founding of our K[nighthood]. I am the only one of the brothers in Petersburg. All the other enlightened (illustres) are on the fields of battle, where I am preparing to return. Tonight, however, there was no meeting as stipulated in the statutes."[91]

On the eve of the war with France in 1812, Durnovo arrived in Vilnus and became very close to the Murav'ev brothers, who invited him to stay at their home. He became particularly close to Aleksandr and Nikolai. Shortly thereafter Mikhail Orlov, Sergei Volkonskii, and Koloshin joined their circle. Durnovo had already become friends with Orlov when they served together in St. Petersburg under Prince Volkonskii. Together with Orlov he attacked Aleksandr Murav'ev's mysticism, and this caused bitter arguments. Meetings, walks and conversations with Aleksandr Murav'ev and Orlov filled the pages of his diary. These are the entries for June 21 and 22: "Orlov returned with General Balashov. They had been to a conference with Napoleon. The sovereign spent over an hour in conversation with Orlov. They say he is satisfied with the latter's conduct in the army of his adversary. He gave a very sharp reply to Marshall Davout who was trying to provoke him." June 22: "What we have foreseen has happened. My friend Orlov, adjutant to Prince Volkonskii and lieutenant in the horseguards, has been designated adjutant to the emperor. He deserves this honor in all respects."[92] Together with Volkonskii's staff, Durnovo and Orlov left the army and followed the emperor to Moscow.

Durnovo's Decembrist connections do not seem to have been broken off in later years. In his diary he records the open aspects of his life in detail but clearly avoids all dangerous references. (For example, the only information about "the Knighthood" occurs in the passages just cited, although the society obviously continued to have meetings, and very often conversations are mentioned with

[90]Lenin State Library, fond 95 (Durnovo), no. 9533, f. 19. (A fragment of Russian typed copy apparently prepared for *Vestnik obshchestva revnitelei istorii*, Central State Archives, fond 1337, *opis'* 1, storage unit 71.)

[91]Lenin State Library, fond 95, no. 9536, f. 7v.

[92]Ibid., v. 56.

no indication of their content.) However, we suddenly find the following entry dated June 20, 1817: "I was strolling in my garden when a courier from Zakrevskii came for me. I thought that the message concerned a journey to remote regions of Russia, but then I was pleasantly surprised to learn that the emperor had ordered me to supervise the movement of troops from outposts to the Winter Palace."[93]

After December 14, Durnovo evidently avoided the imperial favors showered upon those who were near the emperor on the fateful date. Although he had been made an adjutant to Alexander I in 1815,[94] after receiving numerous decorations from the Russians, Prussians, Austrians, and Swedes (Alexander I said of him, "Durnovo is a brave officer"), during the reign of Nicholas I he occupied the modest post of administrator in the Chancellery of the General Staff. But apparently he was uncomfortable even there. In 1828 he requested active duty in the army; upon his transfer he was commissioned a major-general. He was killed at the siege of Shumla.[95]

It is not surprising, then, that Durnovo and Orlov, whom fate had placed at opposite poles in 1825, did not meet as political enemies. If they were not friends, they were at least old acquaintances and conversed quite amicably all the way to the fortress of Peter and Paul.

This complexity of relationships also influenced the Decembrists' behavior during the investigation. The revolutionaries of later periods did not know their adversaries personally and saw them as political forces rather than people. This perspective was conducive to uncompromising hatred. But even in the Commission of Inquiry, the Decembrist could not help but see people with whom he was connected in the service, in society, and through clubs. They could have been either acquaintances or superiors. He could feel contempt for their senile obtuseness, their careerism, and their servility. But he could not see them as "tyrants" and despots fit for the denunciations of a Tacitus. It was impossible to speak with them in the language of political pathos, a fact that disoriented the prisoners.

The poetry of the Decembrists was to a great extent eclipsed by

[93]Ibid., no. 3540, v. 10.
[94]In the publication of the manuscript department of the Lenin Library, Durnovo is referred to as adjutant to Nicholas I, but this is obviously an error (see *Dekabristy: Zapiski otdela rukopisei Vsesoiuznoi biblioteki im. V. I. Lenina*, no. 3, p. 8).
[95]See *Russkii invalid*, no. 304 (December 4, 1828).

the work of their brilliant contemporaries Zhukovskii, Griboedov, and Pushkin; their political concepts had become outmoded by the generation of Belinskii and Herzen. Their unsurpassed contribution to Russian culture lies in the creation of a *type of person* completely new for Russia. In its approximation of an ideal it is reminiscent of Pushkin's contribution to Russian poetry.

Basic to the Decembrist's whole character was a sense of self-respect. This quality was rooted in a highly developed sense of honor and in each participant's belief that he was a great man. We are struck by a certain naivete in Zavalishin's remarks about his classmates who, aspiring to rank, gave up serious theoretical studies "and by so doing almost without exception became ordinary people."[96]

This attitude required that *every* action be viewed as significant, worthy of remembrance by future generations, worthy of the historian's attention, and embodying a higher meaning. On the one hand this produced a certain posturing in or theatricalization of everyday life (note the scene of Ryleev's explanation to his mother, as described by Nikolai Bestuzhev).[97] On the other hand it resulted in the application of exceptionally high standards to everyday behavior. In Siberia, in a period when historicism had become the leading idea of the age, the sense of the political significance of *the entirety* of one's behavior was replaced by a sense of its historical meaning. "Lunin lives for history," wrote Sutgof to Mukhanov. Lunin himself, comparing his own fate to that of the grandee Novosil'tsev, wrote upon learning of the latter's death: "What a contrast in our fates! For one the scaffold and history; for the other a council chairmanship and an almanac." Note that the real-life details of this entry—the scaffold and the council chairmanship— are the signifier of the complex sign that human life was for Lunin (life was something that possessed meaning). The signified was the presence or absence of spirituality, which in turn was symbolized in a particular text: in a line written in history or a line written in an almanac.

Comparing the Decembrists' behavior with poetry is not a rhetorical device; it has a serious basis. Poetry uses the unconscious stratum of language to construct a conscious text with a complex secondary meaning. Everything in a poem is significant, even those

[96]*Zavalishin*, p. 46.
[97]*Vospominaniia Bestuzhevykh*, pp. 9-11.

elements of the language system that in ordinary speech are purely formal.

From the unconscious stratum of everyday behavior character-istic of the Russian nobleman at the turn of the nineteenth century, the Decembrists constructed a conscious system of ideologically signifying behavior, complete as a text and permeated with higher meaning.

Let me give just one example of a purely artistic relationship to the material of behavior. A person can alter his appearance by changing his hair style, his walk, his posture, and so forth. Because they are the result of choice, such elements of behavior are easily saturated with meaning ("a casual hairdo," "an artistic hairdo," a "coiffure à l'empereur," and so on). But facial features and height have no alternatives. The writer, who can grant these features to his hero as he sees fit, makes them the conveyors of important meanings. But in everyday life we usually semioticize not the face but its expression, not the height but the way a person carries himself. (Of course we perceive these unchanging external ele-ments as particular signals, but only when they are included in complex paralinguistic systems.) All the more interesting are in-stances in which an individual interprets his natural appearance as a sign, that is, approaches himself as a kind of message, the meaning of which (his predestination, the fate of humanity, and the like) he must decipher. This is the priest Myslovskii's impres-sions of Pestel', whom he met in the fortress: "He was over 33 years old, of medium height and had a pale and pleasant face with impressive features. He was extremely swift, resolute, and elo-quent. He was an erudite mathematician, a superior military tac-tician. In his gestures, his movements, his stature, and even in his facial features, he strongly resembled Napoleon. This very likeness to a great man, confirmed unanimously by all who knew Pestel', was the reason for all his follies and crimes."[98]

Olenina writes in her memoirs: "Sergei Mur(av'ev)-Apostol was no less remarkable a personality [than Nikita Murav'ev—Iu. L.]. In addition, he had an inordinate likeness to Napoleon which prob-ably played upon his imagination."[99]

It is enough to compare these characteristics with those Pushkin gives Hermann in "The Queen of Spades" to see the general,

---

[98]Myslovskii notebook, p. 39.

[99]"Vospominaniia o dekabristakh. Pis'ma V. A. Oleninoi k P. I. Bartenevu," in *Dekabristy: Letopisi*, book 3, p. 485.

essentially artistic principle. But Pushkin used this principle for the construction of an artistic text and an invented hero. Pestel' and Sergei Murav'ev-Apostol adapted it to entirely real lives: their own. Nevertheless, this approach to one's own behavior as consciously created according to the laws and models of higher texts did not lead the Decembrists to aestheticize the category of behavior as it did the Russian symbolists with their "lifebuilding." For the Decembrists, behavior, like art, was not an end in itself but a means, the external expression of the high spirituality permeating the text of life or the text of art.

There is an obvious connection between the Decembrists' everyday behavior and the principles of the romantic world view. Still, it is important to keep in mind that the highly semiotic nature (posturing, theatricality, literariness) of their everyday behavior never turned into affectation or pompous declamation. On the contrary, it combined strikingly well with simplicity and sincerity. Olenina, who had known many of the Decembrists since childhood, says, "The Murav'evs in Russia were just like the Gracchus brothers," but she also observes that Nikita Murav'ev "was nervous and painfully timid."[100] The broad range of personalities from Ryleev's childlike simplicity and shyness to the refined aristocratic simplicity of Chaadaev shows convincingly that the affectation of cheap theater did not characterize the Decembrist ideal of everyday behavior.

There were two reasons for this. First, the Decembrist ideal of everyday behavior was completely opposed to that of Turgenev's Bazarov. It was not structured as a rejection of etiquette but as an assimilation and reworking of earlier norms. It was behavior oriented not toward Nature but toward Culture. Second, it remained principally the behavior of the nobleman. It required good manners. The genuinely good manners of the educated sector of the Russian nobility implied simplicity in conduct. Educated nobles completely lacked that feeling of social inadequacy and frustration which was the psychological basis for the Bazarov type of plebian affectation. This quality accounts for the striking ease with which the exiled Decembrists entered the world of the common people. (This facility had been lost by the time of Dostoevskii and the Petroshevtsy.) Belogolovyi was able to observe the exiled Decembrists for an extended time with the keen eye of a child not belonging to the nobility. He observed, "The old man Volkonskii—

[100]Ibid., pp. 486 and 485.

he was by then over sixty—passed for a great eccentric in Irkutsk. Having ended up in Siberia, he abruptly broke his ties with his brilliant and illustrious past. He changed into a bustling and practical man, leading a simple life . . . and making friends with the peasants." "The townspeople who knew him were very shocked when, passing through the marketplace on their way home from Sunday service, they saw the prince perched on the box of a peasant cart piled up with grain sacks. He was carrying on a lively conversation with the peasants who had surrounded him, and breakfasting with them then and there on a crust of grey wheat bread." "The prince's guests were most often peasants and his floors were always dirty from boots. Volkonskii appeared in his wife's drawing-room soiled with tar and with pieces of hay stuck to his clothing; he full beard was scented with the aromas of the barnyard or with other not quite drawing-room odors. In society he generally presented an eccentric figure although he was very well educated. He spoke French like a Frenchman, rolling his r's, was very kind and with us, the children, he was always gentle and affectionate."[101] This ability to relate in a natural and completely unaffected manner to visitors in a drawing-room, to peasants at the market, and to children constitutes the cultural pattern of the Decembrists' everyday behavior. It is akin to Pushkin's poetry and forms one of the towering manifestations of Russian culture.

We are now in a position to touch upon one further problem. The question of the Decembrist tradition in Russian culture is usually studied from a purely ideological point of view. But there is also a "human" aspect to the question—the tradition of a particular type of behavior, of a type of social psychology. An example is Tolstoi's ideological relation to Decembrism, a complex question that requires qualification. In human terms, however, the continuity of the historico-psychological type of personality and type of behavior is obvious. Tolstoi himself, in speaking of the Decembrists, distinguished between ideas and personalities. The diary of his daughter Tat'iana includes an extremely interesting entry on this subject: "Repin keeps asking Papa for a subject. . . . Yesterday Papa said that he had thought of one but that it didn't entirely satisfy him. This was the moment when they led the Decembrists to the gallows. The young Bestuzhev-Riumin was captivated by Murav'ev-Apostol, *by his personality more than his ideas*. He walked alongside him the whole time and only broke down right before

---

[101]Belogolovyi, *Vospominaniia*, pp. 32-33.

the execution. He wept, Murav'ev embraced him, and they walked to the scaffold together."[102]

Tolstoi's treatment is very interesting. He was drawn first and foremost to the people who participated in the events of December 14. The people were closer and dearer to him than the ideas of Decembrism.

Within human behavior, as within any form of human activity, it is possible to distinguish strata of "poetry" and "prose."[103] Thus for Paul and his sons the poetry of army life consisted in the parade and the prose in military action. Fet wrote in his memoirs: "Convinced that beauty was a sign of strength, the emperor Nicholas strove to attain in his strikingly disciplined and well-trained troops a nearly unconditional subordination and uniformity."[104]

For Denis Davydov, poetry was associated not simply with battle, but with the irregularity, the *"organized disorder* of armed villagers." "This kind of action filled with poetry requires romantic imagination and a passion for adventure. It is not satisfied with unfeeling, prosaic courage. It's like a stanza from Byron. Let him who is unafraid of death yet fears *responsibility* remain within the sight of the commanders."[105] The clear differentiation between the poetic and the prosaic in human behavior and actions is characteristic of the period we have been considering. Thus Viazemskii criticized Pushkin for making the hero of *The Gypsies* perform with a bear, proposing instead the less prosaic occupation of robbery: "Better to leave him to horse stealing. In that trade, although it is not completely innocent, there is some daring and consequently, poetry."[106] The sphere of poetry in real life was the world of "daring."

The individual living in the age of Pushkin and Viazemskii moved freely back and forth from the sphere of prose to that of poetry. In literature only poetry "counted." Similarly, in judging a person the prosaic sphere of behavior was in a sense discounted, as if it did not exist.

The Decembrists brought unity to human behavior, not through the rehabilitation of life's prose but by filtering life through heroic

[102]T. L. Tolstaia-Sukhotina, "Vblizi ottsa," *Novyi mir*, no. 12, (1973), p. 194 (italics mine.—Iu. L.).

[103]See Jean Galard, "Pour une poétique de la conduite," *Semiotica*, 10 (1974).

[104]A. A. Fet, *Moi vospominaniia*, part 1 (Moscow, 1890), p. iv.

[105]Denis Davydov, *Opyt teoriii partizanskogo deistviia*, 2d ed. (Moscow, 1822), pp. 26 and 83.

[106]Cited in V. A. Zelinskii, *Russkaia kriticheskaia literatura o proizvedeniiakh A. S. Pushkina*, part 1 (Moscow, 1887), p. 68.

texts and removing whatever was not worthy of history. The prosaic accountability to authority was replaced by accountability to history, and the fear of death by the poetry of honor and freedom. "We breathe freedom," said Ryleev on December 14 in Senate Square. Freedoms were transferred from the realm of ideas and theories to "breath," to life. In this is the essence and meaning of the Decembrists' everyday behavior.

Concerning Khlestakov

Iurii M. Lotman

Gogol considered Khlestakov to be the central character of his *Inspector General*. Sergei Aksakov recalls that "Gogol was always complaining because he couldn't find the right actor for the role. He felt that for this reason the impact of the play was lost, and it might just as well be called *The Mayor* as *The Inspector General*."[1] In Aksakov's words, Gogol "regretted very much that the *leading role* [my italics—Iu. L.], Khlestakov, is being played stupidly in Petersburg and Moscow, depriving the play of its meaning.... Returning to Petersburg," continues Aksakov, Gogol "suggested staging *The Inspector General* in his home theater, and he wanted to take the role of Khlestakov himself."[2] This incident is worthy of note, since Gogol cast the roles for his amateur performance with particular care—planning, for example, to have the postal censor Tomashevskii play "the role of the postmaster."[3]

There was in fact some justification for placing the greatest interpretative stress on the role of the Mayor. Such a view was a logical outcome of the idea that the play's central theme is a denunciation of the world of the petty bureaucrat. From this point of view, Khlestakov is indeed a secondary character, a functional figure whose purpose is to hold up the anecdotal plot. This interpretation was first put forth by Belinskii, who saw in the play the idea that "it is only fitting for *a man who is himself only a phantom*

Translated by Louisa Vinton from "O Khlestakove," *Trudy po russkoi i slavianskoi filologii*, no. 26 (Tartu, 1975) pp.19-53.
[1] S. T. Aksakov, *Sobranie sochinenii v chetyrekh tomakh*, vol. 3 (Moscow, 1956), p. 160.
[2] Ibid., p. 166.
[3] Ibid.

to take his punishment from a phantom or ghost, or, to put it more precisely, from the shadow of the fear arising from a guilty conscience.[4] "Many people," writes Belinskii, "consider Khlestakov to be the protagonist of the comedy, its most important figure. This belief is mistaken. Khlestakov is present in the comedy not in and of himself, but as a completely incidental figure, one mentioned only in passing. The protagonist of the comedy is the Mayor, the representative of the world of phantoms."[5] Belinskii's article was written at the end of 1839. In April 1842, however he wrote to Gogol, "I now understand why you feel that Khlestakov is the protagonist of your comedy, and indeed I agree with you."[6] Belinskii's new opinion was never developed as fully as the one laid out in his 1839 article "Woe from Wit," which inspired the traditional perception of *The Inspector General* for both Russian criticism and the nineteenth-century Russian public. Even today, Khlestakov's role remains problematic, although thoughtful observations by twentieth-century scholars and critics and theatrical interpretations by actors ranging from Mikhail Chekhov to Igor' Il'inskii have revealed much about the enigmatic character whom Gogol defined as a "phantasmagorical figure."[7]

Every work of literature can be examined simultaneously from two points of view: as a separate artistic world with an organization all its own, and, in a wider context, as a fragment of a certain cultural or structural unity of a higher order.

The artistic world created by an author is always in some way a model of the real world beyond the text. This extratextual reality is also a complex structural unit—the fact that it is beyond the text does not mean that it is beyond semiotics. The people around Gogol were enmeshed in a complex system of rules and norms. To a great extent, life itself was realized as a hierarchy of social norms: the bureaucracy of the post-Petrine Europeanized state, the semiotics of ranks and service gradations, and the rules of conduct that stipulated behavior appropriate to nobleman or merchant, bureaucrat or officer, cosmopolitan or provincial. The result was a multilayered system in which underlying century-old habits of mind and modes of behavior could be glimpsed through those that were more temporary or even completely transitory.

In this sense, reality itself was a stage on which people were cast

---

[4]V. G. Belinskii, *Polnoe sobranie sochinenii*, vol. 3 (Moscow, 1953). p. 454.
[5]Ibid., p. 465.
[6]Ibid., vol. 12, p. 108.
[7]N. V. Gogol, *Polnoe sobranie sochinenii*, vol. 4 (Moscow/Leningrad, 1951), p. 118.

certain roles. The more commonplace the man, the more closely his personal behavior followed the social scenàrio.

The reproduction of life on the actual stage thus acquired the traits of a play within a play, the reduplication of social semiotics in theatrical semiotics. The inevitable result for Gogol's plays was an atmosphere of comedy and puppet theater, for if the theatrical representation of reality can arouse serious responses in an audience, the theatrical representation of a theatrical representation almost always causes laughter.

It is thus appropriate to begin an examination of the nature of the character Khlestakov by analyzing the behavioral norms that made "Khlestakovism" a fact of life in Russia before and after Gogol wrote his text.

One of the main features of post-Petrine Russian culture was a special sort of dualism: what was believed in theory to be the ideal way of life was at the same time not supposed to correspond to reality. The widths of the gap between the world of texts and the real world could vary widely. At one extreme was the belief in an ideal high standard that was corrupted in the realm of base reality; at the other was deliberate government demagogy, which found expression in laws not meant to be put on the books (Catherine's liberal "Instruction" [Nakaz] and legislative bodies that were not supposed to enact real legislation (her Legislative Commission). Although a deep gulf divided the activity of the theorists of the age of classicism from the political practice of the "empire of facades," the two had one underlying feature in common. The moment a cultured man of the latter age took a book into his hands, went to the theater, or appeared at court, he found himself simultaneously in two worlds, which coexisted but at no point intersected: the world of the ideal and that of the real. For a believer in classicism, only the world of ideas and theoretical constructs had any reality; at court, in political discussions, and in the theatricalized festivals demonstrating the advent of Russia's "golden age of Astraea," the rules of the game stipulated that the desired world existed while the real one did not. This world of ideas was a play world associated with social interchange, everyday life, and the entirety of official "facade" life—all areas in which the intrusion of reality was felt most strongly. Here, to call attention to the true state of affairs was an unforgivable violation of the rules of the game. But alongside this world was another world of bureaucratic and state life. In this world, realism was preferred: pragmatists were needed, and not dreamers. The empress herself, in moving from the theater to her study, in turning from a letter to a European philosopher or the writing of her "Instruction" to the routine matters of internal and international politics, instantly became a businesslike pragmatist. Theater and life did not mix for Catherine, as they later did for Paul. Men of Potemkin's generation and position could still unite "dreaming" and pragmatism (especially as Catherine, always a pragmatist and an opportunist, valued in her "best friend" that whimsical imagination her own dry nature lacked, and allowed him to "dream" in politics):

> I spin my thought in chimeras:
> Now stealing prisoners from the Persians,
> Now sending arrows toward the Turks;
> Now dreaming myself Sultan,
> I terrify the universe with my glance;
> Then suddenly developing a fancy for clothes,
> I run to the tailor for a caftan.[8]

Subsequent generations, however, had to choose. They could pursue activity that was practical but contradicted their ideals, or an activity that was ideal but had to be pursued outside of practical life. It was necessary either to renounce one's dreams or to nullify life by living only in the imagination, substituting words, poems, "activity" in dreams and conversations, for actual deeds. The word began to occupy a hypertrophic place in culture. This development led to the growth of creative imagination in the gifted and to "a great talent for lying," as Aleksandr Izmailov expressed it, in the mediocre. The line between them could become faint. Karamzin wrote: "What is a poet? a skillful liar...."[9] Psychology tells us that the tendency to lie arises during the transition from childhood to adolescence, when the development of the imagination coincides with a feeling of dissatisfaction with reality. As a trait of historical, and not individual, psychology, lying indicates infantile tendencies in a mature person, group, or generation. I will use an extreme example, the life of Dmitrii Irinarkhovich Zavalishin, to make this point clear.

Zavalishin was a striking figure. Mark Azadovskii has described him as "an exceptional man of action, wonderfully educated, very public-spirited, but also extremely vain, with abnormally high self-

[8]G. P. Derzhavin, *Stikhotvoreniia* (Leningrad, 1957), pp. 98-99.
[9]N. M. Karamzin, *Polnoe sobranie stikhotvorenii* (Moscow/Leningrad, 1966), p. 19.

esteem and unmistakable traits of adventurism."[10] A full elucidation of Zavalishin's place in Russian history cannot be undertaken
here, especially since his actual political convictions and his role
in the Decembrist movement, as the same authority on Decembrism
has written, "have not been studied at all."[11] We are concerned
here not so much with Zavalishin's political tendencies as with his
psychological makeup, in which we find details whose relevance
extends beyond a study of individual psychology. Among the Decembrists, Zavalishin was a loner. Even the Decembrist most well
disposed toward him, Nikolai Bestuzhev, wrote: "One must know
Dmitr[ii] Irinarkh[ovich] better to stop liking him."[12] Of course, it
was not his exceptional talents, memory, and erudition that set
him apart from his associates in the political struggle and in Siberia;
people more impressive than he were also there. Nor was Zavalishin the only man active in the Decembrist movement who was
distinguished by exaggerated ambition and even adventurism.
Something else made him unique. Dmitrii Zavalishin was an extremely mendacious man. He lied all his life. He lied to Alexander
I, claiming to be an ardent supporter of the Holy Alliance and
monarchical power. He lied to Ryleev and the Northern Society,
claiming to be an emissary of a powerful international secret society. He lied to the Beliaevs and to Arbuzov, recruiting them into
a nonexistent organization and deceiving them with hints of his
own involvement in an attempt to be made on the tsar's life during
the Peterhof celebration. Later, when the celebration passed without incident, he pretended that he had almost been forced to flee
abroad. He claimed that he had even made an agreements with a
ship's captain, but that suddenly everything had changed, as "a
man has been found who needs no urging."[13] Later he lied during
the investigation, portraying all his actions as an attempt to expose
the secret society, an attempt which, he claimed, only Alexander's
unexpected demise had halted. When this version collapsed, Zavalishin presented himself as Ryleev's victim, unabashedly attrib-
uting everything to Ryleev, including poems that he, Zavalishin,
had composed. But the ultimate expression of this mendacity is
achieved in Zavalishin's memoirs, one of the most curious examples of this kind of literature.

[10]*Vospominaniia Bestuzhevykh*, ed. M. K. Azadovskii (Moscow/Leningrad, 1951), p.
787.
[11]Ibid.
[12]N. A. Bestuzhev, *Stat'i i pis'ma* (Moscow/Leningrad, 1933), p. 271
[13]*Vosstanie dekabristov*, vol. 3 (Moscow/Leningrad, 1927), p. 264.

The nature of Zavalishin's lying was by no means simple or trivial. Not only was it unselfish, but it entailed consequences that were frequently grave and, in the end, tragic for him. Moreover, it had one unvarying feature: none of his wild schemes and ambitious pretensions had any connection to even the most optimistic of realistic assessments. As an eighteen-year-old midshipman, he hoped to become head of an international chivalrous order. He viewed the patronage of Alexander I, to whom he had applied with this goal in mind, simply as an obvious preliminary step. At twenty, summoned to St. Petersburg from a round-the-world voyage, he proposed that the government create a vassal state on the Pacific Ocean, with its center in California. (He himself would, of course, become its head.) Simultaneously he prepared to assume leadership of the underground political movement in Russia. There was, naturally, a striking divergence between his global plans and the modest duties of a junior naval officer, albeit one who began his service career brilliantly and who was uncommonly gifted. Zavalishin was a man of the Decembrist generation, a man of action. A voyage around the world, an audience with the emperor, whom he amazed with his eloquence, an association with Ryleev—all of these were *deeds*. But he was born ten years or so too late; he had not taken part in the War of 1812, and because of his age, rank, real potential, political experience, and influence could count on filling only supporting roles in both his government career and the political struggle. And this in no way suited him. Life was too limited for him, so he corrected it systematically in his imagination. Each time his fervent and irrepressible mind gave birth to a new fantasy it immediately became his reality. He was utterly sincere when, in a letter to Nicholas I, he described himself as a man "dedicated to the service of Truth."[14]

Zavalishin wrote his memoirs in old age, as his life, begun so brilliantly, neared its end, all his hopes denied. He thus wrote a narrative which, although rich in information about the Decembrist movement (his memory was astounding), does not describe an actual life, disfigured and marred by failures. It describes instead the splendid life *he could have lived*. He recreates his life as an artist would. Nothing happens as it did in fact. Favorable omens accompanied his birth; his military school labeled him "a small fellow, but a great wonder." After his examinations, "they said straight

---

[14]Ibid., p. 224.

out" that he "had nothing to learn from our teachers."[15] He was "first in the entire school."[16] In Sweden, when Zavalishin was fourteen, "Bernadotte took a great liking to me and would keep me near him when he played chess with our ambassador."[17] "I achieved astounding success in everything; too many witnesses and too much evidence will attest to this. I wish here to dwell upon the circumstance which induced me to take part in the political movement: the fact that, long before I took up politics I was already what is called a 'reformer' in all the fields of service in which I had been called upon to act."[18]

Thus does Zavalishin's time at the military academy appear in his memoirs. Subsequently he describes his round-the-world voyage under Lazarev's command. During preparations for the voyage — the other officers "were almost all still on leave"—"I quickly set off for Kronstadt, and the two of us, senior lieutenant Lazarev and I, got down to work. But then Lazarev loaded me with commissions, one after the other. I was charged with all that had to be done at the Admiralty because the senior lieutenant understood only the workings of a frigate. I helped him even with that. I was ordered to install the artillery according to a new plan, which then served as a model for the entire fleet; then the construction of galleys was assigned to me." In his own words, Zavalishin was "in charge of all the paper work." He was "a regimental adjutant, a purser, and a permanent inspector of all the departments—provisioning, commissary, piloting, artillery, and navigation." Such an abundance of duties "astonished everyone" and "a formal inquiry was made." In response to this inquiry, Lazarev explained that "since, by general acclaim, I was one of the fleet's brightest hopes, and was already regarded as a future commander, he considered it his duty, for the good of the service, to acquaint me with all branches of command."[19]

Naturally, it was Zavalishin, not Lazarev, who really led the expedition of the *Cruiser*, one of the most renowned voyages ever made by a Russian ship around the globe. When Zavalishin was called away, all fell to ruin.

New triumphs follow. During the Petersburg floods, Zavalishin organized special rescue efforts. Recognizing their own helpless-

[15]D. I. Zavalishin, *Zapiski dekabrista* (St. Petersburg, 1906), p. 21.
[16]Ibid., p. 22.
[17]Ibid., p. 31.
[18]Ibid., p. 41.
[19]Ibid., p. 54.

ness and Zavalishin's organizational talents, the senior officers willingly followed his orders. The sovereign thanked him; his proposals and projects evoked universal admiration. Mordinov was astonished, "as he himself expressed it, by my unusual command of the subject matter and my foresight with respect to the colonies.... In the meantime, the top officers of the R[ussian]-A[merican] Company had long been eagerly awaiting a chance to deal directly with me."[20]

Zavalishin's memory transforms the secret society he encountered in Petersburg into a sort of underground parliament, whose committees were constantly at work and whose general meetings were loud and well-attended. At these meetings, Zavalishin's voice resounded loudest of all: "Although many praised my oratorial talents, my eloquence, and, in particular, as many have commented, my invincible logic and dialectical skill, I really didn't care very much for these crowded and noisy meetings, which many attended only to 'hear Zavalishin.' I preferred the smaller gatherings—committees, they were called—in which specific questions were discussed."[21] It should be remembered that Zavalishin was never a member of the Northern Society or of any Decembrist circle whatsoever; even if the network of "gatherings" and "committees" about which he writes had existed, he would not have been allowed in. Ryleev even "advised great caution in dealing with Zavalishin," for "he was, by his own admission, prejudiced against him."[22]

Ryleev and Zavalishin were on unfriendly terms. Ryleev and Aleksandr Bestuzhev suspected that Zavalishin's stories abut the "Society for Restoration" were pure bluff (they were right). His correspondence with the emperor aroused their misgivings. We do not know if there was a connection between these circumstances and a puzzling episode in Zavalishin's life. After writing his usual letter to Alexander I, Zavalishin left St. Petersburg and went to Moscow. There, news of the emperor's death reached him. He set off from Moscow for Kazan' and Simbirsk, where a courier sent from Petersburg arrested him at his estates. In Zavalishin's memoirs, this affair has an entirely different character; it becomes a gripping tale of adventure. Ryleev and Zavalishin are engaged in a struggle for the leadership of the Northern Society. Most of the ordinary members are on Zavalishin's side, and Ryleev decides to

[20]Ibid., p. 87.
[21]Ibid., p. 97.
[22]*Vosstanie dekabristov*, vol. 3, p. 237.

get him away from Petersburg. To this end, Zavalishin is sent on a mission to inspect the work members of the secret society are doing in the provinces. He discovers that the Moscow group has disintegrated. In Simbirsk, however, where members of "his" branch somehow turn up, everything is going well. Their activity is so vigorous, their anticipation of his arrival so great, that "members of the society . . . had been waiting . . . at the city gates" to meet him. Although we know that there were never any members of a secret society in Simbirsk, Zavalishin's tale is by no means a cheap lie. Someone apparently did meet him (most likely one of his relatives) to warn him that an officer with a warrant for his arrest was already waiting for him in Simbirsk. But Zavalishin's imagination transformed reality in the same way that Don Quixote's fancy made shepherds into knights.

Zavalishin's memoirs raise complex questions for the researcher, because they offer a great many facts, some unavailable in any other source. But every time he recalls an actual situation, Zavalishin, like a director dissatisfied with a piece of film, demands a "retake" and creates a new version of the plot. It is as though he were avenging himself on life. We can discover from his memoirs what conflicts took place, but not how they were resolved.

Zavalishin was a man of a transitional era. One of the traits most characteristic of the "regularized state" created by Peter was the abolition of any sort of regularity in the real course of public life. Just as the "Law of Succession" of February 5, 1722 put an end to the automatic inheritance of power and, by unleasing secret ambitions, initiated a series of court coups, so the liquidation of *mestnichestvo* in 1682 and the government's refusal to assign state posts "by lineage"[23] transformed the psychology of the gentry. The "Table of Ranks" replaced the old order with a new one, which, by linking advancement to merit, gave some room to those with initiative and ambition. The Table of Ranks, however, was never the sole determinant of service advancement. In addition to its prescriptions, which required that everyone shoulder the yoke of service ("children of the nobility must . . . be promoted from the lowest ranks"[24]), there was a second regulating force: "fortune." "Fortune" promised rapid advancement, from the lowest grades to the very highest in disregard of all rules and regulations. In *War and Peace*,

---

[23] A. Romanovich-Slavatinskii, *Dvoriantstvo v Rossii ot nachala XVIII veka do otmeni krepostnogo prava* (St. Petersburg, 1870), p. 11.
[24] *Polnyi svod zakonov*, vol. 6, no. 3890.

Tolstoi expresses extremely succinctly the notion that we are dealing here not with a system of infractions and anomalies, but instead
with two constant mechanisms, at once united and contradictory.
Their interaction produced the real conditions of state service experienced by a Russian noble of the eighteenth and early nineteenth
century.

> At this moment, Boris saw clearly that . . . above and beyond the
> system of seniority and discipline that was stipulated by the regula-
> tions and followed in the regiment, there existed another, more es-
> sential seniority. It was this second seniority that had made the tight-
> laced red-faced general wait respectfully while the captain Prince An-
> drei found it convenient to engage in conversation with Lieutenant
> Drubetskoi . . . Now he felt that on the sole merits of having been
> recommended to Prince Andrei, he was already above the general—
> a man who in other circumstances at the front, could destroy him, a
> mere lieutenant of the guards.
>
> [*War and Peace*, book 3, ch. 8][25]

The civil service had come to resemble a game of cards. On the
one hand, one could play stodgy games of skill—ombre or boston—
and, through "moderation and thoroughness" advance through
the ranks. On the other hand, one could gamble (the term *sluchai*,
"fortune," used in reference to careers is a direct translation of the
card-players' *hasard*). The gambler in service still weighs risk against
ambition, either playing for small stakes or wagering double or
nothing in an attempt to break the bank. Favoritism dates back to
Peter the Great ("cases in which men of undistinguished family
advanced to high government posts were rare and usually occurred
through the patronage of Peter himself," writes Professor K. A.
Safronenko,[26] and his observation should be kept in mind: the
peculiar "democratism" of service promotions in Peter's reign was
inseparable from favoritism). Peter's favoritism evolved into a distinct state-economic organism under Catherine. Ia. L. Barskov
writes:

> Favoritism is a curious page in the history of economic, as well as
> court life. It was one of the most important factors in the eighteenth-

---

[25]L. N. Tolstoi, *Sobranie sochinenii v chetyrnadtsati tomakh*, vol. 6 (Moscow, 1951),
p. 306.

[26]K. A. Safroneko, *Pamiatniki russkogo prava*, no. 8, *Zakonodatel'nye akty Petra I*
(Moscow, 1961), p. 163. It is revealing that Pushkin, in "My Genealogy," dates
the beginning of favoritism from Men'shikov ("My grandfather didn't sell
pancakes . . . ".)

century Russian nobility's acquisition of great riches. The resources accumulated by the favorites themselves, or with their help, substantially surpassed the age-old holdings of the original noble families. It took dozens, even hundreds of years for the latter to amass several thousand desiatins of land or several hundred thousand (let alone a million) rubles in capital, while a favorite, even one as insignificant as Zavadovskii, could become a millionaire in two years. It is true that these enormous, easily acquired sums, could just as easily be squandered, and many favorites died without heirs. Nonetheless, the most famous wealthy men of the late eighteenth and early nineteenth centuries owed their fortunes to favoritism.[27]

To contemporaries, it seemed that the development of favoritism was the outgrowth of the empress's personal eccentricities. Paul's reign, however, proved quite the opposite. His desire for extreme "regularity" in everything did not abolish favoritism, but instead led to its equally extreme development. Paul's love of order, his aversion to luxury, his personal abstemiousness (in comparison to Catherine) changed nothing for the root of favoritism was the principle of unlimited personal power, and not the character of the individual who wielded it.

Combined with the collapse of feudal monarchies and the expansion of the role of money and individual initiative then underway throughout Europe, favoritism engendered a monstrous growth in adventurism and spread seemingly infinite horizons before personal ambition.

The psychology of ambition underwent substantial alterations around the end of the eigtheenth century. Side by side with the idea of self-assertion, of changing one's own status in an unchanging world (the protagonist of the picaresque novel had this aspiration) arose the ideal of activity in the name of changing the world. Models from antiquity and later the experience of the French Revolution were taken as paradigms of historic behavior. Using them as a guide, the most ordinary man could win himself a few lines, a page, or an entire chapter in history. Finally, the fate of Napoleon Bonaparte somehow became a symbol of man's boundless power

[27]Ia. L. Barskov, "Pis'ma imp. Ekateriny II k gr. P. V. Zavadovskomy," *Russkii istoricheskii zhurnal*, book 5 (1918), pp. 240-241. Cf. *Karlik favorita: istoriia zhizni Ivana Andreevicha Iakobovskogo, karlika svetleishego kniazia Platona Aleksandrovicha Zubova, pisannaia im samim* (Munich: Slavische Propyläen, Texte in Neu- und Nachdrucken, vol. 32, 1968). Here, for example, we learn about Platon Zubov: "Of silver coin alone, he left in the range of 20 million rubles when he died, although he admitted that 'he himself did not know why he amassed and hoarded money' " (p. 300).

over his own destiny. Pushkin's line "we all imagine ourselves Napoleons" was not hyperbole; thousands of the younger officers in all the armies of Europe asked themselves if the hand of fate were not poised over them. Faith in one's own destiny, in the notion that the world is filled with great people, was a feature of the psychology of young nobles early in the nineteenth century. Pushkin's words "And are there not among my friends / Two, three who'll meet great ends?" ("Ezerskii," XII) sounded ironic when they were written in 1832. In the early 1820s, however they would have been accepted as completely serious. People were willing to see a physical resemblance to Napoleon in Pestel' and Sergei Murav'ev-Apostol.[28] Whether there really was such a resemblance is not important; what matters is that people were looking for it. They had learned from Plutarch that one could discern the essential nature of one's contemporaries by finding in them even the most external and incidental points of resemblance to historical figures.

In spite of the striking difference between them, the egotistical ambition of an eighteenth-century adventurer and the self-sacrificing love for glory of an early-nineteenth-century "liberal" had one trait in common—ambitious designs were inseparable from activity and found fulfillment in deeds. Zavalishin, however, was one of the last representatives of his generation (he was born in the summer of 1804). His was the lot of those who "visited this world in its fateful minutes," but "rose late—and on their way were taken unawares by the fall of Rome," as Tiutchev wrote in 1830. Not only did he miss out on the Napoleonic wars, he was unable even to join a secret society. His ambitious dreams found their outlet not in practical acts, but in imagined deeds. Hypertrophy of the imagination was his compensation for an unsuccessful life.

It would, however be a serious error to forget that Zavalishin and Khlestakov belong to different eras. Despite the appearance of similarity, they represent contrasting psychological types.

There is a great difference between the lying of Khlestakov, the lying of Griboedov's Repetilov, and the self-deception of Zavalishin. Zavalishin was imbued with the deepest admiration, even tender love, for himself. When he lied, he invented and attributed to himself circumstances and actions, words and situations, all at

[28]On Pestel': "In his gestures, his movements, his height, even his face he very much resembled Napoleon" (*Shchukinskii sbornik*, no. 4 [Moscow, 1905], p. 39). On Sergei Murav'ev-Apostol: "he bore . . . an unusual resemblance to Napoleon I" (*Dekabristy: Letopisi*, State Literary Museum, book 3 [Moscow, 1938], p. 485).

variance with reality. In these imaginings, his ego burst forth with the glory and genius he was convinced formed the essence of his personality. He recreated the world through the force of his imagination. Yet even as he fictionalized his surroundings because their reality displeased him, he himself remained Dmitrii Irinarkhovich Zavalishin. Repetilov does not glorify himself; he confesses. Nevertheless, in an ecstasy of self-denunciation, exaggerating the traits of his own personality he remains himself. When he says that he "kept a ballerina! and not just one, three at once!" we can assume that he had had some sort of theatrical fling. When he says about himself "I spurned everything: laws! conscience! faith!" it is likely that some drawing-room style free-thinking really did take place.

Khlestakov is another story. The source of his lying is an unremitting contempt for himself. Lying intoxicates Khlestakov because, in his imaginary world, he can *cease to be himself*, escape from himself, become someone else. He can exchange first person for third, for he is deeply convinced that only "he," and not "I," can truly be of interest. The combination of self-hatred and escape lends Khlestakov's bragging its character of neurotic self-assertiveness. He extols himself because he is filled with a secret self-contempt. The split personality which was to become the central focus of Doestoevskii's *Double*, but which was completely alien to men of the Decembrist era, was already present in Khlestakov: "I only stop by the department for two minutes, just to say 'I want this done such a way and that done such a way,' and before you know it this little rat of a copy clerk has gone for his pen (*makes sound of scratching pen*) and started writing."[29] In this striking pas-

[29]Gogol, vol. 4, p. 48. Further references to Gogol's work are supplied in the text. In a letter from Viazemskii to Zhukovskii dated December 13, 1832, we find an exceptionally interesting piece of evidence on the relation between a situation of social humiliation and the psychological reaction of self-hatred and the aspiration to be reborn, to stop being oneself, including even the mythological thirst to "change one's name." (This is not the same as the Tolstoyan thirst for "regeneration," which is linked to an entirely different ideological-psychological complex.) Viazemskii was not "small fry" and the possibility of being humiliated socially was entirely foreign to him. In 1826 he wrote: "They say that men are egoists / Where is egoism? Who is the full I? / Who is not in debt to this word? / In the new edition of the dictionary / It looks like an anachronism." How acute, then, must have been his feelings of being a featureless cog in the wheel when government pressure compelled him to enter state service. Viazemskii wrote to Zhukovskii: "Here's a good plot for Russian tale of the fantastic dans les moeurs administratives: a clerk loses his mind over his name, his name pursues him, wavers in front of his eyes, echoes in his ears, boils in his saliva; his own name makes him choke, he secretly and silently takes on another name, that of his boss, for example, he signs this other name to some important document, which moves through the usual channels and leads to serious consequences; for his unintentional deception, he is brought to trial and so on.

sage, Khlestakov, soaring off into the world of lies, invites his companions to have a laugh at the real Khlestakov: for this "little rat of a copy clerk" is none other than himself in his true Petersburg office existence.

It is revealing that Gogol meticulously sought out the most venomous, the most loathsome formulations for his protagonist's self-characterization. At first (in the so-called "second version"), Khlestakov, as Khlestakov sees him, appears as follows: "I arrive at just the right time. And I see this young man waiting in the drawing room, the kind they call (*waves his hand; whistles*) in a cap as jaunty as they come. So I walk in, and I'm thinking, well, what a dandy we've got here" (IV, 292). Note also the "Observations for Actors," in which Gogol describes Khlestakov: "the sort of person who, in the office, will be called a total addlehead" (IV, 9). Later, in the first printed edition, Khlestakov brings up the "copy clerk" who

There's a plot for your free time. I won't take it up out of superstition, out of fear that it would happen to me" (*Russkii arkhiv*, vol. 38, book 1 [1900], p. 367). There is a striking similarity between many features of this "Russian tale of the fantastic" and Gogol's "Diary of a Madman." Since Viazemskii's letter coincides chronologically with the date Gogol began work on the story, we can hypothesize that Gogol's idea for the plot came through Zhukovskii.

In many ways, "Diary of a Madman" is a tragic parallel to *The Inspector General*. The deliverance from self and flight to life's summits that Khlestakov receives from "an uncommon addleheadedness in thinking" and a potbellied bottle of provincial Madeira, Poprishchin experiences as the price of insanity. The basic parallel is obvious, however. Oppressed by his social humiliation, Poprishchin does not aspire to change the world. More significant, the world is, in his consciousness, so unshakable that it is precisely news of social changes—a revision in the law of succession and the vacancy of the Spanish throne—that drives him out of his mind. He wants to make himself into an "anti-self" and, carrying this wish to its extreme, elevates himself into a king. (Khlestakov, acting under Russian conditions and in circumstances of censorship, draws the line at field marshal and leader of the state council; cf. the plot of Pushkin's "Golden Fish.") The scene of the name change and the signing of the document ("in the most important place, where the director of the department signs . . . Ferdinand VIII," III, 209), as in Viazemskii's version, marks the moment of Poprishchin's reincarnation. The conviction that real life is just behind a door engenders first a passion for spying, a passion that is the psychological source of informing, and then a desire to become an oppressor and witness the humiliation of others ("to watch them dance attendance on me"—III, 205). The aspiration to become an "anti-self" in order to humiliate one's present self is an attribute shared by other Gogol characters. Cf. the Mayor's speech: "Why is it good to be a general? Because if you happen to be traveling somewhere your couriers and adjutants are always galloping out ahead, shouting "Horses!" And at the post stations, nobody's getting horses, everyone has to wait, all those titular councillors, captains, mayors and you don't give a damn. You have dinner at some governor's, and let the mayor cool it. Ha, ha ha. (*Doubles over with laughter*) What a way to go!" (IV, 82).

The simultaneous awakening of the human being in Poprishchin, as G. A. Gukovskii has described it, makes him a hero of tragic disjunction.

"goes right to it with his pen (*sound of scratching pen*), that's how fast he goes" (IV, 412). But Gogol was seeking still harsher terms of self-evaluation, and in the final version he added the words "little rat."

The liar of the 1820s strove to escape from the conditions of life; Khlestakov strove to escape from himself. Gogol emphasizes the poverty of Khlestakov's imagination as he attempts to dream up a fantastic change in the external conditions of his life. His soup is still soup, and, "though it came by ship direct from Paris," it is still served in a pot; his watermelon is still watermelon, even with a price of "seven hundred rubles." Contrasted to this is the variety of incarnations Khlestakov would like to assume: famous writer, man about town, habitue of the theater, director of a Department, commander-in-chief, even the Turkish ambassador and General Dibich-Zabalkanskii. Even with the "office rat's" mediocrity of fantasy, manifested in the way he imagines the nature of each of these roles,[30] the contrast here is very substantial. In his imaginary world, the surroundings remain those of a clerk's true existence, but assume quantitatively enormous proportions. Observe the use of numerals: a watermelon costs seven hundred rubles, a bottle of rum, one hundred; Khlestakov pays eight hundred rubles for a "little flat" that is fantastic only in price—its features suit the average clerk's existence perfectly: "three rooms and nice ones too" (IV, 294). But the roles Khlestakov chooses are constructed on a different principle. First, they must be exotic in the extreme; they must represent a way of life *as remote as possible* from Khlestakov's *real life*. Second, they must be the acme of their type: if a writer, then a friend of Pushkin, if a military personage, then the commander-in-chief. This links Khlestakov not only to Poprishchin, hero of Gogol's "Diary of a Madman," who metamorphosizes into a Spanish (the world of the exotic!) king (the highest degree!),but also to the Karamazovian devil, who wishes to turn into a merchant's 235-pound wife and "light a candle with a pure heart." If the protagonist of Dostoevskii's *Double*, like Gogol's characters, pictures his ideal alternate existence as the summit of an ascending

---

[30]Cf. his idea of the creative process: "And Pushkin composes in such a funny way. Just imagine: in front of him there's a glass of rum, the finest rum, a hundred rubles a bottle, the sort that they keep for the Austrian Emperor alone [this assumes that the Austrian Emperor's rum is also bought in a liquor store, and is distinguished merely by its especially high price—Iu. L.]. And right away he starts to make a sound of scratching pen . . . Recently he wrote a piece called cholera medicine that makes your hair simply stand on end. One clerk (*variant*: one division director) no sooner read it than he went off his rocker" (IV, 294).

scale of social values, the Karamazovian devil constructs his according to a descending scale.

Their aspiration to escape from themselves makes characters of this type divide the world into *their own* space, which is devoid of social value, and *foreign space*, which is highly prized. All their vital forces are directed toward penetration into that *foreign space*. A symbol of this urge is the firmly shut door, and the attempts of Gogolian heroes to peep through. Poprishchin writes: "How I'd love to have a closer look at the life of those gentlemen, with their politesse and courtly tricks, to see how they behave and what they do among themselves. How I'd love to glance into the drawing-room, which you usually see through a slightly open door, and beyond the drawing-room, into yet another room" (III, 199). In *The Inspector General*, Bobchinskii says, "Give me just a little peep through a crack in the door, so I can see how he does what he does" (IV, 22). As if afraid that the audience would fail to appreciate this moment Gogol emphasized it with a bit of slapstick: "*At that moment the door swings open and the eavesdropper Bobchinskii is catapulted onto the stage*" (IV, 38). This passion for spying is related psychologically to the conviction that one's own life is dull and uninteresting, and is akin to the wish to see "the beautiful life" on stage, in books, or on the screen.

These features appear with unusual clarity in the scene of Khlestakov's drunkenness. The use of alcohoic beverages (or other chemical means of altering individual behavior) is a subject too broad, raising too many age-old questions, for me to touch on it here, even superficially. It may be noted, however that from the point of view of "festive" or "ritual" behavior there are two possible positions on the use of alcohol, which correspond to two cultural types. The first is oriented to the use of the weakest alcoholic beverages—hence the Greek and Roman rule that wine be diluted with water, and the notion that undiluted grape wine was a beverage unacceptable in cultured surroundings. The second is oriented to the use of the strongest alcoholic beverages possible. The emphasis in the first case is on extended use, on the *process* of drinking; in the second on the *result*, the effect of drink on consciousness.[31] The objective of the first is to fortify personality traits, to emancipate personality from all that prevents an individual from being himself. Consequently, it entails the accentuation of the

[31]Cf. Roland Barthes, the chapter "Le vin et le lait" in *Mythologies* (Paris: Seuil, 1957), pp. 83-86.

memory of what one is like in a "nonfestive" situation. The only personality traits that suddenly gain freedom are those denied development by the surrounding world. As in Zavalishin's type of fantasizing the reality of the external world at once loses its rigidity and begins to yield to the deforming influence of the imagination. Life lifts its hand from the intoxicated man; his stifled potential is realized. He becomes more himself than when he is sober.

The second orientation aims to alter personality itself. Oblivion thus becomes the chief goal of chemical behavior modification; the memory of one's previous (usual) condition and of the essence of one's personality must be smothered. One of Khlestakov's distinctive traits is his short memory (a quality which, among other things, makes him incapable of complex calculations of self-interest and greed and gives him that "ingenuous simplicity" which Gogol reminded his actors was an essential feature of Khlestakov's personality). When Khlestakov is drunk, his short memory makes him utterly unable to preserve the unity of his personality. His consciousness crumbles into isolated moments each of which retains no memory of the one preceding it. It is as if Khlestakov is born anew with every passing minute. He lacks any conservatism or traditionalism, for he has no memory. Moreover, perpetual change is his natural state. This is the law by which he behaves when he declares his love and when his condition suddenly changes from that of a hounded debtor to that of a grandee who has drawn the winning card. A reverse transformation likewise poses no difficulty for him. Ideas of evolution and the logic of internal development cannot be applied to Khlestakov, despite his perpetual motion. Adopting a new mode of behavior, he instantly attains in it a perfection that would cost a man who had to develop it internally his entire life's effort (undoubtedly, Khlestakov has a talent for impersonation). But this instantaneous acquisition vanishes without a trace, just as instantaneously. He falls asleep a Very Important Person, only to awaken an insignificant clerk once again, "an addlehead and a nobody."

At this point is is appropriate to pose a question about the purpose of this essay. We are not considering Gogol's comedy as an artistic whole. In that sense, Khlestakov would only be a textual reality, an inhabitant of an internal world, a single element in the architectonics of a created work. Our analysis really belongs to the elusive field of textual pragmatics. It is no accident that this field has attracted very little scholarly attention. First of all, the concept of pragmatic relations formulated by C. S. Peirce and Charles Morris is fairly vague when applied to complex semiotic systems. The relationship between the sign and the people who receive and send information is not readily definable. The word "relationship," used here in a sense that differs from the usual semantic or syntactic definition, is far from precise, and behind the concept "people" lies the question of whether the individual is the object of a semiotic, sociological, psychological, or some other type of description.[32]

The question becomes even more complex when historical material is being studied. In this case, difficulties arise not only from conceptual fuzziness, but also from the absence of sufficient recorded data to permit us to evaluate the attitudes of diverse groups toward the texts that circulate in their midst. Even when critical opinion is well documented, information on the response of readers is, as a rule, sparse and fragmentary. For example, in the case of the Middle Ages, the information we have tells us mainly not how people responded to certain texts but instead how they should have responded. Of course, even this meager information is valuable material for reconstructions. But a methodology for making them has not yet been developed.

Research into what is called the pragmatic approach is nonetheless a matter of vital interest. The difficulties discussed above should be regarded as a stimulus, and not as a retardant, to further research in this field.

It would make sense to replace the concept of "people" with the idea of a group organized according to the structural laws of a certain culture. The group can be regarded as a type of text in relation to the culture. Pragmatic relations can then be interpreted as the correlation between two texts, organized differently and occupying hierarchically different places, but functioning within a single corpus of cultural texts. To narrow our task further, we will isolate one aspect of the cultural group: the structure of the behavior of a group which is historically distinct and culturally definable. This behavior can be studied both as a distinct language and as the sum of certain historically recorded texts.

Stated in this form, our task is within the realm of possibility for semiotic study. It also more closely resembles the traditional aesthetic problem of the relationship between art and reality. If we

---

[32]Chaplevich's "pragmatic poetics" is an example of the muddle that can be produced under the guise of research into pragmatics. See Eugeniush Chaplevich, *Voprosy literatury* no. 7 (1974).

examine the structure of behavior intrinsic to any culture as a complex hierarchical organization which creates for its characteristic social roles both norms of correct behavior and admissible deviations from these norms, then we can identify the significant and insignificant elements in the real deeds of historical figures and groups. We can reconstruct invariant types of historical behavior. In so doing, we should keep in mind that when a given cultural era establishes typological norms for "correct behavior" in order to organize the behavior of group members, it is engaging in a similar task. We can use metatexts created by the culture itself as a basis for our reconstructions. It must be remembered, however, that any description of behavior in a text contemporary to it, be it the driest legislative order or the most realistic work of art, is not our ultimate object of study, but only a source for its reconstruction. The manner in which it is encoded is determined by the specifics of the text. This distinguishes our method from the impressionistic approach, popular around the turn of the century, which dealt with literary characters as "types from Russian life." A work of art can be studied from numerous viewpoints. One approach regards such a work as the result of its author's creative act. Another views it as material for the reconstruction of patterns of cultural behavior in a given era. The naive confusion of these approaches is all the more intolerable for its constant occurrence.

Imagine an observer completely unacquainted with nineteenth- and early twentieth-century European culture confronted with a statue by Rodin. He is seriously mistaken if, on the basis of this text, he tries to imagine the clothing, gestures, and behavior of the people who were the sculptor's contemporaries. He must apprehend what he sees as an integral artistic act, which embodies the translation of the concepts of a certain age into the language of a particular artistic structure. But imagine that this work has been done in the most exhaustive manner imaginable. Now, taking the statue, it should be possible to decode the era in it. One could even discover the era's everyday face, though no longer in the initial naive sense.

The goal of this essay is not an examination of Khlestakov's image as part of the artistic whole of Gogol's comedy. I aim instead to use this complex creation of an artist's synthesizing mind to reconstruct some of the behavioral types that form the larger historico-cultural context. An examination of this context may open the door to an understanding of the pragmatics of Gogol's text.

Khlestakov, the hero of *The Inspector General*, is distinguished by certain traits that belong to a more generalized model, a model that was present in Gogol's consciousness on a high level of abstraction, which became variously realized as different characters in his texts. This creative archetype is a fact of Gogol's artistic consciousness. But it is possible to detect in it elements which bear a fairly clear resemblance to the behavior of certain historical figures. These elements are very stable and tend to be repeated with minor variations. Thus we can see, both in Gogol's creative consciousness and in historical documents, manifestations of a more general historical configuration, a cultural mask or pattern of behavior which had taken shape historically within a specific culture. From the fairly numerous examples available, I have selected the most revealing.

In 1812, Roman Medoks, a seventeen-year-old junior cavalry officer, squandered two thousand rubles of treasury funds and deserted from his regiment. Hoping to avoid punishment, he devised a plan that combined adventurism, "extraordinary addleheadedness," dreams of heroic enterprises, and the most ordinary swindling. Medoks first forged documents in the name of a certain Sokovnin, a lieutenant in the Horse Guards and an adjutant of Minister of Police Balashov. He then furnished himself with falsified orders, signed by the minister of war, in which His Imperial Majesty invested him with broad and unlimited powers for activity in the Caucasus. With these orders, he intended, like a second Minin, to form a militia from Caucasian mountain people and lead it to a thunderous assault on Napoleon. He hoped in this way to earn himself a pardon.[33]

Upon his arrival in Georgievsk, Medoks was allocated 10,000 rubles on the basis of a counterfeit order from the minister of finance. The two experienced administrators there, Baron Vrangel' and General Portniagin, the commander of the Caucasian front, trusted him completely. It is significant that when one of the office clerks expressed doubt that such an important mission would be entrusted to an officer so young and so low in rank, and the revenue department withheld the funds, Vrangel' pulled both up short and insisted that the requested sum be disbursed. Medoks was welcomed as a figure invested with imperial powers. He reviewed parades; balls were given in his honor. Attempting to postpone

[33]Cf. S. Ia Shtraikh, *Provokatsiia sredi dekabristov: Samozvanets Medoks na Petrovskom zavode* (Moscow, 1925; 2d rev. ed. S. Ia Shtraikh, *Roman Medoks: Pokhozhdeniia russkogo avantiurista XIX veka*, (Moscow, 1929); 3d ed. Moscow 1930).

exposure, he informed the local post office that he had been empowered to examine the governor's correspondence. He told General Portniagin that he had been instructed to conduct covert surveillance of Baron Vrangel', who, he claimed, was not trusted in Petersburg.

Completely losing any sense of reality Medoks sent Balashov a report, authored by the imaginary adjutant Sokovnin, which described Medoks's own activities. He enclosed with this a letter exposing his own fraud, in which he stressed his patriotic motives and requested the protection and patronage necessary to carry the militia "levies" to their conclusion. At the same time, claiming to be an official under Balashov's protection, he appealed to the minister of finance, Count Gur'ev, for further funds. The brashness and scope of the affair perplexed the central authorities, substantially delaying the arrest of a man whose tactics consisted in implicating the widest possible circle of the most highly placed individuals. When finally arrested, he called himself Vsevolozhskii, and later Prince Golitsyn, apparently listing in succession all the aristocratic names he knew.

By the emperor's order, Medoks was imprisoned for life in the Peter and Paul Fortress. In 1826 his fortunes suddenly changed. In his Shlussel'burg cell, he became acquainted with a few of the men sentenced in the Decembrist affair. We can safely assume that he immediately applied to the appropriate agencies to offer his services as an informer. In any case he was freed unexpectedly in March 1827 and sent to a settlement in Viatka, through which sentenced Decembrists passed on their way to Siberia. As he traveled through Viatka, the Decembrist Ivan Pushchin wrote his family, "At that point I discovered that a certain Medoks, sentenced at age 18 to the Shlussel'burg fortress and held there for 14 years, was now in Viatka, living in freedom. I met him in the fortress."[34] Medoks escaped from Viatka, procured a passport under a false name, and set off for the Caucasus, only to be detained again in Ekaterinodar. The tsar ordered him sent as a private to Siberia but he escaped once more. From Odessa, where he was living under forged documents, he appealed to Nicholas for pardon in a letter written in English. The crowning touch in all these reversals of fortune occurred when Medoks, officially a private in the Omsk regiment, turned up—without the knowledge of his immediate military superiors, but clearly with the sponsorship of the secret police—in

[34]I. I. Pushchin, *Zapiski o Pushkine: Pis'ma* (Moscow, 1956), p. 100.

Irkutsk, where he showed a suspicious interest in the exiled Decembrists and their families in Siberia. He wormed his way into the home of Aleksandr Murav'ev, who had been exiled to Siberia with his title intact, and who had received permission, through imperial clemency, to enter state service as the mayor of Irkutsk.

In the opinion of S. Ia. Shtraikh, Medoks was acting as an agent provocateur from the moment he appeared in Murav'ev's home. This belief is groundless: in the files preserved from this period, there are neither reports written by Medoks nor documentary evidence of his ties with the secret police, even though these files comprise, as far as is known, a relatively complete body of documents. In general, Shtraikh tends to rationalize Medok's behavior and portray him as a purposeful man following his own course. But Medoks's personality, as it appears from the documents, was in fact quite different.

While still in Shlussel'burg, Medoks, by then a convict who had served fourteen years and had no hope of release, met the Decembrists Iushnevskii, Pushchin, Mikhail and Nikolai Bestuzhev, Pestov, and Divov. After his subsequent transfer to the Peter and Paul Fortress he managed to meet Fonvizin and Naryshkin, and in Viatka became closely acquainted with Iushnevskii, Shteingel', Shveikovskii, and Bariatinskii. The mystery surrounding his appearance in Viatka and his later move to Irkutsk seems to suggest that he had some dealings with the secret police. It should be remembered, however, that, first, no documentary evidence of such dealings is available, and, second, the Decembrists themselves, who were in this respect extremely cautious, saw nothing strange in his presence among them. There seem to have been more mundane explanations for his arrival in Irkutsk.

Medoks probably aspired to gain entry to Decembrist circles in Siberia for many reasons. He enjoyed meetings and discussions with sympathetic and highly educated people (as was remarked upon even at the time of his first arrest, Medoks himself was distinguished by his fluency in French, German, and English, "his knowledge of literature and history, his skill at drawing, his clever conversation and his other accomplishments characteristic of a well-bred man, in particular his solid command of his native tongue and great skill at expressing himself fluently and precisely in it."[35]). In addition, he was completely without means and relied on the financial support he received from Aleksandr Murav'ev and the

---

[35]Shtraikh, *Provokatsiia*, p. 31.

Decembrist "ladies" (most notably Iushnevskaia). The amounts were generally trifling, although to a man in his position they were significant. But the most important factor seems to have something else: with the Decembrists, Medoks felt that he had entered the aristocratic world of the "Sokovnins, Vsevolozhskiis, and Golitsyns," which had always been the outer limit of his fantasies. The size of the sums sent by the Volkonskiis, Trubetskois, and Sheremet'evs to their exiled relations simply took his breath away. It seemed to him (especially after the failure of his attempt to secure a pardon from Benkendorf, the head of the secret police, through the scholar P. Shilling, at which point he began to concoct his own escape plan[36]) that he could use the exiles to make aristocratic connections which might prove useful to him. A trait he shared with Nicholas I was an exaggerated opinion of the power, solidarity, and wealth of the forces he thought the exiled Decembrists represented.

Soon after he was accepted into Murav'ev's home, Medoks met Princess Varvara Shakhovskaia, whose sister was married to the founder of the Union of Salvation. For many years Shakhovskaia had been linked with Petr Mukhanov in an ill-fated love. First parental opposition and then Mukhanov's arrest and exile prevented their union. Shakhovskaia went to her sister's home in Irkutsk to be nearer her beloved, and also in the hope that Nicholas I would allow their marriage (close kinship was an additional impediment: Mukhanov's sister was the wife of Shakhovskaia's brother). Permission was not granted, and Shakhovskaia soon returned to Moscow where, shortly thereafter, she died.

As soon as he saw Shakhovskaia, Medoks conceived a burning love for her. There is no reason to believe, as Shtraikh suggests, that he had no feelings whatsoever for her, and played the role of lover only to fulfill his dutes as police provocateur. Medoks's diary proves the contrary: he was truly in love. Nonetheless, his love was expressed in terms that could have come straight from the diary of Gogol's Poprishchin, with its famous "his daughter—oh, Goddamn it" or from Benediktov's poetry. "Thinking," writes Medoks, "that she would not be wearing a bonnet, I was carried away beforehand by the vision of her beautiful black hair, coiffed with the taste of Raphael. I was all aflame with the thought that I would

---

[36]The notation in Medoks's diary for April 28, 1831: "If Shilling's assistance is unsuccessful, I will have to make my own arrangements, without waiting for clemency" (ibid., p. 42).

see the woman I adored in all her finery.... She was wearing her bonnet; her breast, uncovered in the ideal I had conjured up just a minute before, was completely invisible beneath her fur tippet."[37] It is true that he tried to initiate a liaison with Iushnevskaia at the same time, but he explains this away in his diary as his weakness for "plump dames."

Medoks's hopes, however, were frustrated. Benkendorf rejected Shilling's petition. He was received merely as an acquaintance in Murav'ev's home. He enjoyed the confidence of the female Decembrists, who used him instead of official channels to transmit correspondence, and the exiles willingly conversed with him, reminiscing about their past lives and deeds, but things went no further than that.

Having realized that a rather lively exchange of letters, conveyed by women, was taking place through unofficial channels between Petrovskii Zavod in Siberia and European Russia, Medoks then undertook a grandiose provocation. He wrote to Benkendorf, and through his mediation, to the tsar, with information about a colossal new plot hatched by the Decembrists. According to his reports, the conspiracy was centered in Moscow. The participants were closely associated with the exiles and were preparing a new insurrection. Medoks's information on the secret correspondence with Russia was accurate, but he supplemented it with fictitious documents, and with ciphers and codes which, he claimed, were used in exchanges between the political prisoners and their confederates in St. Petersburg and Moscow. These falsified documents, like any sort of forgery, are extremely interesting. A forgery dis-

---

[37]Ibid., pp. 36-37. Medoks's diary, published by Shtraikh in the 1930 revised edition, (*Roman Medoks: Pokhozhdeniia russkogo avantiurista XIX veka*), does not support the editor's contention that Medoks's feelings for Varvara Shakhovskaia were feigned, and that his only object was to obtain information for a denunciation. To make his version persuasive, Shtraikh claims arbitrarily that the diary was written for show in the Murav'evs' home, and that pieces of it were intentionally "forgotten" in their drawing-room. All this is arbitrary conjecture. It is as groundless as the assertion that the renowned scholar Shilling was an agent provocateur for the Third Department. (On Shilling, see M. P. Alekseev, "Pushkin i nauka ego vremeni," in *Pushkin: Sravnitel'no–istoricheskie issledovaniia* [Leningrad, 1972].) Medoks was not the kind of early-twentieth-century police agent that Shtraikh makes him out to be. He was a "Gogolian man" who stumbled into the cultured world of Pushkin's generation. He was dazzled by its civilized refinement, its spirituality and moral elevation. The material security of the Murav'evs' impoverished Siberian existence stunned him. He was both attracted to this world and keenly envious of it. Falling in love with Vavara Shakhovskaia and informing on Aleksandr Murav'ev were "natural" consequences. Both inclinations were equally genuine and to an equal degree the predictable fruits of Medoks's psychological makeup.

closes the nature of a document as a fact of culture in the same way that a parody reveals the nature of a work of art.

Just as Khlestakov's stories about Pushkin mirror a bourgeois understanding of the nature of poetic creation, Medoks's forgeries reflect trite notions about Decembrism that were widespread in his time. He sharply exaggerated the secret conspiratorial character of the imaginary "Union," including reports on Masonic rituals, discussions about the seven degrees, references to knights templars, and sham ciphers. On the other hand, Medoks skillfully utilized actual conversations conducted in his presence; he merely transferred to the future what had been said about the past. He was thus obviously repeating someone else's words (and this is interesting for reconstructing the content of exiled Decembrists' discussions) when he wrote about Mikhail Orlov, "No one knows better than he how to attract people to himself. In his time, he was a unique [i.e., "irreplaceable"—Iu. L.] man."[38] But, by adding to this the information that Orlov was "not at all disheartened, and probably could be useful," he tried to suggest that Orlov was involved in a new conspiracy.

It is hardly a matter of chance that Medoks's cipher designates Orlov by the graphic mark for lightning. No less interesting is Iakushkin's appearance there as a dagger. Reporting Iushnevskii's supposed statements about the distribution of roles in the impending insurrection, Medoks characterizes Iakushkin as follows: "Iakushkin and Iakubovich are daggers that have long been sharpened." While this description fits with Iakushkin's conduct during the "Moscow conspiracy" of 1818 (in Pushkin's words, "He seemed in silence to unsheath the regicidal dagger"), it bears no relation to his mood in 1832. Iushnevskii could have attributed these characteristics only to the Iakushkin of days gone by. Medoks altered the tense, and transformed a story about the past into an informer's denunciation in the present.

All the same, Medoks's denunciation does echo some statements accurately. His evidence on the penetration of the exiles' writings into foreign publications merits attention, for his report on the subject bears traces of the lively intonations of real discussions. "Iushnevskii was beside himself with laughter, saying that, in the copies of this journal [*Revue Britannique*—Iu. L.] that they'd received, their own articles had been cut out, for fear that they'd be enlightened by them." Medoks comes across like a historical nov-

[38]Shtraikh, *Provokatsiia*, p. 63.

elist of average ability, who, having thought up a romantic context, puts comments recorded in sources into the mouths of historical figures. He invented the situation, but he probably heard the words somewhere in Decembrist circles.

Also interesting is the scheme for a journal called *Mitridat* (the name inspired by the legend that Mithridates inured himself to poison, thereby ridding himself of the fear of poisoning), a publication in French which would refute the official lies of the Russian government. Medoks undoubtedly heard a conversation about the desirability of such a journal, but transformed an insubstantial discussion into a carefully considered political project.

The group of people Medoks implicated is revealing in another sense. He was convinced that the Siberian exiles enjoyed support within the highest aristocratic circles, the same circles that he, with his keen feeling of social envy, had longed all his life to join.[39] In the same way that Khlestakov lists his Petersburg connections, Medoks named in succession all the titled names that came to mind: Count Sheremet'ev, Prince Kasatkin-Rostovskii, Countess Vorontsova, Countess Orlova. To these names he appended those mentioned by the "state criminals" as members of secret societies who had escaped punishment: Mikhail Orlov, adjutant general Shipov, Lev Vitgenshtein (to this last, Medoks "entrusted" the publication of *Mitridat*). It is revealing that Medoks "enlisted" in the conspiracy not the most stalwart and politically active of the Petrovskii prisoners, but the richest and most celebrated: Trubetskoi, Nikita Murav'ev, Fonvizin, Iushnevskii, Shveikovskii. He also implicated Iakushkin and Iakubovich as "regicides" and added Mukhanov, probably out of jealousy.

According to a familiar rule of psychology, Medoks's denunciation implicated Varvara Shakhovskaia, the object of his love, and Aleksandr Murav'ev, who had rendered him material support and hospitality.

---

[39]Envy generally played an important role in Medoks's motives. There is a hint of it, for example, in his denunciation of Iushnevskii, when he states that, instead of the death he deserved, Iushnevskii "enjoys his life, enjoys his wife, who remains a noblewoman, lives in a dungeon which is a dungeon in name only, and in fact is virtually an academy" (Shtraikh, *Provokatsiia*, pp. 62-63). Those last words are characteristic; they once again convey to us the atmosphere of conversation in the Petrovskii Zavod era. The Decembrists could not understand the spite and envy with which Medoks observed their few indulgences—Medoks, who had never received a single kopek from anyone, who had spent fourteen years in a cell without the slightest aid, and who, in Irkutsk, penniless and in a soldier's greatcoat, was consumed by boundless ambition.

The Petersburg authorities reacted nervously to his denunciations. The fact of the matter was that Medoks's ideas about the nature of Decembrism were essentially shared by Nicholas I. Convinced, like Medoks, that aristocratic conspirators stood behind the protagonists of December 14, Nicholas was compelled to sit through a lecture on contemporary politics in which Mikhail Orlov explained to him the "truly democratic" nature of the Decembrist movement.[40] Later in this article, I will discuss the reasons for their seemingly peculiar credulity which supplied the Khlestakovs of the time with a receptive audience.

The government dispatched to Siberia a cavalry captain by the name of Vokhin, who, with Medoks's help, was supposed to collect proof of the existence of a conspiracy. Medoks was asked to produce proof. He prepared a false paper, written in an imaginary code. Upon presentation of this paper in Moscow, Medoks claimed, the conspirators' secrets would be revealed. The ruse got Medoks what he wanted, a summons from Siberia to European Russia. What lay ahead he seems not have been inclined to guess, counting, perhaps, on the discovery of a real conspiracy, in the existence of which he himself had begun to believe. Or perhaps he was not thinking at all, and simply pinned his hopes on the "off chance."

In Moscow he immediately began to spend money, which he now had in abundance: he settled in at the best hotel, ordered six hundred rubles worth of clothing from a French tailor, requested— and received—money from Benkendorf and Moscow's governor-general, and married advantageously, claiming a fair-sized dowry. Medoks's conduct raised the suspicions of General Lesovskii, the head of the Moscow region secret police. General Lesovskii shared his qualms with Benkendorf, but the authorities in Petersburg stubbornly continued to believe in the idea of a conspiracy, even as the falsity of Medoks's denunciations became more and more evident. When, at last, after half a year's delay, Lesovskii demanded positive results from Medoks, the latter fled, telling his wife he was leaving to visit his sister, and carrying off the remains of her dowry.

He departed on a journey around Russia, passing himself off first as a functionary with important orders, and later, when he called on the relatives of exiled Decembrists (for example, Vladimir Raevskii's brothers in Staryi Oskol), as one of their suffering cohorts. During his travels, he wrote a letter to Lesovskii, assuring him of his devotion, but not telling him his whereabouts. When

[40]*Krasnyi arkhiv*, no. 6 (1926), p. 160.

his money ran out, he returned to Moscow on the sly, hoping to receive additional funds from his wife. His wife's relatives, however, turned him in to the police, and he was sent back to Petersburg under arrest. He tried to extricate himself through a new series of denunciations. This time he informed the government that the conspiracy had made its nest in the corps of the secret police: the head of the Third Department, Aleksandr Mordinov had impeded investigation into the conspiracy because he was a first cousin of Aleksandr Murav'ev. The main reason for Medoks's failure was Lesovskii's opposition. Medoks even tried to convince the authorities that in order to expose the conspiracy, it was essential for him to live in luxury and even to have his own coachman. Without this provision, he said, the conspirators would not trust him and would not reveal their secrets. He also requested an audience with the tsar. None of this, however, did any good: Medoks ended up in Shlussel'burg once again, and remained incarcerated until the amnesty of 1856. He died in 1859.[41]

Some other facets of this historical-psychological type are revealed in the life of Ippolit Zavalishin, brother of Dmitrii.

On June 22, 1826, Ippolit Zavalishin, an artillery school cadet, approached Nicholas I as he strolled on Elagin Island. The cadet proffered a deposition in which he denounced his own brother Dmitrii, who had signed a confession regarding his involvement in the Decembrist affair and was in the fortress, waiting for his fate to be decided. Ippolit Zavalishin accused his brother of high treason and of having received enormous sums from foreign powers in return for conducting subversive activity in Russia. A new case was opened. Ippolit Zavalishin lived beyond his means and had large debts. In addition, the hope of an instantaneous, and, as it seemed to him, guaranteed "fortune" glimmered before him. Dmitri Zavalishin writes the following about the nature of the affair:

> Of course, he could not have seen in my possession any secret papers whatsoever. However, in connection with my work in provisioning a voyage around the world, I had a multitude of official documents which were in no way secret, and for this reason, lay uncovered on the table.... As has subsequently become clear, these were the papers

[41]In connection with the psychology of social inadequacy, Medoks and the main character of Bulat Okudzhava's novel *Mersi, ili pokhozhdeniia Shipova* (*Druzhba narodov*, no. 12 [1971]) seem comparable. English translation: *The Extraordinary Adventures of Secret Agent Shipov in Pursuit of Count Leo Tolstoy in the Year 1862* (London: Abelard-Schuman, 1973).

that he looked through. Among the documents were many written in foreign languages; there were many consular accounts for the various items procured for the voyage and for the transfer of bills of exchange. Ippolit knew no language other than French, and could not have understood the contents of these papers. But when he subsequently saw the government's irritation with me, its manifest unfairness toward me, this thoughtlessness led him to imagine that, with a government so disposed, any testimony whatsoever would be accepted without investigation. He realized that, with his poor schooling, he could not hope to rise by a legitimate route, and took it into his head to obtain advancement by means of a false denunciation of his brother.[42]

The falsity of the denunciation was discovered, although Ippolit rushed to fortify it with a second, in which he implicated a large number of completely innocent people. Under arrest for the duration of the investigation into his denunciation, Ippolit Zavalishin informed General Kozen that he "expected to be a field adjutant."[43] One must indeed have needed Khlestakov's imagination to believe that such a leap from among the cadets of an artillery school would be possible. Fate, however, settled the matter differently: the emperor ordered him reduced to the ranks, and sent to the Orenburg garrison.

On arriving in Orenburg, Zavalishin soon discovered the existence of a circle of freedom-loving youth.[44] He proposed that they establish a secret society, for which he himself composed the statutes, and then promptly turned them in to the authorities. This second attempt to make a career by means of denunciations likewise proved unsuccessful. Ippolit Zavalishin received an even stiffer sentence than his victims: life at hard labor. He served his time in the company of the Decembrists.

Although the adventures of Roman Medoks make a better picaresque novel, the life of Ippolit Zavalishin provides our historical-psychological invariant with some essential features. According to

[42]Zavalishin, *Zapiski dekabrista*, p. 252.
[43]Cited from an introductory article by P. E. Shchegolev in V. P. Kolesnikov, *Zapiski neschastnogo, soderzhashchie puteshestvie v Sibir' po kanatu* (St. Petersburg, 1914), p. xii.
[44]Cf. Kolesnikov, published with several excisions by the censor; full text—Manuscript Division of the Institute of Russian Literature, fond 60 (the Bestuzhevs), storage unit 18 (5587); M. D. Rabinovich, "Novye dannye po istorii Orenburgskogo tainogo obshectva," *Vestnik AN SSSR*, no. 7 (1958); Iu. Lotman, "Matvei Aleksandrovich Dmitriev-Mamonov—poet, publitsist i obshchestvennyi deiatel'," *Uchenye zapiski Tartuskogo gosudarstvennogo universiteta*, no. 78 (Tartu, 1959).

the evidence available to us, Ippolit Zavalishin was an immature youth (at the time he offered his first denunciation, he was seventeen). He had already learned how to get into debt and boasted that "he knew all the taverns and bars in Petersburg well, even before he entered military school."[45] But in this same evaluation, written by General Kozen from the words of Ippolit Zavalishin himself, it is reported that "he is well-read beyond his years; possessed of a good memory, he knows much poetry by heart."[46] Something else, however, is more astonishing: Zavalishin felt compelled to declare to the same General Kozen that he was a passionate admirer of the Decembrist Ryleev. He made this declaration some time at the end of June or the beginning of July, 1826, when Ryleev's death sentence had already been decided, and, perhaps, even carried out. True, we cannot say to what degree the formula "declaration" suits Zavalishin's words. Perhaps they were only the ecstatic chatter of a narcissistic adolescent. It is nonetheless noteworthy that *this* was how he chattered.

V. P. Kolesnikov, in his memoirs, provides more psychologically intriguing details. He describes how the victims of the Orenburg provocation and the provocateur himself were dispatched to Siberia. At one point in this procedure a notation was made of any distinguishing marks on the prisoners. The officer in charge, Bulanov, an acquaintance of the condemned who had served with them in the same regiment, "was so discreet and considerate, that he wanted neither to undress nor to measure us, but wrote down the marks and height of each prisoner on the basis of what he said," Kolesnikov writes. Then, unexpectedly, Zavalishin demanded that under distinguishing marks it be entered "that he had a birth-mark shaped like a crown on his chest, and one shaped like a sceptre on his shoulders. This made everyone laugh."[47] For all our natural distaste for Zavalishin, a man of utter moral perversity and ugliness,[48] as historians we cannot dismiss his words

---

[45]Kolesnikov, p. xi.

[46]Ibid.

[47]Ibid., p. 22.

[48]It is nonetheless of interest to the cultural historian that Ippolit Zavalishin's deed is universally appraised as an abnormality. Neither Nicholas I, nor the presiding judge in the case of the Orenburg secret society, General Essen, nor the Orenburg merchants, soldiers, and peasants could conceal the repugnance they felt for him. Even in surroundings which were far from moral, among minor provincial functionaries, he aroused disgust. Kolesnikov has preserved the following scene for us: when, after being transported in shackles from Orenburg to Ufa, the arrested men were led into provincial headquarters—a half-ruined building where clerks

with laughter. What we are unexpectedly confronting here is a superstition with which the history of pretenders has well acquainted us: the persistent folk belief that the body of the true tsar must bear the congenital "tsar's marks." The root of this belief is the deep-seated mythological idea that existing power is "counterfeit" ("counterfeit tsar," "antichrist," "werewolf"), while the true sovereign is disguised, and may himself not discern his own royal nature immediately. Note the following, from 1732:

> There appeared in the village a beggar who proclaimed "I am no peasant, no peasant's son: I am an eagle, an eagle's son, an eagle it is mine to be [cf. the fable of the eagle and the raven in *The Captain's Daughter*—Iu. L.] I am Tsarevich Aleksei Petrovich . . . on my back I have a cross and on my thigh is a birthmark in the form of a sword." The peasants took him to a shaman famed for his ability to recognize people [this is an interesting notion: there exists a special facility for "recognizing people," i.e., for discerning their true nature from certain marks—Iu. L.]. The shaman identified him as the true tsarevich.[49]

Pugachev's confederates demanded that he show them the "tsar's marks" on his body: "You call yourself a sovereign, and sovereigns have tsar's marks on their bodies."[50] And Pugachev showed them the "eagles" on his body (probably scars from boils).

The folkloric form in which Zavalishin's belief in his chosenness is expressed may sound stunningly foreign on the lips of a cosmopolitan nobleman and officer, albeit a demoted one, in the 1820s. (That he did so believe shows once again that the consciousness of an educated nobleman was not so widely removed from the world of folklore as is commonly thought.) We should remember,

---

and scriveners with ragged elbows crowded around pomade jars serving as ink wells, "all the clerks instantly stopped scratching their pens and turned to us with unconcealed curiosity. One put his pen behind his ear, another held his between his teeth, a third kept his in his hand; but at once all rose from their places and surrounded us. Their first question, pronounced by several voices at once, was: 'Which one of you is Zavalishin?' . . . Assuming a theatrical air of importance, he stepped forward and, smiling caustically, answered, 'What can I do for you? I am at your service!' The scriveners looked him over from head to toe and immediately withdrew. One of them said: 'Nothing, we only wanted to see what sort of creature you were' " (ibid., p. 64). It is important to remember that the very existence of Kolesnikov's notes is due to the initiative of the Decembrist Shteingel', who took steps to see that the conscience of posterity retained this unparalleled incident. It is no accident that Kolesnikov's notes are one of the earliest examples of Decembrist memoir literature: they were written in 1835.

[49]K. V. Chistov, *Russkie narodnye sotsial'no-utopicheskie legendy XVII-XIX vv* (Moscow, 1967), p. 126.

[50]Ibid., p. 149.

however, that the notion of great destiny seems to have been cultivated in the Zavalishin family. It was thus the encyclopedically erudite Dmitri Zavalishin, and not the half-educated boy Ippolit, who in his declining years opened his memoirs by informing the reader with the utmost seriousness: "They say that my christening was accompanied by exceptional solemnity. I was christened in a hall of banners, under signs [the wordplay with "banner (*znamia*) and "sign" (*znamenie*) characteristic of the esoteric texts of prophecies—Iu.L.]; in attendance were the archbishop, important city officials, and deputations from various peoples: Persian, Indian, Kirghiz, Kalmyk [it is hard to believe that Zavalishin, who had carefully studied Holy Scripture for many years and had translated the entire Bible from the original "for his own use" while in the labor camps, was not thinking of the adoration of the Magi when he wrote this—Iu. L.]. . . . In my household, they were always telling me about these portents, which, they thought, had something to do with a brilliant future. One of the prophecies was made by a phrenologist." At this point in the text, Zavalishin adds the following footnote: "As late as 1863, my sister wrote me that the inscrutable fates of Providence were clearly conducting me toward some exceptional goal."[51] And although the form in which the aged Dmitrii Zavalishin tells his story dissociates him from these prophecies, his entire life was, without a doubt, spent in expectation of their fulfillment. It is entirely possible that even Ippolit Zavalishin considered the moment in which he described his "distinguishing marks" as his "fateful hour"; he thought he would finally be "recognized" and his fate would change abruptly. It is extremely interesting that these naive notions, derived from folklore, were united in Ippolit Zavalishin's mind with romantic Napoleonism, the cult of a chosen man who is beyond moral prohibitions. Of course, this occurred in a primitive form, corresponding to the intellectual level of a seventeen-year-old cadet, in whose head folklore and Western culture were muddled in the most peculiar way.

Kolesnikov describes the following tragicomic scene: Ippolit Zavalishin, sentenced to life at hard labor, his head shaved, is shuffling in irons and "on the chain" (an iron bar or thick rope, to which bound convicts were fastened in pairs—the "Orenburgers" were treated with far less ceremony than the Decembrists, who traveled to Siberia in private wagons). Thus arrayed, he declares

[51]D. I. Zavalishin, *Zapiski*, p. 10.

"with comic arrogance" to his companions, whom he himself has
ruined:

> "You do not understand me! You are incapable of comprehending
> my destiny!" Taptikov and Druzhinin, laughing, said: "You're not
> thinking of becoming a Napoleon, are you?" "And why not?" he
> answered angrily. "You know, if I am successful, I will pave a road
> from Nerchinsk right to the palace with people's corpses, and the first
> step to the throne will be my brother!"[52]

Ippolit Zavalishin had an astounding talent for instantaneous
change. At one moment he was a gloomy demon and a Napoleon;
at the next, a free thinker who banished from his cell the priest
who had come to comfort him: "Longhaired priest, how could you
possibly understand this high and sacred idea? [the idea of life as
the bearing of a cross?—Iu. L.] Out with you!"[53] And within a half
an hour is he dancing in his chains between the bunks, repeating
to his fellow unfortunates, "You want to sleep, but I want to dance
the galop,"[54] or whistling lightheartedly as he marches into exile
under guard. One moment, in a letter to the emperor, he characterizes his denunciation of his brother in this style: "Seeing my
high feelings of devotion and of love for the fatherland spurned,
and my unprecedented sacrifice come to nothing, I am in a fever
of indignation and various feelings which perturb me greatly." And
the next moment, he discusses this same letter—and with whom?—
with the general sent to guard him: "If having read my documents,
His Majesty the Emperor could read what is in my heart, he would
send me to the devil."[55]

I would like to note one more trait that links this group of characters: they are all, according to their subjective self-consciousness,
romantics. I have noted elsewhere that the romantic model of behavior is a particularly active generator of imitation. Easily reducible
to simplistic stereotypes, it is actively apprehended by the reader
as a program for his own behavior. If, in a realistic situation, art
imitates life, then, in a romantic one, life actively impersonates
art.[56] It is no accident that such fictional characters as Goethe's
Werther and Lermontov's Demon gave rise to an epidemic of im-

---

[52]Kolesnikov, p. 76.
[53]Ibid., p. 75.
[54]Ibid., p. 76.
[55]Ibid., p. xi.
[56]Lotman, *Stat'i po tipologii kul'tury* (Tartu, 1973).

itations, which cannot be said of Natasha Rostova or Konstantin Levin, Raskolnikov or Ivan Karamazov. Nonetheless, the man who has chosen romantic norms as a program for behavior, who plays the role of demon or vampire, does not have the power to change the stage on which his life's play if performed. Deeds transferred from the ideal space of a romantic text to Russia's far from ideal reality engendered strange hybrids. G. A. Gukovskii was probably the first to see romantics in Gogol's bureaucrats: the protagonist of "Diary of a Madman," he writes, "is also, if one may say so, a romantic, and Poprishchin's romantic pose is a parody of romanticism. It would be hard to devise a parody more savage."[57] Of course, we have more than just parody here. What is parody in a text intentionally created by a writer appears in the real text of human behavior as a deviation in a person's attitudes conditioned by external circumstances. This deviation leads to the sharp disparity in characters of this type between self-appraisals and appraisals made by some outside observer. A text which from a subjective point of view reads "demon" can appear a Khlestakov or an Ippolit Zavalishin in the eyes of an outside observer.

In romanticism of the type exemplified in Lermontov's Grushnitskii, behavior typically does not spring from the organic needs of personality, and is not at one with it. Instead, behavior is "selected," like a role or a costume, and is, so to speak, "put on" over the personality. This facility makes possible quick changes in behavior and the total lack, in any given state, of memory of the one that preceded it. While the skin preserves a memory of its previous form during all of its changes, a new costume has no memory of the preceding costume. There are eras when not only individuals but whole cultures at a certain stage of their development can replace organic evolution with "costume changes." The price for this is a historical and cultural loss of memory.

We have discussed examples in sufficient detail to make it unnecessary to multiply them. We already have the grounds to claim that the literary Khlestakov is related to a certain historico-psychological type. But what are the historical conditions that caused this type to arise?

The first is the cultural and historical proximity of a highly developed centuries-old culture, from which a man of Khlestakov's type can assimilate ready-made texts and patterns of behavior. Earlier, we linked khlestakovism with romanticism. It must be em-

---

[57]G. A. Gukovskii, *Realizm Gogolia* (Moscow/Leningrad, 1959), p. 310.

phasized that khlestakovism is not a generator of romanticism (it does not act as a cultural generator at all); it is rather a consumer of romanticism. Because it parasitizes a highly developed culture, simplifying it, khlestakovism requires a specific medium: a situation in which a fully formed, highly developed culture is in collision with an immature culture in a superdynamic state.

Second, against this background of dynamism, fluidity, and the absence of dominant conservative elements in a culture, it is essential for the organic development of a society to have been at least inhibited or, at some instant, completely halted. This happened, for example, when Russia's social development, which had received its dynamic impulse in the Petrine period, was frozen under Nicholas I. The absence of any ingrained tradition in the bureaucratic culture of the time created in certain circles an uncommon frivolity of thought, and the sense of "no barriers" and "unlimited possibilities." The make-believe nature of state bureaucratic activity readily permitted the substitution of "lies" for real activity. Transferred to the psychology of an individual personality, it produced khlestakovism.

Third, khlestakovism is linked with a high degree of semiotization in society. Only when a dominant role is played by various kinds of social fictions or "pretendings" will there be the requisite disjunction between activity and results. Without this, the khlestakovian confusion—the confounding of both one's own self and others as a form of existence—becomes impossible.

Fourth, khlestakovism presupposes a despotic authority. Khlestakov and the Mayor, Medoks and Nicholas I (or Benkendorf), are not antagonists, not deceivers and the deceived; they are inseparable pairs. Only a situation of autocratic arbitrariness, in which even the state's own norms of "regularity" are violated, can produce an atmosphere of instability and, simultaneously, of the illusion of unlimited possibilities, which fuel the unlimited amibition of the Khlestakovs and the Ippolit Zavalishins. Moreover, although autocracy puts immense effort into depriving itself of real sources of information on what is in fact happening in the society it governs, it still needs this sort of information.[58] Stifling the press, falsifying statistics, transforming all forms of official record-keeping into ri-

---

[58]Cf. the words of the Decembrist Mikhail Lunin: "The people are thinking in spite of their deep silence. As proof, one need only look at the millions being spent to eavesdrop on opinions which the people are prevented from expressing." Both the desire not to allow the people to express their views and the measures taken "to eavesdrop on" these thoughts are equally characteristic of autocracy.

tualized lies, the autocracy of Nicholas I left itself a single source of information—covert surveillance. In so doing, however, it put itself into a situation reminiscent of a tragic farce. It would be a mistake to believe that Nicholas I's government, including his secret police civil service, was staffed by obtuse, uneducated, or completely incompetent people. Even in the so-called Third Department, there were energetic and completely reasonable functionaries. There were those not totally lacking in education. But however we judge their intellectual abilities, it is clear that their viewpoint was broader than that of the insignificant individuals— the assorted Medokses—who served as their sources of information. By relying on ambitious juveniles, ignorant fantasizers, and idle scandalmongers, the administration inevitably lowered itself to their outlook.

How is it that the stupid and simple-hearted Khlestakov manages to deceive the Mayor, a man who, in his own way, is intelligent and experienced in the ways of the world? How is it that the simple-hearted, empty-headed, outwardly insubstantial[59] Medoks is able to deceive all those with whom fate brings him into collision, Benkendorf and Nicholas I as well as the generals and governors in the Caucasus? When a single source of information is used, it is impossible to rise above it.

In the fable "The Razors," published in 1829 (Gogol read it as a reference to people of the Decembrist circle, who were kept from government posts), Krylov wrote:

> My razor is very dull!
> Of course I know! It's not that we're so dumb
> But I'm afraid I'd cut myself on a sharper one.
>
> . . .
>
> People are afraid of intelligent men;
> They're happier keeping their fools around them.[60]

The blockhead and the adventurer became two faces of Nicholas I's state system. But by recruiting adventurers as its servants, Nicholas I's bureaucracy became a servant to adventurers. It enmeshed itself in the circle most inclined to indulge in hare-brained schemes. At the same time as it concentrated the main features of

---

[59]"His face is white and open, the hair on his head and his eyebrows are light brownish, somewhat scant, his eyes are gray, his nose small and somewhat pointed, he stammers when he speaks" (Shtraikh, *Provokatsiia*, p. 32).

[60]I. A. Krylov, *Sochineniia*, vol. 3 (Moscow, 1946), p. 238-239.

the era in one character, khlestakovism, in rising from the bottom to the very summit of the state, shaped the image of its time.

Gogol insisted with reason that Khlestakov, who embodies the idea of lying not in abstract moralizing, but in its concrete, historical, sociocultural appearance—"this phantasmagorical figure who, as lying deception personified, whirled away with the troika God knows where" (IV, 118)—is the protagonist of *The Inspector General*. It is hardly necessary to remind the reader of the emotional associations that the troika image had for Gogol. The question of how his consciousness transformed a realistic, historical type, is, however, another matter. Its treatment exceeds the limits of this essay; it calls for an examination of Gogol's comedy as an independent text.

Earlier, we discussed the active nature of romantic texts. Of course, I do not mean that the literature of realism is passive with respect to the reader's behavior. Nonetheless, its activeness is of a different sort. The reader perceives romantic texts as a straightforward program for behavior. Realistic images are in this respect less directive. Nevertheless, they *give a name* to patterns of behavior that are present as spontaneous and unconscious elements of a particular social fabric, and in so doing they bring these elements to the level of the social and conscious. Khlestakov, "a type composed of much that is scattered in various Russian characters" (IV, 101), is established, named, and given definiteness beneath Gogol's pen. Once this happens, khlestakovism is brought into the world that exists beyond the boundaries of Gogol's comedy. It now appears on an altogether new level, in the category of culturally recognized forms of behavior.

In some respects, it may be said that realism is more conventional[61] than romanticism. In depicting typified forms, a realistic work treats material which has already undergone a certain amount of cultural processing beyond the limits of an artistic text. The man who stands beyond the text has already selected a cultural role for himself; he has placed his own individual conduct in some category of social role. Introduced into the world of an artistic text, he emerges twice encoded. Coding himself as "the Demon," "Cain," "Onegin," "imagining herself to be the heroine of one of her beloved bards" (*Onegin*, VI, 5)—the character is at the same time a functionary, a

---

[61]On our understanding of the problem of the conventional in art cf. Lotman and Uspenskii, "Uslovnost' v iskusstve," *Filosofskaia Entsiklopediia*, vol. 5 (Moscow, 1970), pp. 287-288.

minor officer, a provincial noble's daughter. The realistic text is, in theory, oriented to the situation of "a representation within a representation." Thus it is specifically in realistic literature that quotations, reminiscences, "new designs on old canvas" occupy such a prominent place (it is significant that Pushkin's *Tales of Belkin* marks the beginning of Russian realistic prose). In the same way, realistic painting gives prominence to the themes of the mirror and the painting within the painting, and realistic theater gives prominence to the "stage within the stage." In romantic art (if we exclude the peripheral field of romantic irony) these situations are substantially less common. But though systems of citation are characteristic of realistic art only during the stage in which it is working out its own language, the orientation to a double semiotic coding is its fundamental feature. A side effect is that realistic texts are a valuable source for evaluating the pragmatics of various types of social signs.

Thus, if a romantic text refashions the actual behavior of an individual then a realistic text refashions society's attitude to the behavior of the individual, organizing various types of behavior into a hierarchy on the basis of the culture's scale of values. Its active nature is manifested in the organization of an integral system of conduct for this culture. Of course, such a system of influences is extremely complex. And just as we have already observed that research into the pragmatics of artistic texts presents one of the most complex problems now confronting contemporary literary criticism, we should also mention that the pragmatics of realistic texts (in contradistinction to the pragmatics of folklore or medieval texts, where special rules apply, and the pragmatics of romanticism, where a relatively strict pragmatic usage is in force) is a particularly complex task for research.

The "Human Document" and the Formation of Character

LIDIIA IA. GINSBURG

The liberalizing movement in nineteenth-century Russia was the work of a variety of social groups, and it assumed a variety of forms: sometimes reaching the point of near revolution, and sometimes weakening, but never ceasing to develop. All Russia's great writers in one way or another responded to the issues it raised—regardless of their attitudes toward revolutionary methods of resolving them. This is the source of the extraordinarily intense development of Russian social thought, of the quick and decisive way in which one generation was replaced by the next, imparting to each decade a particular ideological atmosphere. These conditions made possible the succession of historical character types against which each generation's self-image was measured. It is difficult to find a sharper and more conspicuous alternation of models of social man than the transition from the heroic personality of Decembrism in the 1810s and 1820s to the nihilists of the 1860s.

The method of Russian psychological prose emerged in the spiritual life of the intelligentsia of the 1830s and 1840s, the life of that era's famous circles, whose membership included Herzen, Turgenev, and Dostoevskii (the method had other sources too, of course). The ideological bent, the wish to comprehend all phenomena philosophically, the intense and demanding analysis and self-analysis in which the psychological was inseparable from the moral and the civic—all these tendencies of the intellectual life of

Translated by R. Judson Rosengrant from " 'Chelovecheskii dokument' i postroenie kharaktera," *O psikhologicheskoi proze* (Leningrad, 1971), pp. 37-75, incorporating author's corrections. Translation copyright © 1985 by R. Judson Rosengrant.

the circles of the 1830s and 1840s were later to characterize the Russian novel in the second half of the nineteenth century.

The great figures of Russian culture in the middle and second half of the nineteenth century drew certain conclusions, and moreover different ones, from circle life. It is clear what significance the overheated intellectual atmosphere of the Petrashevskii Fridays must have had for Dostoevskii's novel of ideas; that in his denunciation the police agent Liprandi called the Petrashevskii circle a "conspiracy of ideas" is no accident. The structure of the Turgenev novel is another matter. These are not novels of ideas, yet at the center of each, from *Rudin* to *Virgin Soil*, there stands a hero-ideologue. This approach to man was nourished in the young Turgenev by close association with Belinskii, Bakunin, Herzen, Stankevich, and Granovskii. For his part, Herzen took from the experience of the philosophical discussions of his youth the historical method and dialectical skills that came to define his entire oeuvre, including his greatest creation, *My Past and Thoughts*.

The conception of man worked out by the Russian intelligentsia in the 1830s and 1840s progressed through several stages. First was a romantic idealization of personality. Then came an intensive investigation of that personality in terms of philosophical categories. And finally there was the transition, especially clear-cut in Belinskii, to realistic determinism—the analysis of man in relation to his social conditioning.

The Herzen-Ogarev and Stankevich circles were formed almost simultaneously as student circles at the beginning of the 1830s.[1] Their subsequent fates, however, were quite different. Herzen's circle was destroyed as early as 1834 (at the height of its romantic and Saint-Simonian enthusiasms), and its members scattered, the close relationship among them never to be recovered. Indeed, only Herzen and Ogarev remained friends.

The Stankevich circle, which Bakunin, Botkin, and Katkov joined only in 1835-1836, lasted until the very end of the 1830s, surviving even Stankevich's departure abroad, and is therefore of particular theoretical interest. Its intellectual life constitutes a kind of juncture of two periods in Russian culture. The fates of its members bear witness to the obsolescence and eventual demise of the romantic

[1] For a discussion of the Herzen-Ogarev circle and of the problem of personality as the young Herzen perceived it, see my *Byloe i dumy Gertsena*, (Herzen's *My Past and Thoughts*) (Leningrad, 1957), in particular the chapter "Evoliutsiia geroia" (Evolution of the hero).

man and his replacement by another type, the *real* man, as Belinskii called him.

We are faced here with something like a psychological projection of the transition from romanticism to realism. Epochal character types, successively embodying romantic emotionalism, Hegelian introspection, and the sober-mindedness of the 1840s, replaced one another. The same person could, if he were someone conspicuously shaped by history, pass through all these stages.

Characteristic of the Russian romantics of the 1830s were an extraordinarily acute self-consciousness and an intense interest in the idea of personality, both to a degree that had been typical neither of people of the Decembrist stamp, nor even of the romantic idealists of the 1820s. The "wisdom-lovers" of the 1820s were interested in *Naturphilosophie*, but their main concern was aesthetics and the romantic philosophy of art.[2] In the Stankevich circle, the ideological focus shifted to the question of man's purpose. Ethics rather than aesthetics began to assume primary importance. Corresponding to this development was the need to create an image of personality that would have broad historical meaning. That image derived from every conceivable form of circle social life, but its chief means of cultivation was the letter.

Was this moral and at the same time psychological self-analysis an essentially new phenomenon in Russian culture?

Sentimentalism, oriented toward a uniform ideal of the natural and sensitive man, had also cultivated a heightened interest in the inner life. As is well known, the special character of Russian sentimentalism came from the fact that it had been formulated not by the bourgeoisie, the group that had produced Western sentimentalism, but by the social stratum that later came to be called the "educated nobility."

The members of this stratum were military officers and bureaucrats, sometimes very prominent ones (I. I. Dmitriev, for example, was an actual privy councillor and a minister of justice), and of course they could not conduct themselves according to the rules governing sensitive hearts.[3] But no one expected them to. Their

[2]The wisdom-lovers of the 1820s would become the slavophiles of the 1840s. A fundamental anti-individualism became part of the slavophile world view; it follows that elaboration of the problems of the contemporary reflective personality was impossible for that group.

[3]The most sentimental of the sentimentalists, Prince Shalikov, commanded the military unit that was most cruel in suppressing a peasant uprising in the Tula province in 1797.

way of life was determined by other norms based on class. But the history of Russian cultural awareness at the end of the eighteenth century and the beginning of the nineteenth contains phenomena of another kind as well. There was, for example, the intimate circle of the Turgenev brothers, which included among its members the young Zhukovskii, Voeikov, Merzliakov, and Andrei Kaisarov. In his book on Zhukovskii, subtitled "the poetry of feeling and 'sincere imagination,' "[4] Veselovskii notes the characteristic features of the spiritual life of that circle: an intense interest in the inner man, as well as in self-enrichment, the ideal of self-perfection, the moral significance of diaries and confessions (which Zhukovskii would continue to insist on), and friendship conceived as a means of self-knowledge and mutual cultivation. All these features anticipated the forms of circle social activity in the 1830s.

The freedom-loving, civic frame of mind that caught up some of the members of the Turgenev circle did not immediately supplant the mental habits inculcated in their youth by Prokopovich-Antonskii, the disciple of Freemasonry who headed the university Nobility Pension where the Turgenev brothers and Zhukovskii had studied, and by Ivan Petrovich Turgenev, whose moral authority was beyond question not only for his sons, but for their comrades as well.

In 1783 Ivan Petrovich Turgenev, who was one of the most important representatives of Moscow Freemasonry, translated and published John Mason's popular *Self Knowledge*. The young Zhukovskii read it carefully, and it served him as a practical course in self-improvement. The book is a typical mixture of Masonic mysticism, political conformism, and practical moral-psychological excursions into the realm of self-knowledge, including a description of appropriate exercises and various techniques for the examination of mental life. The purpose of all the exercises is the religious purification of the soul and mystical atonement with God, but the suggested means are frequently marked by a kind of psychological concreteness. Thus are mentioned the necessity of knowing one's own temperament or "constitution" and of acting "decently and in keeping with" one's own character. The book is rife with appeals for a cultivated and skeptical self-examination, which is compared to the examination of things "through a magnifying glass." "For in order to a true *self knowledge*, the human mind, with its various

[4] A. N. Veselovskii, *V. A. Zhukovskii: Poeziia chuvstva i "serdechnogo voobrazheniia"* (Petrograd, 1918).

powers and operations, must be narrowly inspected; all of its secret bendings and doublings displayed. Otherwise our self acquaintance will be but very partial and defective; and the heart after all will deceive us."[5] Accordingly, Chapter XII of the first part is entitled "Everyone that knows, is in a particular manner sensible how far he is governed by a Thirst for Applause." Chapter XI of the first part is called "Concerning the secret springs of our Actions." "Another considerable branch of self acquaintance is, to know the true motives and secret springs of our actions. . . . It is not only possible, but very common, for men to be ignorant of the chief inducements of their behavior; and to imagine they act from one motive, whilst they are apparently governed by another" (Part I, chapter XI, pp. 88-89).

There are other statements of the same kind in the book: "We may meet with frauds and faithless dealings from men; but after all, our own hearts are the greatest cheats; and there are none we are in greater danger from than ourselves" (Part III, chapter I, p. 161). "Would you know yourself, you must very carefully attend to the frame and emotions of your mind under some extraordinary incidents. Some sudden accidents which befal [sic] you when the mind is most off its guard, will better discover its secret turn and prevailing disposition than much greater events you are prepared to meet" (Part III, chapter VII, p. 188).

If we turn from these reflections to the diaries of the young Zhukovskii, the latter's provenance becomes obvious. "What am I? What is good in me? What is bad? What is the product of circumstances? What of nature? What can be acquired and how? What must be corrected and how? What can neither be acquired nor corrected? . . . What kind of happiness is possible for someone of my character? These are questions on the solution of which some (much) time must be spent. They will be solved little by little in the course of my journal" (entry for June 13, 1805).[6]

The entry for July 30, 1804 begins: "I passed the day most unpleasantly. I was dissatisfied with myself, upset, depressed." Later on there is an analysis of "today" in the form of a conversation between two interlocutors, which defines the psychological consequences of the most fleeting impressions. This too is a theme of

[5]John Mason, *Self Knowledge: A Treatise Showing the Nature and Benefit of That Important Science and the Way to Attain It* (Boston, 1800), p. 21; published in Russian as *Ionna Masona poznanie samogo sebia* (Moscow, 1783). All references in the text are to this reprint of the original English version (published in 1745—Tr.).
[6]*Dnevniki V. A. Zhukovskogo* (St. Petersburg, 1903), p. 12.

Protestant religious-moralistic and Masonic literature. The author of *Self Knowledge* frequently reminds us that in the evening "we should review and examine the several actions of the day, the various tempers and dispositions we have been in, and the occasions that excited them" (Part III, chapter I, pp. 164–165). The diaries of the young Zhukovskii are a monument to the early attempts of Russian thought to analyze the inner man. The moral program of that self-analysis was oriented toward a kind of universal ideal of the sensitive and virtuous man. The merits or shortcomings of any human being were measured against this preestablished ideal; they were not individualized. In his early diaries and letters, Zhukovskii dwells on such personal deficiencies as sloth, idleness, and lethargy—deficiencies that had been anticipated in a Masonic literature that demanded an active effort in self-understanding. In John Mason's book the chapter "Self Knowledge promotes our Usefulness in the World," is devoted to the question of the maximum utilization of one's personal gifts. Discussed there are those who "live away whole days, weeks, and sometimes months together, to as little purpose, . . . as if they had been asleep all the while" (Part III, chapter VII, p. 147). On August 26, 1805, Zhukovskii wrote in his diary:

> In my present frame of mind I don't even feel the need to think: such moments verge on nothingness and indeed are worse than nothingness, for you feel something unpleasant. . . . How was my youth passed? I lived in complete idleness. . . . No one showed any particular concern for me, and . . . whatever concern was shown seemed like charity to me. I was not abandoned or cast out, I had a place to call my own, but . . . I did not feel anyone's love; consequently, I could not be grateful from genuine feeling but only from a sense of obligation. . . . That made me cold. . . . Whoever is isolated from others has no subject for reflection. . . . His character becomes timid, indecisive, listless, indolent, for character too is formed through activity.[7]

The important thing here is the circumstances in which Zhukovskii's character developed; they are biographically concrete, but not individualized. Social disadvantage—in particular, an illegitimate birth—an unhappy childhood, and a lonely youth are all traditional motifs of sentimentalism. They had indeed been a part of Zhukovskii's real experience. But Zhukovskii, working from that experience, selected and gave expression only to those elements

[7]Ibid., pp. 476-477.

that fit already existing general formulas, in the same way that the poetry of sentimentalism had fit them.

The theme of activity, of the struggle against idleness and sloth, is also present in Zhukovskii's early correspondence."How splendid it would be if we could all live together—I do not call living *breathing, sleeping,* and *eating,* but *acting* and taking pleaure in one's activity; it follows that that activity must lead to something higher, or else how can one take pleasure in it?" (letter to Aleksandr Turgenev of September 11-16, 1805).[8] The same thing appears in a letter written five years later (November 7, 1810): "All my past life is shrouded in a kind of fog of mental inactivity through which it is impossible to discern anything.... So, my dear friend, activity and its object, utility—these are what inspire me now."[9] It is clear from all the letters taken together that activity was conceived as inner work on the self and as the occupation of the writer.

Zhukovskii reflects a great deal in his early letters on the nature of true friendship. It is very difficult for a lonely person to be both active and virtuous. Friendship understood in a particularly moralistic way is the central act of spiritual life. It is at once the condition and the consequence of action and virtue. "We must labor, we must act in concord so that we may be worthy of friendship and, thus, become friends. Friendship is a virtue; it is everything, and not for just one person, but for two (or even for three or four, but the more the better). If it should be said of me, 'He is a true friend,' that will be the same as saying, 'He is a virtuous, noble person who is animated by a *single* flame with another being who is equal to him, who sustains him, and who is sustained by him.' That is what friendship means to me" (letter of September 11-16, 1805).[10]

The forms of social intercourse, so diverse in different periods and milieus, are an important indication of the prevailing conception of man, of his psychological structure and purpose in life.

Still another line in the development of the Russian educated nobility was taking form at the beginning of the century, one leading to Decembrism (broadly understood) and the generation of Pushkin. These latter were people who were either associated with the noblemen's rebellion or were on its periphery, people who (before the Decembrist catastrophe) had been faced with practical tasks, and who preferred the legacy of the French and Russian

[8]V. A. Zhukovskii, *Sobranie sochinenii*, vol. 4 (Moscow/Leningrad, 1960), p. 453.
[9]Ibid., pp. 476-477.
[10]Ibid., p. 454.

Enlightenment to the traditions of Anglo-German sentimentalism. Both civic zeal and Voltairean skepticism were characteristic of people of this stamp, as was a hidden inner life. That life was revealed neither in friendly conversation, nor in letters and diaries (as evidenced by the diaries of Pushkin, the notebooks of Viazemskii, and so on). It was opened only by the key of poetry, where it became, in aesthetically transmuted form, the possession of all who could read. These people could have applied to themselves the words of Montaigne: "Many things that I would not want to tell anyone, I tell the public; and for my most secret knowledge and thoughts I sent my most faithful friends to a bookseller's shop."[11] Neither the psychic hardships of Batiushkov, which led to mental illness, nor the severe hypochondria of Viazemskii, nor the tempestuous emotional life of Pushkin left much trace in their voluminous correspondence. People of the Pushkin era used coarse language in their letters as a matter of course, but they kept hidden the secrets of their hearts with stubborn modesty. They would have turned away with amazement and repugnance from the incredible admissions of the familiar correspondence of the 1830s and 1840s.

The cult of friendship remained intact from the circle of the young Zhukovskii and the Turgenev brothers to the Pushkin circle, and thence to the Stankevich circle, although its forms underwent conspicuous change. Friendship for Zhukovskii had been a means of self-improvement and the achievement of moral perfection. For Pushkin, friends were the comrades of one's childhood games and youthful banquets, one's soulmates and boon companions: "Chedaev, you remember how it was?"[12]

In the 1830s friendship was hard, demanding, and utterly candid. It cultivated the skills of psychological analysis. It was a kind of reciprocal reflection that answered the need of the mature personality for continuous self-perception and self-revelation.

Post-Decembrist romanticism was marked by an intense interest in the inner life of the personality—the *elite* personality, needless to say. Later it will be necessary to go more deeply into the paradox of romantic individualism, in consequence of which its elite personalities were not individual but reproduced a shared model: that of the Byronic demon, say, or the Schellingian poet.

Authentically individual analysis, individual treatment of universally significant moral values, emerged at the end of the 1830s

---

[11] *The Complete Essays of Montaigne*, trans. Donald Frame (Palo Alto, 1965), p. 750.
[12] From Pushkin's "Chaadaevu" ("K chemu kholodnye somneniia?").

and the beginning of the 1840s at a time of transition, of severe crisis in the Russian romantic mind. It emerged in the circles of that era, the outposts of the passionate intellectual life of young Russia.

Romanticism as such is not self-analytical. It is the image of personality, not the mechanism that sets it in motion, that is important. Of course, minds raised on the Enlightenment and rationalist philosophy had not delved very deeply into examination of the "inner man" either. Zhukovskii had resolved that inner man into predetermined virtues and shortcomings. For the later positivism, already pervasive in the Russia of the 1840s, life was not primarily an ethical fact. That is why the Stankevich circle, with its romanticism in retreat before Hegelianism (in a peculiarly Russian version), is of such interest. It was here that the question of personality as a historical phenomenon and as an individual psychological entity was first posed in earnest, as were the issues of destiny, of behavior, and of the personality's moral responsibility in regard to its own qualities. Reality was regarded as the embodiment of the spirit of Reason, and therefore everything that took place within that reality, everything that happened to a person, could have philosophical and ethical significance.

Three extraordinary personalities stand at the head of the intellectual life of the circles: Bakunin, Stankevich, and Belinskii.[13]

The striking thing about Mikhail Bakunin's biography is that this man seemed to live several lives. The Bakunin of the 1830s was a romantic, a Fichtean, a Hegelian, a member of the Stankevich circle, a friend and adversary of Belinskii, and the inspirer of the "Premukhino Idyll." The 1840s were for Bakunin years of study, wandering, and association with the international revolutionary movement: he was one of the organizers of the Dresden uprising in 1849. The 1850s saw him in Austrian and Russian jails, in exile in Siberia, and finally, in 1861 (when he was forty-seven), escaping from Siberia abroad, where he became an active collaborator in Herzen's publishing ventures, and, later on, the leader of world anarchism.

The young Bakunin was one of the last and most brilliant flashes of Russian romanticism. The numerous letters that have survived from the 1830s bear witness to the way in which he himself shaped

---

[13]Belinskii is the subject of the next section of Ginsburg's book, not translated here—Tr.

his own personality, as well as to the way in which his image was refracted in the minds of his family and friends, especially the members of the Stankevich circle. There were many different perceptions of Bakunin, but all agreed that his personality had an especially structured quality, with sharply delineated features that tended toward clear-cut historical and moral definitions. Indeed, it was for this reason that literature did not neglect him. He became the prototype (in one case certainly, in the other probably) of heroes of novels by Turgenev and Dostoevskii. The Bakunin archives show very clearly how this young man, whose lot till then had been that of a merely private being, at a certain point identified himself with the historical life of his time.

Premukhino, the name of the Bakunin family estate in the Tver district, has a permanent place in the history of Russian culture. The "Premukhino Idyll," the "Premukhino Harmony" was a whole system with its own ideology and style. Moreover, that style had a dual manifestation. In the 1810s and 1820s it was something quite consciously, even deliberately, created by Aleksandr Mikhailovich Bakunin, Mikhail Bakunin's father and the head of the immense patriarchal family. Later, in the 1830s, the spiritual life of Premukhino came to be dominated by the young people under the inspiration of their eldest brother, Mikhail, and Premukhino then became one of the focal points of Russian romanticism, in particular of the romantic cult of femininity. Bakunin's four sisters became the objects of that cult, which was maintained by their brothers and by their oldest brother's friends, including Belinskii, Stankevich, Botkin, and Kliushnikov.

In 1828, the fourteen-year-old Mikhail Bakunin was appointed to the Artillery School in Petersburg and left Premukhino for five years. In the letters of the young military school pupil there is as yet no evidence of either individual or historical identity. Rather one finds a politically conformist youth who obviously lacks those intellectual interests with which Herzen and Ogarev were familiar at an earlier age, a youth with rather naive literary tastes and ideas who spoke of the historical novels of Bulgarin with esteem and at the same time remarked of the recently published *Boris Godunov* that "Pushkin's passionate admirers see only beauty in it. But there are deficiencies too."[14] In any case, the mental experiences that figure in Bakunin's early letters (1832-1833) are oriented on a def-

---

[14]M. A. Bakunin, *Sobranie sochinenii i pisem*, vol. 1 (Moscow, 1934), p. 42; subsequent references to this edition are given in the text.

inite literary model: they are formulated in accordance with the rules of sentimentalism.

Bakunin wrote to his sister Varvara:

> Your letter, dear Varen'ka, disappointed me. It proved to me that my thoughts and hopes are an empty chimera, that that tender friendship, that precious gift from above, does not exist for me, poor wretch, since I could not find it in a sister, one whom I adored.... For it is she who has destroyed my fascination. But what is to be done? That is the way of the world, and I am only now beginning to understand the full truth of something Aunty once said: "How many more times will you be disappointed, dear Michel, how many more times will your hopes and dreams be dashed, how much longer will it be before you begin to see the world as it really is!" [I, 98-99]

It is no accident that a Karamzinian flavor, one obviously dated by the early 1830s, predominates in the letters of the young Bakunin. It was indeed that cultural legacy he received from his parents. Aleksandr Mikhailovich Bakunin was a free thinker (there is even a suggestion that in the most circumspect way he took part in the drafting of the charter for the Union of Welfare[15]) who with time had mellowed and exchanged his nonconformism for moderately conservative views. He was an enlightened late-eighteenth-century Russian nobleman, and it followed that he viewed the literature of sentimentalism as the most advanced.

He instilled that style of life and literature in the numerous members of his family too. The Premukhino way of life was conceived as the embodiment of a kind of sentimental and enlightenment—and, at the same time, feudal—utopia. Its program was set forth by the dilettante poet Aleksandr Mikhailovich Bakunin in the 1820s, in a long poem (preserved in the family archive) called "Osuga," the name of the small river on which Premukhino was situated.

> I see the peaceful village filled
> With labor-loving peasant folk;
> I haven't any notion why
> Our intellectuals call them slaves!
> With labors well within their strength
> They render our established share.
> . . .

[15]The Union of Welfare (*Soiuz Blagodenstviia*), a Masonic secret society formed in 1818 and dissolved of its own accord in 1821, advocated a number of liberal social reforms; it was a forerunner of Decembrism—Tr.

The house is large, without parquet,
No lavish carpets spread around,
Nor other cherished bric-a-brac,
Not even tables set for *cards*.

. . .

When at the turn of eventide,
The family comes to gather round,
Like swarming bees within the hive,
I'm more contented than the tsar.

I'm surrounded by familial love,
The Tsar by courtly masquerade;
To me fly honey-laden bees,
But drones consume the Tsar's largesse.[16]

The poem expresses very definite sociopolitical and moral assumptions and ideals, stylistically shaped under the direct influence of Derzhavin's "life at Zvanka" and the sentimental correspondence of the elder Karamzinians.

Sentimentalism in essence permanently shaped the mode of life and epistolary style of the Bakunin sisters—despite all the romantic features that later accumulated. Mikhail Bakunin too was for a long time unable to cast off the view of life of the *man of sensibility*.

In a long letter to his father written in December 1837, Bakunin reviewed his past, returning to the values and standards prescribed by the Premukhino utopia. His childhood had been a time of sacred love and friendship linking all the members of the family, a time when the children's inquisitive minds had been nurtured under the enlightened and humane guidance of their father. Then came the years of study at the Artillery School, a period of mental contamination and devastation yielding to a new moral fervor. Of course the Bakunin of 1837 already understood the world differently, but in this letter he was singling out certain aspects of his complex mental life. He appears here as the man of sensibility, clad in the appropriate style, one familiar to his father and easily understood by him. A blissful childhood, youthful lapses, impulses to purification—all this is very generalized and could be characteristic of any disciple of the sentimentalists; it does not pretend to be exceptional at all. Nevertheless, awareness of his own exceptional nature developed in Bakunin with extraordinary force—

[16]Quoted in A. A. Kornilov, *Molodye gody Mikhaila Bakunina* (Moscow, 1915), pp. 9, 30-32.

to the same degree that he came to grips with romanticism and with romantic philosophy in the process of finding his own historical identity.

The intellectual life of the 1830s was varied and chaotic. Romanticism at that time covered the widest spectrum—from the academic, where it flourished in the soil of intense study of contemporary philosophy, to the philistine, where it was transformed into a mindlessly fashionable craving after effect. The elasticity of the boundaries between the various "romanticisms" fostered the eclecticism of the period. The young had already absorbed the romantic legacy in its entirety, simultaneously adopting Pushkin and Marlinskii, Zhukovskii and Ryleev, Byron, Schiller, and Hugo, although to the preceding generation these had been not only diverse, but frequently incompatible or even diametrically opposed phenomena. The contradictory times offered the younger generation a broad selection of images of epochal personality. There was the demonic hero, in which the tradition of revolutionary romanticism (Polezhaev, Lermontov) survived; it had its vulgar manifestation too, as immortalized in Lermontov's Grushnitskii. There was the Schellingian exhalted poet, who signaled the post-Decembrist shift toward the "absolute" and the transcendental. Added to these varieties of romantic imagery were certain modifications, that took root in the soil of new philosophical and sociological enthusiasms. Thus, in the romantic epistolary "poem," as exemplified by the correspondence of the young Herzen with his fiancée, an image combining "demonism" with social-utopian aspirations, took shape, transforming the demonic theme. Herzen's hero was demonic not because it was his metaphysical essence to be so, but because he had been driven to it by social injustice, the hostility of the "mob," the persecution of authority, separation from his beloved, and so on. Remove these causes, and you will restore the hero to harmony. But to do that, it is first necessary to change reality.

This was but one of the philosophical modifications of the romantic image in the 1830s. It remained for Bakunin to create another soon after associating himself with contemporary romanticism.

In January 1834, while still in his "pre-philosophical" period, the twenty-year-old Bakunin wrote to his sisters that he had experienced an "intellectual revolution" and had "made a definite decision" about his future, that he was disenchanted with "society" and saw the acquisition of knowledge as the only goal worthy of a man. This vague scheme would take on substance later, together with that philosophical romanticism which Bakunin was introduced to in 1835 by the Stankevich circle. It was at that time that the young Bakunin began to shape his new personality, the image of the militant seeker after spiritual values and the advocate of philosophical ideas.

As is well known, Russians of the 1830s and 1840s understood German philosophy in a most idiosyncratic way, submitting it to the imperatives of their own intellectual life. This was true of Bakunin to an even greater extent than it was, say, of the more academic Stankevich. After attempting to master the philosophy of Kant with little success, Bakunin immediately turned to Fichte, although not to his major works (*The Science of Knowledge*, *The Vocation of Man*), but to his late treatise *Admonition for a Happy Life*, where it is argued that life is a continuous striving for happiness, and that life, happiness, and love form a unity. Fichte's doctrine of love was taken up by the members of the Stankevich circle at the time of their most intense ethical reflections, and they expounded it after their own fashion. In this idiosyncratic interpretation, the doctrine determined much of Stankevich's world view and for a time captivated Belinskii. For Bakunin, however, more was involved: he was attracted by the emotional and hortatory features of Fichte's doctrine and temperament. A peculiar messianism was fast becoming the basis of his own position.

Messianism was, generally speaking, an active element of romantic culture, as students of romanticism have noted. Viktor Zhirmunskii has indicated the significance of the conceptions of the hero, the teacher, the prophet, the the "poet-warlock" for the world view of the Jena romantics (especially Friedrich Schlegel and Novalis).[17] Not only was this romantic elite not governed by private passions and infatuations; it also had to be continually ready to sacrifice itself and perish in the name of the higher truth whose bearer it was, and for the sake of those to whom it had brought that truth. The Jena romantics were little known in Russia during the first half of the nineteenth century, but their ideas were in the air. Furthermore, those ideas were reinforced by the principles of Schellingian aesthetics with its image of the divinely inspired poet, which was quite familiar to Russian educated society of the 1830s. At the same time, Russian romantic messianism during the same decade, with its intense awareness of its own calling and destiny,

---

[17]V. M. Zhirmunskii, *Nemetskii romantizm i sovremennaia mistika* (St. Petersburg, 1914), pp. 109-110, passim.

was tied to political and social aspirations that, to a greater or lesser degree, were already manifest.

For Herzen and Ogarev those aspirations naturally assumed a social-utopian character. In 1833 Herzen informed Ogarev of a sharp exchange with a university comrade suspected of some base act. Ogarev anxiously wrote in reply, "For heaven's sake, don't get yourself into a duel; remember *who* you are and *why* you exist."[18]

The romantics of the 1830s strove to impart grandeur, a more exalted and universal meaning, to even the most intimate of experiences. These experiences were intertwined both with dreams of the liberation of humankind and with the religious rhetoric so characteristic of the early phase of utopian socialism (whether Western or Russian). Ogarev wrote to his fiancée, "Our love, Mariia, contains in itself the seed of the liberation of humankind.... Our love, Mariia, will be spoken of from generation to generation, and all who live after us will preserve our memory as something holy. I make this prophecy to you, Mariia, for I am a prophet, for I sense that God, who lives in me, is whispering my fate to me and rejoicing in my love."[19] Still earlier, Ogarev had written to Herzen, "I have prayed to God to destroy me if I am not destined to accomplish what I desire...."[20] The intensity of Ogarev's self-consciousness, though he was a much more passive person than either Herzen or Bakunin, is very characteristic. It is already obvious that we are dealing here with something not only of a psychological but above all of a historical order—with the typically romantic sense of the relationship between the public and the private.

Personality incessantly and insatiably nourished itself by drawing upon the whole content of public life. Science, art, social activity—all were elements in the growth and enrichment of the individual being. The result was the principled dilettantism (as Herzen, with good reason, named it at a critical juncture), the concealed contempt for the object. The objective world was dissolved and transmuted in the crucible of the "romantic spirit," and at the same time the romantic extracted from the wellsprings of

[18]N. P. Ogarev, *Izbrannye sotsial'no-politicheskie i filosofskie proizvedeniia*, vol. 2 (Moscow, 1956), p. 262.

[19]*Russkaia mysl'*, 1889, book 10, pp. 7-8; M. Gershenzon has adduced data demonstrating that while a student in St. Petersburg at the beginning of the 1830s, Pecherin [a philologist, poet, early socialist, and eventual convert to Roman Catholicism—Tr.] was experiencing similar moods: M. Gershenzon, *Zhizn' V. S. Pecherina* (Moscow, 1910), p. 11, and passim.

[20]Ogarev, vol. 2, p. 273.

his consciousness those truths that he believed to have universal significance.

In a letter to Herzen in 1840, Ogarev recalled in a remarkably lucid analysis the youthful ideology of their circle: "The first idea that really got into our heads when we were boys was socialism. First we attached our "I" to it, and then we attached it to our "I," and our main goal became, 'We shall build socialism.' Don't deny it. It's true. Don't you feel that there's much that is distorted in this, that it's egoism, well-concealed egoism, but egoism never-theless?"[21] The romantic personality was remote from vulgar ego-ism (which is poorly concealed); it contained within itself a whole world, but that whole world of philosophy, science, art, politics, and religion was made into a means of nurturing the personality itself, and everything was suddenly turned on its ethical side to-ward the problem of destiny and individual behavior.

Herzen's and Ogarev's youthful messianism was directly linked to their revolutionary aspirations and thereby to the transformation of life. From this came the idea of preparing oneself for appropriate action. The young Bakunin also sensed an activist in himself, but in essence he still did not know what kind and in what field of action. For the time being, he expounded philosophical under-standing and religious and moral self-improvement, and the ded-ication of the self to science, although these peaceable goals were obviously inadequate for someone of his mental stamp. "I am a man of circumstance, and the hand of God has inscribed in my heart the following sacred words, which embrace my whole exis-tence: 'He shall not live for himself.' I want to realize that beautiful future. I will make myself worthy of it. To be in a position to sacrifice everything for that sacred purpose—that is my only am-bition" (I, 169). This 1835 letter to the Behr sisters is the first con-scious formulation of Bakunian messianism, as well as one of the most clear-cut. One finds here a remarkably vivid manifestation of that psychological mechanism which Ogarev called the romantic's "well-concealed" egoism. The young romantic was ready to accept any burden or sacrifice, but on one condition: the greatest universal values must come into the world through him, must be realized in his personality.

In a letter to his sisters written in 1836, Bakunin says frankly that he is following "a mission ... indicated ... by Providence" that consists of "raising the earth to the heavens" (I, 219). And in an-

[21]Ibid., p. 306.

other letter: "It is necessary to smash everything false ruthlessly and without exception, so that the truth may triumph; and it shall triumph, its kingdom shall come, and all who were weak, all who were afraid of the pitiful demons that fettered them, all who stopped halfway, all who made deals with the truth, shall not be permitted to enter. They shall repent their mistakes, and they shall bewail their weakness" (I, 224). This is the language of homily and admonition undisguised.

Bakunin's spiritual life in the 1830s and the beginning of the 1840s was quite confused: it included a number of different elements in a condition of great ferment. But in searching for his own historical self-realization, Bakunin made a rigorous selection. The idea of being chosen, of being intended for some great purpose (it was still unclear what kind), completely dominated the image the young Bakunin was forming. All other qualities were peripheral and subordinated to it.

In addition to the demonic model (which at the beginning of the 1830s was very important for the romantic art of living [*zhiznetvorchestvo*]), there was also the image of the prophet. This theme had been elaborated in various ways in the poetry of the Decembrists with their use of biblical motifs to express a love of freedom, in the verse of the wisdom-lovers (Venevitinov, Khomiakov), and finally in Pushkin's celebrated poem.

For the wisdom-lover poets, the image of the prophet was still detached from personality. Thus, though Khomiakov had worked out this theme in his verse, he made no attempt to attribute the characteristics of the prophet to his own image of himself. It was just this, however, that the young Bakunin strove to do. A schema for the future life of the prophet was emerging, a schema that anticipated blows of fate as yet unfallen. In 1835 Bakunin wrote to Aleksandr Efremov:

> I want to see *her*, I want to reassure myself that she is merely a simple woman, kind, clever, educated, and that the image in which she has been raised above all those qualities, the image that has placed her in an ideal world, belongs to me, belongs to my imagination. My friend, this experience is an essential one for me. I have as yet little suffered the blows of fate; I have emerged from the fray unscathed. I require one more final blow, which would grant me the right to tear asunder all my ties with the external world and yield to desecrating it.... You see how reasonable I am: others flee from the blows of fate, but I seek them out in order to secure my independence forever (I, 187).

Bakunin's attitude, as we see, is a fully conscious one. The elements he includes in his personal image are few in number, and they are repeated persistently in letter after letter. There is the celebration of single-minded will and the stern renunciation of mundane benefits and pleasures, as well as of one's external "I," for the sake of enriching that same "I" by means of the higher life of the spirit (again the romantic dialectic of the universal and the personal): "I think *my personal I* has been killed forever; it no longer seeks anything for itself, and its life will henceforth be lived in the absolute, where my *personal I* has found more than it has lost" (I, 398).

Such statements had little connection with the disordered empirical existence of the young Bakunin. But that did not disconcert him in the least. In shaping his personality, Bakunin proceeded not from psychological particulars, but from his theories, intentions, and ideals. He proceeded from all that deeply moved him, that claimed his passionate attention, and that he therefore saw as the highest reality. His self-affirmation was accomplished entirely on an ideal plane, and it therefore knew no limits: "Great storms and thunderclaps, shaken earth, I do not fear you, I despise you, for I am a man!... I am a man, and I shall become a god!" (I, 262). And in another letter, written later: "Jesus Christ began as a man-animal and finished as a man-god, such as we all must be" (I, 384-385). In his own way, the twenty-three year old Bakunin anticipated the problematics of Dostoevskii: Kirillov's basic idea in *The Devils* is that whoever has overcome the fear of death becomes a god.

In creating his "man-god," Bakunin performed something like an artistic act. His titanic conception of himself had its own style, one nurtured on the stylistic norms of 1830s romanticism. It was an amalgam of many romanticisms which, however, omitted those elements not necessary to its system—for example, the irony of the early German romantics and the folkloristic interests of the late. But above all it was an amalgam of sensibility and enthusiasm, the sources of which were manifold: there was the still unexhausted legacy of sentimentalism, there was Jean-Paul, narrowly interpreted without his irony, there was Schiller, and there was the uninhibited writing of the French, especially the novels of George Sand, who was becoming increasingly popular. The emotional style of the young Bakunin's letters was much more monotonous than that of Herzen's letters of the 1830s, and this was so for two reasons (in addition to the psychological ones). In the first place, Herzen, unlike Bakunin, was already emerging as a major writer who was involuntarily breaking stylistic molds; in the second, Herzen was writing to his fiancée and to his friends in his native language, while most of Bakunin's letters to his sisters were written in French, so that their style was deprived of its creative source.

The young Bakunin formed the titanic image of the prophet and the "man-god" (for the most part) in letters to his sisters and to their friends Aleksandra and Natal'ia Behr, as well as in some of the letters to his younger brothers. In the 1830s Bakunin's messianism was primarily of a private variety, as has frequently been observed in the biographical literature devoted to him.

Herzen was no stranger to romantic messianism in everyday life either. It was a phenomenon characteristic of the epoch and followed predictably from the whole philosophy of the art of life. Thus, while in exile in Viatka, Herzen was surrounded by young friends whom he introduced to the higher spiritual life. Natasha Zakhar'ina[22] had her acolytes too. She was the object of devotion for several young girls whom she educated in a spirit of religious romanticism.

There were, of course, not a few heterogeneous admixtures in this private messianism: inborn imperiousness was combined with youthful conceit and even with lordly habits. As if anticipating such a reproach, Herzen wrote in 1836 to his fiancée about the serf Sasha Vyrlina, her lady's maid and companion: "Tell your Sasha, so she won't lose hope. I give her my word as a nobleman that, as soon as it is possible, I will purchase her freedom, and she can serve you her whole life—for serving you is no humiliation; if you were merely a noblewoman, I wouldn't advise it, but you are an angel, and if the whole human race were to fall down on its knees before you, it would not be demeaned, but would only do what it had already once done before another Virgin."[23]

For the young Herzen, however, private romantic propaganda merely accompanied more important ambitions. He had already had a taste of the practical work of social struggle, even suffering imprisonment and exile. The idea of a calling, of a mission, already possessed for him the meaning of historically significant behavior. The Bakunin of the 1830s was another matter—an actor in a cause that was still unknown to him, someone entirely preoccupied with his inner life and with questions of moral perfection. For Bakunin, one's private world was just as much the realm of the absolute spirit as the universe itself.

---

[22]Herzen's first cousin, later his wife—Tr.

[23]A. I. Herzen, *Sobranie sochinenii v 30-ti tomakh*, vol. 21 (Moscow, 1959), p. 106.

The future leader of the Dresden armed uprising and future defender of world anarchism expended enormous energy to ensure that the lives of the members of his domestic circle developed according to the program he had set out. Since the relationships in that circle were distinguished by a remarkable intricacy, there were numerous opportunities to exercise that energy. Bakunin's sister Liubov' was betrothed to Stankevich, though he had ceased to love her, a fact that he made an effort to conceal from her until her death. For a time Belinskii was unhappily in love with Aleksandra Bakunina, who subsequently had an unfortunate romance with Botkin. Bakunin himself regarded his sister Tat'iana with a tenderness that patently exceeded the bounds of brotherly feeling and that rendered him vulnerable to pangs of jealousy. Particularly great storms and family shocks accompanied the struggle for the "liberation of Varen'ka," Bakunin's attempt to obtain the divorce of his sister Varvara Aleksandrovna from her husband, D'iakov, because their marriage did not meet the philosophical demand for ideal spiritual harmony between husband and wife.[24]

Extraordinary disarray and confusion reigned in the Behr household in 1836. Aleksandra Behr planned to enter a convent. Natal'ia Behr, who not long before had been hopelessly in love with Stankevich, suddenly confided to Bakunin that she was in love with him, although until then it had been thought that she cultivated an adoration of him only on philosophical grounds. All these upheavals were accompanied by tiffs and reconciliations between the Behr sisters and their friends at Premukhino. Bakunin and his friends busied themselves with the philosophical interpretation of these reversals, although such reversals would have elicited only ridicule from people of Pushkin's day. But one must take into account the great interest the Russian romantics of the 1830s took in the hidden inner life of those around them, and how they searched for ways to evaluate and explain it—to take into account, that is, everything that would subsequently form the basis of Russian literary psychologism. Nervous noblewomen also had their value. Indeed, much was relevant that in its initial domestic manifestation could only have seemed ludicrous or tiresome. "It was utter chaos," wrote Natal'ia Behr to the Bakunin sisters in connection with her encounter with Michel, "an abyss of sensations and ideas that utterly astounded me.... There were moments (oh, for me those

---

[24]All of these episodes have been elucidated in detail in the Bakunin literature, especially in Kornilov.

moments were truly hellish) when I wanted to purchase with all the most terrible of misfortunes the power to revive him, or to be destroyed myself and by my death to bestow a new life on a new woman, one who could give him happiness, who could take care of him and be his guardian angel. At those moments I wanted to have the power of God."[25]

It was just this ecstatic milieu that accepted without modification the image of the prophet and the "man-god" that Bakunin created. He would never have dared to present it in pure form to his friends in the Stankevich circle; he would have met with a harsh rebuff.

Great ideological movements usually have not only their vulgarizers, but also their parasitical following, which transforms their ideas into fads or games. Before us is a phenomenon that might be called feminine romantic parasitism. Rationalistic culture produced a number of famous women, from La Fayette and Sévigné to Mme. de Staël. In the literary conditions of the seventeenth and eighteenth centuries, a woman had to have her own gifts and achievements in order to receive recognition. In this sense she was faced with demands that were, so to speak, broadly human. German romanticism also brought forward a number of talented women: Caroline Schlegel, Rahel Varnhagen, Bettina von Arnim (although, except for Bettina, they wrote almost nothing but letters). Yet romanticism put the question differently. Romantic culture presumed and required the presence of woman as beautiful lady, as bearer of the principle of the eternal feminine, and so on. This prompted women of romantic circles to play a specific role independent of their personal accomplishments and gifts, resulting in the occasional ideological mimicry and the distorted and banal imitations of the complex spiritual life of the true ideologues. Natal'ia Aleksandrovna Herzen was beyond a doubt both a talented writer and a talented person. One cannot say the same about the Bakunin sisters, with their exhaltation learned from Michel. As far as the Behr sisters are concerned, exhaltation had already become hysteria.

In Turgenev's story "Tat'iana Borisovna and Her Nephew," which appeared in 1848, there is a character who, while not directly involved in the action, is nevertheless important for an understanding of the narrative. She is "an old maid of about thirty-eight and a half, the kindest sort of creature, but warped, strained, and given to displays of enthusiasm." She "fell in love with a young student who was passing through, and at once began a vigorous and pas-

[25]Quoted in Kornilov, pp. 155-156.

sionate correspondence with him. As is customary, she gave him her blessing in her missives for a sacred and beautiful life, sacrificed her "whole being," asked only the name of sister, gave herself up to descriptions of nature, alluded to Goethe, Schiller, Bettina, and German philosophy—and of course drove the poor youth to black despair." These lines are known to be a pitiless depiction of Tat'iana Aleksandrovna Bakunina; they refer to her unhappy romance with Turgenev, which began in 1841. The style of Tat'iana Bakunina's love letters (and those of all the women of that circle) is portrayed very accurately.[26] Perhaps Turgenev dealt especially harshly with that style because he himself had in fact been forced to pay it tribute. Entering the Premukhino world, he behaved in accordance with its romantic precepts. Here are some lines from a farewell letter he wrote to Tat'iana Bakunina (March 20, 1842):

> ... You alone will understand me: it is for you alone that I would be a poet, for you, with whom my soul is in some miraculous way conjoined, so that I hardly need see you at all, or feel the need to talk to you ... ; and in spite of that, never, in hours of creativity and deep and solitary bliss, do you leave me; to you I read whatever issues from my pen, to you, my excellent sister.... Oh, if only once I could walk with you some spring morning down that long, long avenue of limes, if only I could hold your hand in mine and feel our two souls merging.[27]

A passage in German then follows using "blessing," "sister," and "best and only friend." Thus not only the enthusiastic "old maid," but also the "young student passing through"—that is Turgenev himself—is answerable for the parodied style. The romantic milieu required accommodation even from those natures that were little suited to it.

One should say that the world of Premukhino remained true to its precepts in even the most tragic circumstances. In 1840, Varvara Aleksandrovna Bakunina met Stankevich abroad. They came to an immediate understanding and declared their love for each other. Five weeks later Stankevich died. For Varvara Aleksandrovna this

---

[26]Tat'iana Bakunina's letters to Turgenev have been published by N. L. Brodskii in his article " 'Premukhinskii roman' v zhizni i tvorchestve Turgeneva," *I. S. Turgenev*, no. 2 (Moscow/Petrograd, 1923); see also L. V. Krestova's article, "Tat'iana Bakunina i Turgenev," *Turgenev i ego vremia* (Moscow/Petrograd, 1923).

[27]I. S. Turgenev, *Polnoe sobranie sochinenii i pisem v 28-mi tomakh* (Moscow/Leningrad, 1961), *Pis'ma*, vol. 1, pp. 220-221; subsequent references are to Turgenev, *Sochineniia* or *Pis'ma*.

was a catastrophe in which all her hopes for happiness and a new life perished. Yet the very next day, while seated next to Stankevich's body (he had died during their joint trip from Rome to Milan), she wrote down her thoughts and feelings in keeping with all the canons of the Premukhino style. The page with these notes in German (the language of romanticism) has been preserved in the Bakunin family archive:

> Oh, no, no, my beloved, I have not forgotten your words; we met and we recognized each other! We are joined together for eternity; separation is brief, and that new kingdom which has already been revealed to you—it will be mine too: there love is eternal, there the power of the Spirit is eternal!. . . This faith was yours! It is mine too. Brother, do you recognize me? Does the voice of a sister reach you in eternity? I shall recognize you in your new strength and beauty. . . . and you also will recognize, you will divine her—your sister left far behind!

Following this is a frankly philosophical discourse through which the voice of Michel is clearly heard:

> The material world in and of itself is nothing, but only through its internal union with the spirit has my being, my *I* received its reality. Only through this incomprehensible conjunction of the infinite and the finite has my *I* become an *I*, a living independent being. When I say "I," I become conscious of myself, I become known to myself. Through a reverse convergence with the Universal, I must lose this consciousness of myself—my individuality disppears; I am no longer I, for only the Universal remains, Spirit for its own sake. Thus I am nothing! What then is death? There's little comfort in this.[28]

These words were written by a woman sitting next to the body of her beloved who had just died. If romantic philosophy in that circle was a fashion imbibed secondhand, it was nonetheless one that was lived with great seriousness. And that is why Bakunin relied so heavily on the audience of young ladies and adolescent brothers he had trained. Among his friends, however, Bakunin's preaching assumed forms that were much more cautious and less consistent with his inner sense of himself. The style of his letters to his friends is accordingly of a different kind too. It is more colloquial, simpler, and philosophical matters are expounded in a

[28]Quoted in Kornilov, pp. 666-667.

dry and specialized language.[29] Bakunin obviously feared Stankevich with his sober judgments and unquestioned authority in the circle, and in the letters to Stankevich there is neither the edifying nor the oracular tone. On the contrary, there are even complaints about his own spiritual inadequacy: "To end my life [if he does not manage to go to Berlin to study—L. G.] as an artillery lieutenant or as an actual state councillor is quite the same to me: I am neither the first nor shall I be the last who has been stopped short of his ideal aspiration, which anyway is very often just the agitated movement of young blood. I have remained the same decent and absurd fellow that you knew.... And so you see, dear Stankevich, that neither my external nor my inner life is worthy of great attention" (II, 297).[30] From prophet to lieutenant of artillery—such was the range of Bakunin's self-definition. No less variegated were the ways he was perceived by those around him. The proselytes bowed down to the prophet, but the father, irritated by his son's philosophical experiments, declared that Michel was puffed up with egoism and "blind self-regard," that he liked only flatterers and longed "to hold sway in the family."[31]

Granovskii was frightened by Bakunin's "abstract energy" ("for him there are no subjects, only objects"). In 1840, he confided to Neverov: "I've never encountered such a monstrous creature before. Until you get to know him better, it's enjoyable and even useful to talk to him, but on more intimate acquaintance, it becomes oppressive—*unheimlich* somehow. I am afraid he'll run into Stankevich again somewhere. He'll torment him just as he did Botkin."[32] But the Botkin who in his time (1838) had been tormented by Bakunin wrote to him, "All the hostility I felt for you is gone, and reborn are those sacred moments when for me you were the bearer of the secrets of a higher life."[33] The juxtaposition of these judgments makes a case for the linking of Bakunin with Dostoevskii's

---

[29]An extremely small number of Bakunin's letters to his friends and acquaintances in the 1830s have survived. Obviously, the addressees or their families destroyed his letters after he was declared a state criminal. Lost too is an immense quantity of letters to Belinskii, documents of great importance for the history of the spiritual development of both figures. One must base one's evaluation of the young Bakunin's correspondence on a few extant letters to A. Afremov, Stankevich, Ketscher, Neverov, and S. N. Murav'ev (see Bakunin, vols. 1, 2).

[30]Letter of 1840. One should mention that Bakunin's letters not infrequently had an ulterior purpose. In this instance he needed to elicit Stankevich's sympathy, because he looked to him for help in connection with a propoosed trip abroad.

[31]Kornilov, pp. 162, 165.

[32]T. N. Granovskii i ego perepiska, vol. 2 (Moscow, 1897), pp. 375, 383, 403.

[33]Literaturnoe nasledstvo, vol. 56 (Moscow, 1950), p. 117.

Stavrogin, who either ruined those who crossed his path or acquainted him with the "secrets of a higher life."

Bakunin's personality breaks up into a series of disparate images created by himself, by the members of his family, by his friends, and ultimately by the memoirists and writers for whom he served as a prototype. Furthermore, his friends perceived him differently at different times in the course of their association. It follows from this that there was no ready-made, stable Bakunin personality that had only to be taken from reality and depicted. But it in no way follows that his personality had no objective features. Bakunin's psychological makeup manifested itself in multifarious ways, and interpretations and evaluations of it were just as diverse, yet at the basis of everything—if one looks closely enough—was a rather consistent behavioral mechanism. Whether praising Bakunin or excoriating him, his contemporaries returned repeatedly to the contradictions between the strength of his speculative mind and the insufficiency of his concrete grasp of life, between the indefatigable energy of his spirit and a sort of deficiency in humanity. Belinskii termed Bakunin a prophet and a thunderer "whose organism was devoid of warmth." It was enough to weaken or remove one of the elements of that contradiction for the mechanism of Bakunin's behavior to break down.

It is for precisely this reason that Turgenev failed to capture Bakunin when he used him as the prototype for Rudin. Turgenev retained the abstractness, the hortatory fervor, in Rudin, but he deprived him of force. The vast logical speculations of the young Bakunin were turned into the impotent introspection of the superfluous man. Lack of resemblance was the immediate result. Herzen said in this regard, "Turgenev, taken with God's practice in the Bible, created Rudin in his own image and likeness; Rudin is a second Turgenev who has been thoroughly exposed to the young Bakunin's philosophical jargon" (XI, 359). Chernyshevskii, who called Rudin a "caricature," added, "as if a lion were fit for caricature."[34] In revising the novel, Turgenev gradually moved away from the attempt to render Bakunin's portrait (the original, obviously more portraitlike versions have not survived). Nevertheless, Turgenev never repudiated the parallel. With Bakunin in mind, he declared in a letter in 1862, "I presented a rather true portrait

---

[34]N. G. Chernyshevskii, *Polnoe sobranie sochinenii*, vol. 7 (Moscow, 1950), p. 449.

of him in Rudin: now he's the Rudin *not* killed on a barricade."[35] Turgenev imparted a number of individual Bakunin traits to Rudin, but he upset the basic principle underlying his personality, the essential contradiction between the inner coldness, the deficient humanity, and that "leonine quality" that Belinskii spoke of even in moments of sharpest conflict with him.

The Bakunin problem assumes a different form in Dostoevskii's *Devils*. Leonid Grossman maintained that Bakunin was the prototype of Stavrogin, and enumerated some twenty points of resemblance. Viacheslav Polonskii and other opponents of Grossman (V. Borovoi, N. Otverzhennyi) have endeavored to refute these points and to demonstrate that Stavrogin has a much greater affinity with the Petrashevskian Speshnev.[36] This is true, but it does not completely dispose of the question. The loud, indefatigably active Bakunin has no reflection in Stavrogin's behavior. Nonetheless, there is in the Dostoevskii character a structural contradiction between power of intellect, and the deficiency of an abstract, ungrounded nature. And there is also Dostoevskii's utilization of what Bakhtin has called "prototypes of ideas."[37] Bakunin's views on the tactics of revolution, especially during the time of his association with Nechaev, must have served as the "prototype" for those of Stavrogin's ideas that inspired Petr Verkhovenskii.

The most remarkable image of the young Bakunin in all his dynamism and theatricalism belongs neither to the artists nor the memoirists. That image was created by Belinskii in his letters to Bakunin and to their common friends. He created it and destroyed it, and then created it anew. Reflected in the microcosm of that amity and enmity, that love and hate, are dislocations of an epochal significance: the breakup of the romantic consciousness and the establishment of a new one. Russian culture was moving ineluctably toward a conception of man that was concretely historical, social, and psychological. On this path—the path from the young to the mature Herzen, from Bakunin to Belinskii—there was one other important transitional link: Stankevich.

Everyone who has written about Stankevich has noted the paradoxical disparity between the meagerness of his philosophical and

---

[35]Turgenev, *Pis'ma*, vol. 5, p. 47; cf. N. Ostrovskaia's *Vospominaniia* (Petrograd, 1915), p. 95, for similar statements by Turgenev.

[36]See L. P. Grossman and V. P. Polonskii, *Spor o Bakunine i Dostoevskom* (Leningrad, 1926) and A. Borovoi and N. Otverzhennyi, *Mif o Bakunine* (Moscow, 1925).

[37]M. M. Bakhtin, *Problemy poetiki Dostoevskogo* (Moscow, 1972), pp. 151-54.

literary legacy and the power of his influence on his contemporaries. Herzen speaks of it in *My Past and Thoughts* (IX, 7), and Annenkov goes into it in particular detail in his biography of Stankevich, where he calls him "one of those remarkable active people who have left nothing behind." "The reason," Annenkov writes, "for Stankevich's complete and irresistible influence lay in his lofty nature, his ability to forget himself completely, and, without the slightest sign of boasting or self-regard, to carry everyone away with him into the realm of the ideal."[38]

Stankevich really was surrounded by a very special atmosphere of love and enthusiastic veneration. "It is impossible to convey in words," Turgenev says in his recollections of Stankevich, "what sort of respect, even reverence, he inspired."[39] Belinskii's letters abound in reverential judgments. Stankevich was summoned to "a great cause." "I have met only one person in my life whom I have unconditionally deferred to, whom I now defer to, and whom I shall always defer to." After his death, Belinskii called Stankevich "a divine personality" and declared that he was beholden to Stankevich for everything human in himself. "Think only what each of us was," he wrote to Botkin, "before we met Stankevich or people imbued with his spirit."[40] Granovskii responded to Stankevich's death with a similar admission: "He was our benefactor, our teacher, a brother to us all; each of us owes him something. I more than anybody."[41]

Herzen, Turgenev, and Annenkov sought the reasons for Stankevich's significance and influence in the fact that he was the conscience of the people in his circle, the purest embodiment of their moral ideals. But there was more to it than that. The meaning of the distinctive Stankevich cult becomes clear only in relation to the profound intellectual crisis that took shape at the end of the 1830s and the beginning of the 1840s. Bakuninian romanticism had by this time become obsolete. The idea of concrete reality entered Belinskii's purview in 1838, perhaps even in the fall of 1837, when he first became acquainted with the aesthetics of Hegel. The year 1838 was also crucial for Lermontov: it saw the beginning of his work on *A Hero of Our Time*. And Herzen, Ogarev, and Botkin had all abandoned romanticism by the bginning of the 1840s (the fact

---

[38]P. V. Annenkov, *Vospominaniia i kriticheskie ocherki* (St. Petersburg, 1881), p. 382.
[39]Turgenev, *Sochineniia*, vol. 6, p. 393.
[40]V. G. Belinskii, *Polnoe sobranie sochinenii*, vol. 11 (Moscow, 1956), pp. 193, 265, 547, 554.
[41]*Granovskii*, vol. 2, p. 101.

that people of the 1830s retained certain elements of romantic consciousness for the rest of their lives is another issue).

The powerful new intellectual movement, already termed *realism* by Herzen, was above all distinguished by its universality. It involved a new method, which was applied to the most varied spheres of human activity, and it therefore also involved the formation of the realistic man.

The demand for a new order of consciousness, for a new epochal personality, was intense. For the moment, however, that personality was characterized by amorphousness. Indeed, the very term *realism* remained for a time vague and elastic, since it had not yet broken free of its purely philosophical meaning, the speculative formula opposing the ideal and the real. A model for the new personality had still not been found, and the requirements for it during the transitional period were for the most part negative ones. The first order of business was to get rid of the characteristics of the obsolescent romantic idealism—stiltedness, illusion, and rhetoric. Stankevich satisfied these increasingly pressing demands through his own personality. He was an early and in a certain sense a negative embodiment of the sought-after realistic man, and in this fact lies the solution to the question of his unerring power and authority over other minds.

Stankevich was a *man without rhetoric.* Annenkov spoke of this quality, and so did Konstantin Aksakov in his reminiscences of his student days.[42] Belinskii's perception of him was the same. "There wasn't a trace of rhetoric in him," Turgenev wrote in his memoirs of Stankevich; "not even Tolstoi would have found any."[43] Turgenev's memoirs were written in 1856. He of course has in mind here the relentlessness of moral demands and psychological disclosures that was already characteristic of Tolstoi in his early works. The remarkable thing, however, is that Tolstoi himself sensed a peculiar inner affinity with Stankevich. In 1858, after reading Stankevich's correspondence, which had just been published by his brother, Tolstoi wrote, "Never has any book made such an impression on me. Never have I liked anyone so much as this man, whom I never met. What purity, what gentleness, what love he was imbued with."[44]

[42]Konstantin Aksakov, *Vospominanie studenstva* (St. Petersburg, 1911), p. 19.
[43]Turgenev, *Sochineniia*, vol. 6, p. 394.
[44]Letter to A. A. Tolstaia, in L. N. Tolstoi, *Polnoe sobranie sochinenii*, vol. 60 (Moscow, 1949), p. 274; in a letter to Chicherin written at the same time, Tolstoi also said of Stankevich, "Here's someone I could have loved as I do myself" (ibid., p. 272).

Tolstoi was only ten years old when in a letter to Stankevich (1838) Belinskii attempted to define the almost "Tolstoyan" basis of Stankevich's personality. "Friend, a great change has taken place in me. At last I understand what you call (and have long called) *simplicity* and *normality*. You were just as vulgarly idealistic as we were, but you always retained a vigorous sense of your own vulgar idealism and idealistic vulgarity, as well as the need to escape into *simple*, normal reality (XI, 307).[45]

With his common sense, the clarity of his abstract thought, and his appetite for practical action (however modest), with his joviality, his ready sense of humor, and his fondness for jokes and "farces" remembered by all who knew him, Stankevich was indeed perceived by his contemporaries as one who had escaped into "normal reality."

Stankevich evolved from idealism to sober realism in conjunciton with the other remarkable people of his generation. His development differed from theirs in important aspects, however. It seemed to lack a material expression. It was embodied not in written works, but in his personality itself. And that personality lacked any imprint of the romantic mold according to which—in its several varieties— so many of his contemporaries had shaped their own personalities. Stankevich had a nonromantic character. Unlike many others, he did not try to force it into the romantic forms provided by the times. He left his personality in a state of rather amorphous freedom and elegant simplicity. And it was these qualities especially that captivated those who were tired of obsolete yet still persistent molds.

Stankevich belonged to an intermediate, transitional stage, and one that was not all that clear-cut. He took upon himself the spiritual legacy of romanticism, above all the problems of the ideal and of all-embracing love. The foundations of his thought had been laid by romanticism and by German idealist philosophy.[46] Even the philosophy of the real, which completely captivated Stankevich

---

[45]Stankevich's letters attest to steady movement toward "simplicity and normality." A heightened romantic phraseology still breaks through in the earliest of his letters (especially in those to Neverov written in the first half of the 1830s), but thereafter it rapidly diminishes, and if it reemerges, it does so only in relation to specific situations and addressees, for example, in the 1840 letter (to V. A. D'iakova) in which Stankevich's last love is reflected. Generally speaking, the language of Stankevich's letters is the language of uninhibited friendly conversation, in which humorous "chatter" alternates with philosophical reflection.

[46]Stankevich's attempts at verse (he abandoned them early) are typical, if rather unsuccessful, specimens of the romantic poetry of the 1830s.

at the end of his life, revealed reality to him in Hegelian logical categories, without those great rifts in the social and the concrete that from the beginning were characteristic of Belinskii's Hegelianism.

The very application of ideological formulas to life, their biographical substantiation, reveals Stankevich as someone who was linked in many ways to romanticism. Even the particular things that the romantic was supposed to experience, such as a simultaneously earthly and ideal love, happened to him. Yet all those romantic concerns and even practical experiences left his personality free, instead of forging the emerging features of the new man into a romantic mask. At the moment of that new man's maturation, certain negative achievements proved to be very important— such things as the absence of a mask, of rhetoric, of a pose, or of a typological mold. Stankevich was not only a man without rhetoric; he was also someone who lacked a role, and who therefore demonstrated to his contemporaries that a historically active spiritual life was possible even without a role, even without a set, easily recognized form.

Unlike Bakunin, Stankevich did not consciously shape his personality; his friends, his contemporaries shaped it for him. They gave it a one-dimensional form: the ideal of the lofty mind and pure heart. This image of Stankevich served them as a weapon in the struggle against illusion, stiltedness, and rhetoric. He himself, amazingly free of self-love and intellectual coquetry, was inclined to critical self-analysis and stern self-appraisal. Hence the striking disparity between Stankevich seen from without and the same man viewed from within. The idealized image of him was necessary to his contemporaries for their own spiritual maturation. That image was formed by means of a rigorous selection, a sifting of complex and contradictory mental experience. The person immersed in that experience, however, could not—unless he was a Foma Opiskin[47]— recognize his inner self in those one-dimensional, idealized categories.

Inner self-realization was more likely for the forms of romantic demonism, which, even in its undeveloped guise, assumed, or even presupposed, contradiction. Moreover, the romantic character could in the process of its self-realization eliminate as ines-

---

[47]The principal character in Dostoevskii's burlesque *Selo Stepanchikovo i ego obitateli* (Stepanchiko village and its denizens) (1859); Constance Garnett translates this work as *The Friend of the Family*—Tr.

sential or empirically insigificant anything not subsumed in its preconceived exalted formula. This in fact was how Bakunin proceeded. Stankevich, however, was the sort who could brush nothing aside: he wanted to account for the full plenitude of his experience. He knew that a person passes through a great number of impulses, desires, and momentary reactions before he reaches the point of action or behavior that is apparent to those around him. If the person is of an analytical bent, he judges, condemns, and justifies those impulses, but by no means does he ever discount them as irrelevant to any ideal definition of himself.

A person cannot see himself from within as a crystalline pure and ideally harmonious personality—and not merely because of modesty or an aversion to the crudeness of that kind of self-admiration, but also because sanctity, purity, and harmony are not psychological definitions of mental states at all; they are completely judgmental formulations of behavior that has been generalized and abstracted from the empirical complexity of inner life. For self-realization of this judgmental kind, it is necessary to get outside oneself and to construct one's image from an external point of view, as an object whose significance is as much aesthetic as it is ethical. For Stankevich this kind of self-realization was not necessary.

Stankevich conceived the transition to a philosophy of reality in terms of abstract Hegelian categories. The objective content of his personality, its set of day-to-day concerns, was in large measure still linked to romanticism. It was for just this reason that the ideal image of Stankevich held by his contemporaries lacked firm outlines. Sharply limned in it was the negation of rhetoric, stiltedness, illusion, and falsehood, but the positive content of the new personality still had not been defined. That recognizable model of the new man from which individual characters are derived, which gives people form and opens up new possibilities for typology and classification, still had not been created. This is why Stankevich was ill suited as a prototype.

That Turgenev was a celebrated master of historical typification is common knowledge. In each of his novels he strove to fix an image (usually the main hero) that would define the characteristics of a generation. Yet his portrayal of two of his famous contemporaries (Bakunin and Stankevich) proved inadequate. And this was no accident. Turgenev's early tale "Andrei Kolosov," although it partly reflects his own unhappy affair with Tat'iana Bakunina, is even more a reflection of the image of Stankevich and his unhappy affair with Liubov' Bakunina. Turgenev had no ready-made form for Stankevich's personality. He blended into Kosolov auto-biographical reminiscences and recollections of Belinskii. These Bel-inskian elements destroyed the personality's structure. Turgenev made Kolosov a plebian intellectual (*raznochinets*), whereas Stank-evich was a typical late product of the Russian educated nobility. It was precisely this social background that Herzen stressed so insistently in his portrayal of Stankevich in *My Past and Thoughts*. Belinskii has left evidence in his letters of the nervous hyperin-tensity produced by the bitter uncertainty of the plebeian intellec-tual's life. In "Andrei Kolosov" Turgenev attempted to combine that difficult, penurious mode of life, which was unhappily familiar to Belinskii, Dostoevskii, and Nekrasov, with the inner freedom, harmony, and clarity of mind that were characteristic of Stankevich.

The forced combinations were unsuccessful. The hero of the tale was apprehended in a number of different ways, even as a petty egoist and vulgarian.[48] Moreover, the underlying personality con-flict was willy nilly supplanted by something else. Stankevich had decided to break with his fiancée, Liubov' Bakunina, because he had become convinced of the inadequacy of his feelings for her, and a marriage without love would, according to the doctrine sub-scribed to by his friends, be a profanation of love, a desecration of the spirit. Looking at Kolosov, who was placed in a similar situ-ation, we find an anticipation of the theory of free love that would later occupy a central place in the world-view of the plebeian in-tellectuals.[49] That idea was still only dimly sketched in the 1844 Turgenev tale. Druzhinin wrote of "Andrei Kolosov" that "the trouble with the story is that its *conception is at variance with its construction*, that the type conceived in the head of the gifted story-teller has in the story lost all its meaning."[50]

This failure of the young Turgenev is of theoretical interest. It attests to the difficulty of creating an integrated literary personality when the structure, the mold, of the corresponding historical per-sonality still has not taken shape or been discerned. It was of course Turgenev who eventually discovered the key term *nihilist* and who created in the character of Bazarov a model for whole generations. The category of the *superfluous man* was just as clear to him. But

---

[48]See the commentary to "Andrei Kolosov" in Turgenev, *Sochineniia*, vol. 5, p. 546, for a discussion of this matter.

[49]An earlier phenomenon was the "George Sandism" of the 1830s and 1840s to which both Belinskii and Herzen and the people of Herzen's circle gave their allegiance.

[50]A. V. Druzhinin, *Sobranie sochinenii*, vol. 7 (St. Petersburg, 1865), p. 307.

the personality of Stankevich eluded Turgenev not only in "Andrei Kolosov," but also in the much later *Rudin*, where the character Pokorskii is modeled on Stankevich, and unsuccessfully so, by Turgenev's own admission. Pokorskii is ideologically a more definite figure, but as a personality he is formed on the same principle that Kolosov was. He is Stankevich with an admixture of Belinskii, a blend of harmony and the mode of life of the indigent plebeian intellectual.

Turgenev was unsuccessful in finding a model for Stankevich's complex transitional nature. Bakunin, however, he relegated to an already familiar classification, one that he himself had formulated, the "superfluous man." Both Herzen and Chernyshevskii objected to this stereotyping of Bakunin. Bakunin was not, of course, a "superfluous man." He was an indefatigably active organizer who was fanatically devoted to his own, not infrequently abstract, goals. Such he had always been, and such he remained in every instance—from the struggle to "liberate Varen'ka" to the leadership of the world anarchist movement. Nevertheless, Rudin—and everyone has noticed this—is endowed with a number of Bakunin's more identifiable features. As if afraid they might go unnoticed, Turgenev brought them all together in Lezhnev's famous characterization of Rudin: "He is a remarkably intelligent man, though essentially an empty one.... He is an intellectual despot, he is lazy, and he is not particularly knowledgeable.... He likes living at other people's expense, he plays roles, and so on ... ; all that is perfectly normal. But the bad thing is that he's as cold as ice. ... As cold as ice, and he knows it, but pretends to be full of passion." Descriptions of all these qualities may be found in letters by Belinskii, Botkin, and others written in the midst of struggle and polemic with Bakunin. In becoming qualities of Rudin, however, they lost their basic motivating principle. Turgenev gave them a different structure, that of the "superfluous man."

A number of Stankevich's more recognizable traits are ascribed to Andrei Kolosov too—from his ability to inspire all-embracing love to his jovial character and even humorousness combined with an elevated spiritual life. Andrei Kolosov is distinguished by "a clear, simple view of life" and "the absence of any indulgence in rhetoric." It was these very features that formed the basis of Stankevich's image in his circle of friends. Nevertheless, neither Kolosov nor Pokorskii really resembles Stankevich. The crossing of Stankevich and Belinskii in a single image brings together phenomena possessing different social natures and belonging to different (if chronologically very close) stages in the movement of Russian culture toward realism.

Belinskii went much further than Stankevich had. And that was why the idealists of the 1830s regarded Stankevich as their teacher and exemplar. Stankevich was for them a guarantee of clarity and harmony. Belinskii's extreme solutions, his terrible consistency, his whole spasmodic, torturous development frightened and repelled other minds. Stankevich judged himself to be unemotional and made no attempt to conceal that trait. It is a motif that recurs in his letters with extraordinary persistence.

> I don't know whether to call my mind empty to begin with or made empty. Made empty? What was in it then?... My friend, there was something in it once, and there still is, but it's so poor and meager. And I had hoped for such a rich and fulfilling life. That was my mistake, my error.... Love is a religion, the only one possible, and a religion must fill up every moment, every instant of one's life, or else the person who knows himself a little bit cannot love; but in order to be capable of such love, one has to be more highly developed, one has to be a spirit, whereas I was only a mind, and moreover one that suffered from starry-eyed idealism.[51]

This May 1837 letter to Bakunin (the original is in German) explains a great deal not only about Stankevich's own ethical position, but also about the whole temper of his circle. Above all, it explains how Stankevich, though revered by his comrades, was nonetheless able to judge himself unsparingly and without the slightest trace of play-acting or posing. He advocated an unattainable ethical idea— a love that would fill "every instant of one's life." Actual moral practice could not help but fall short. It is for this reason that there emerged in the minds of Stankevich and Belinskii the moral categories of *apathy, lethargy, coldness,* and *unlovingness* [*bezliubovnost'*], which were understood as defects, as sins against the soul. Emotional aridity and apathy were inimical to the requirement of love, indolence to the requirement of an intense spiritual life, and lack of will to the requirement of perfection of the self. Thinking in these categories already marks a departure from the romantic conflict engendered by that embarrassment of spiritual riches that separated the hero from the mob and prepared the way for romantic disenchantment. Now, on the contrary, the source of evil was

[51]*Perepiska N. V. Stankevicha (1830-1840)* (Moscow, 1914), pp. 626-627; subsequently page numbers of this edition are given in the text.

spiritual insufficiency. In a letter to Granovskii, Stankevich says that "human nature . . . needs to have demands made upon it. It needs to rise to them" (449). This means that the highest demands made upon the mind do not come to it in ready-made form.

The most concrete expression of love proves to be love for a woman (so Stankevich declares in his letters). On this level, the philosophical conflict, while remaining philosophical, acquires additional psychological features. Stankevich took his infatuation with Liubov' Bakunina to be an ideal love that opened up the possibility of an ideal marriage. He soon realized that he was mistaken. According to the ethical code accepted in his circle, a marriage without love was the greatest possible sin against the spirit. The cruelty of a break seemed the lesser evil. But since Bakunina was seriously ill, it was necessary to postpone that break; it was necessary to deceive (a role to which Stankevich was particularly ill suited).

According to the rules of honor observed by the nobility, Mikhail Bakunin ought to have challenged Stankevich to a duel for deceiving his sister. Instead, he submitted the episode to philosophical scrutiny, and Stankevich, for his part, analyzed himself in a letter to the brother of the unloved fiancée:

> I have never loved. For me love was always a whim of the imagination, a game of self-love, a crutch for faint-heartedness, the only interest that could occupy a mind devoid of base desires, but lacking too any real, substantial content (speaking in the language of philosophy). The field of action for the person who is truly strong is reality. The weak mind lives in *Jenseits*, in striving, in uncertain striving; it needs *something* (since there is nothing definite in itself to shape its nature and its head). As soon as that indefiniteness has been made *etwas*, has been made definite, then the mind once again goes beyond the bounds of reality. This is my story, and it's obviously the reason for all the trouble. What Belinskii regards as genius is merely vileness. [650]

Stankevich rejects the ideal personal image foisted on him by his friends, and from within constructs another image, in which aridity, apathy, and coldness predominate.

> I have kind friends [he wrote to V. A. D'iakova in 1837] who are inclined to say that my needs are too broad to be satisfied and too strong to leave me in peace. It isn't true! My head was befuddled, my mind was empty and weakened.... I had no definite desires, so there was nothing to satisfy; I wanted a regeneration that would give

me the desires themselves.... Was it possible for such a weak and broken mind to love? Isolated from the world—*die schöne Seele*—it created pale images for itself and sought their likenesses among people.... Encounters, mistakes, contradictions, crises were necessary. I understood my predicament, my former insignificance, without changing it in the least; I cursed that *Schönseseeligheit*, but was not reconciled to the world. From this comes that arid struggle that has taken up so much of my time and energy, and even now I'm still unable to free myself from this servile doubt, these tormenting thoughts that revolve so agonizingly and dully in my mind. [723]

Aridness and *dullness* for Stankevich were at once ideological sins and agonizing physical conditions. In a letter to the same D'iakova written three years later, Stankevich declared that she would find in him "a homunculous hovering between heaven and earth, who is aware of his glass dwelling and yet has not the strength to break it" (738). He has in mind here the homunculous hatched in the retort, the artificial man in the second part of *Faust*. Nonetheless, the image of an ineffectual creature "hovering between heaven and earth" is also very close to Baratynskii's "Nedonosok' (the still-born), a poem that was first published in 1835 in *Moskovskii nabliudatel'* (the Moscow observer) (and later included in the collection *Sumerki* (twilight) and that was certainly known to Stankevich.

> I come from the race of spirits,
> But not of the empyrean tribe,
> For scarcely had I reached the clouds
> Than I weakened and plummeted down.
> So small and poor, how shall I live?
> Beyond the undulant clouds, I know,
> Lies paradise; I hang suspended,
> A winged sigh twixt earth and sky.

Who was right then, Stankevich's contemporaries, who saw in him an exemplary chevalier of the spirit, or he himself with his baring of his faults? Stankevich was undoubtedly what his friends knew him to be, a man of great rectitude and elegant simplicity. But he was not given to playing up his own virtues; he was concerned with something else. He continuously measured himself against the idea of an all-pervasive love and of all-consuming desires, and he found himself wanting. He discovered in himself aridity, coldness, and paucity of spiritual energy and will, and regarded these as ethical deficiencies. Triumphing over these deficiencies became the starting point for the personal psychological and moral program that he worked on till the end of his life.

Stankevich's spiritual life and the forms in which it found realization were clearly gravitating toward later Russian psychologism with its set of peculiarly moral problems. Belinskii proceeded even further in that direction. He regarded himself as immensely obligated to Stankevich and returned to him repeatedly in the practical concerns of his own "inner life." But in Belinskii the contradictions had become so intolerable that they demanded an outlet and solutions, and those solutions were always extreme ones. Belinskii's letters of the 1830s and 1840s are for this reason a unique record of the maturation of the new historical consciousness.[52]

[52]Devoted to Belinskii's letters in particular are: "Perepiska Belinskogo (kritiko-bibliograficheskii obzor)," in *Literaturnoe nasledstvo*, vol. 56 (Moscow, 1950), and Mark Poliakov's article, "Vsia zhizn' moia v pis'makh," in Poliakov, *Poeziia kriticheskoi mysli* (Moscow, 1968).

Index

Library of Congress Cataloging in Publication Data

Main entry under title:
The Semiotics of Russian cultural history.

 Translated from the Russian.
 Contents: Binary models in the dynamics of Russian culture / Iurii M.
Lotman, Boris A. Uspenskii—The poetics of everyday behavior in eighteenth century Russian culture / Iurii M. Lotman—The Decembrist in daily
life / Iurii M. Lotman — [etc.]
 1. Russian literature—History and criticism—Addresses, essays, lec-
tures. 2. Literature and society—Soviet Union—Addresses, essays, lec-
tures. 3. Soviet Union—Civilization—Addresses, essays, lectures.
4. Soviet Union—Intellectual life—Addresses, essays, lectures. I. Lotman,
IU. M. (Iuriĭ Mikhaĭlovich), 1922- . II. Ginzburg, L. (Lidiia), 1902-
III. Uspenskiĭ, Boris Andreevich. IV. Nakhimovsky, Alexander
D. V. Nakhimovsky, Alice S.
PG2986.S45 1985   891.7'09   84-45152
ISBN 0-8014-1183-1
ISBN 0-8014-9294-7 (pbk.)